D0409116

PAST IMPERFECT
An autobiography

PAST IMPERFECT
An autobiography

Joan Collins

W.H. ALLEN · LONDON
A Howard & Wyndham Company
1978

W.H. Allen & Co. Ltd,
44 Hill Street, London W1X 8LB

First published 1978
Copyright © Joan Collins 1978

This book or parts thereof may not
be reproduced without permission
in writing

Set in Compugraphic Paladium by
Yaleset Ltd, Norwood, London

Printed and bound in Great Britain by
Redwood Burn Ltd.
Trowbridge & Esher

This edition published
by arrangement with Warner Books, Inc.

ISBN 0 491 02014 7

ACKNOWLEDGEMENTS

Grateful thanks to Judy Bryer, Sally Paulson and Amanda Girling, who managed to decipher the hieroglyphics with which they were presented!

Grateful thanks also to TRO Essex Music Ltd, for permission to quote from 'I wanna be Rich' and 'What kind of Fool am I?'; to MCA Music Inc., for permission to quote from 'Chalk and Cheese' and 'I'm all I need' from the film *Can Hieronymus Merkin ever forget Mercy Humpe and find true Happiness?*; and to Cynara Music for permission to quote from *'Why do you try and change me?'*

DEDICATION

For my children Tara, Sacha and Katyana, for the past the present and the future, and for Ron, whose support and encouragement got me through it!

Contents

Have you found your life distasteful?
My life did and does smack sweet.
Was your youth of pleasure wasteful?
Mine I saved and held complete.
Do your joys with age diminish?
When mine fail me, I'll complain.
Must in death your daylight finish?
My sun sets to rise again.

Robert Browning

PROLOGUE

Acapulco, 17 January 1977

It has been said that inside everyone there is a book. Waiting to burst upon the world for it to read and relish. Countless times — in New York and Rome by cab drivers, full of anecdotes of hi-jinks in back seats; on the set in London and Hollywood from grips and gaffers, make-up men and hairdressers who understand the world of the film actress perhaps more clearly than anyone else ever could; and in day-to-day encounters in stores, supermarkets, cocktail parties — I have been regaled with the details of someone's life which would 'make a helluva book' (and indeed have often been told that I would be perfect as the lead should the book ever be filmed!). Consequently the idea began to germinate that perhaps I too had a book inside my head, but having started nine novels and never progressed further than Chapter 3 I am dubious about finishing it.

However, with the encouragement of my loving and trusted husband, Ron Kass, and my agent, the redoubtable Irving Swifty Lazar, and my long-term friend Leslie Bricusse in whose Acapulco house these first tentative words are being penned, whilst gazing across the bay at a view of unsurpassable beauty, a magical vista of which I have never tired, with the provocative and mellow sounds of Marvin Gaye in the background to my right and the familiar and incessant wails of the Mexican housekeeper's new baby to my left, I shall attempt to tell my story. And I shall attempt to finish it too!

1

Oh What a Beautiful Baby!

My first appearance before the world is in a photograph taken of my mother and father and Lew Grade at a charity ball seven hours before I was born.

Apart from a slightly glazed and panicked look on my mother's face, no-one could ever tell the lady was about to deliver her first born. She looks smoothly blonde and soignée, flanked by the young dinner-jacketed men beside her.

My father, Joe, and Lew Grade, who were at the time partners in a theatrical agency called Collins and Grade, have the suitably smug expressions of men about to become fathers and godfathers for the first time. Although Lord Lew (as he is today) never became my official godfather, he and my parents were, at that time, and for many years to come so extremely close, both in business and in their personal lives that he was always 'Uncle Lew' to me. And he took a great personal interest in me when I was a child. Mummy and Daddy were bridesmaid and best man after he married a lovely young singer, Kathleen Moody, during the war — and until Mummy's death in 1962 she and Kathy and Kathy's sister, Nora, were the closest of friends, even though the business relationship between my father and Lew had long been dissolved.

My father scared the hell out of me for so many years that it is even now hard to write about him without the feeling he may get mad at me. Throughout my years of analysis and soul searching, with all the intellectual and emotional knowledge of myself and my relationships, Big Daddy has always been a frightening figure rather than a father-figure. No doubt at all that some of my quests to capture the eternal love of impossible men were to get me back Daddy, for there is no doubt also that I had him, but good for at least the first six or seven years of my life.

I was born in a Bayswater nursing home in north west London, on

1

1933 May 23rd, sometime between the end of the Great Depression and
the beginning of the war. 'No woman should ever be quite accurate
about her age. It looks so calculating.' Thus spake Oscar Wilde!

According to my parents and relatives I was the world's most
adorable baby — but not with quite the personality to match.
Gemini children are mercurial and moody, charming and
delightful one minute, a pain in the ass the next. . .and I was
typical. My baby looks were such that my ever-vigilant mother
had a printed sign 'Please do not Kiss Me' displayed in my pram
whenever we took our morning strolls.

Beautiful bonny babies must have been rare in north London
then, for Mummy was constantly fighting off demented women
begging to kiss, hold, steal or adopt me. I was so over protected
that my mother even put ice cream in the oven for a few minutes
before I ate it so the chill should be off.

It was an idyllic infant and early childhood. We lived in a flat in
Maida Vale not far from Regents Park. Daddy worked at the
Collins and Grade Agency with Lew, and obviously adored Baby
Joan and Mummy. One of the reasons I was called Joan was because
they had really wanted a boy, to have been called Joe Jr no doubt,
and my name was the closest feminine equivalent. Throughout the
first fifteen years of my life, whenever my mother called 'Joe' I
would answer and vice versa. I seriously thought of changing it to
Paulette.

My adoration for my father was intense as a young child. At
nursery school I told the other kids that my father was the tallest
and handsomest man in the world. Handsome he was, with jet
black hair, naturally curly (yet he would slick it flat to his head
with three layers of Brylcreem), a Roman nose, and a finely
chiselled profile. Tall, well hardly. When the scales fell from my
eyes, one day, I realised my father was only about five foot nine!
There is a yellowing photograph in an old family album that
epitomises for me the idealistic father-daughter relationship. I am
four or five years old — gap-toothed — large bow in hair and
wearing a pretty sun suit in some far away summer vacationland,
sitting on the grass, legs neatly crossed and smiling happily. He is
suntanned, black-haired and smiling, grey-flannelled and sports-
coated holding in his hand a huge fishing net with which he is
about to catch the little girl. And she sits trusting and happy,
secure in love of the handsome man.

My mother was beautiful too. Blonde and blue-eyed, she had
the perfect Anglo-Saxon looks to complement my father's darkly
Jewish ones. As fair as he was dark, and as gentle and kind as he

2

was stern and strict, my memories of my mother have become fonder through the years. I was always stronger than she, and it irritated me that she was such a slave to my father's ways and whims. When Daddy became angry we all fled. His raised voice made us nervous for days.

My parents sent me to dancing school before I was three, and throughout the rest of my childhood I attended at least nine or ten different dancing academies as well as thirteen different schools. Before I was even old enough to go to kindergarten I would spend part of each morning listening avidly to the radio while my mother vacuumed, dancing and whirling like a dervish to the early morning radio programmes. In the days before radio music was only one continuous juke-box, the variety was infinite, and I would dance greedily to marches, classical music, brass band, Strauss waltzes and best of all, jazz. We would sing too. I had aspirations as a singer, as well as an actress — I think I know most of the words to every popular song ever written until Beatlemania took over!

Each Sunday we would get into Daddy's car. There was usually a new one each year — impeccably tuned, and drive. The boredom of those drives lives with me still. To this day, I'd rather go on a plane, train or helicopter than drive anywhere for longer than two hours. We would drive through the unspoiled English countryside to Brighton, where Daddy's mother lived, or to Bognor where Mummy's mother lived, or to Devon or Sussex or Kent where nobody we ever knew lived but it was 'a nice drive' and throughout all the drives I would sing and sing and sing!

My family was in 'showbiz' from way back. Even as a tiny girl my interest in movies, dancing and theatre was enormous. Later, radio caught my imagination and held me enthralled for years. Dick Barton! Paul Temple! Even now the mention of their names gives me a nostalgic pang. One's fantasies took over completely, listening to the dramatic dialogue and music. The exploits of Dick, Jock and Snowy were fodder for my bedtime thoughts.

My father was born in Cape Town, South Africa, in 1902 to a successful theatrical agent Will Collins and a saucy soubrette and dancer Henrietta Collins. Hetty must have been an early emancipated woman since she continued dancing with her sister act 'The Three Cape Girls' right up until a month or so before young Joe's birth. Considering Queen Victoria was still sitting stiffly on the throne this showed a remarkable lack of concern for convention, something I obviously inherited from her.

Photographs of her — hand on hip or posed in daring can-can costumes show a beautiful , strong-featured young brunette with a wilful look about her and a twinkle in her eye.

I remember Grandma Hetty as a lovely, laughing, gutsy lady, who taught me to dance and do the 'splits' and high kicks, and was always full of life, laughter and fun up until her death when she was in her eighties, and still vigorous. She encouraged me in my youthful aspirations as singer-dancer-actress, I still wasn't sure which it would be. She regaled me with stories of backstage life, and made it sound wonderfully exciting. A world peopled with clowns, dancing and make-believe. I could almost smell the greasepaint and the musty, dank backstage odour of the scenery when she talked.

She had two other children, Lalla and Pauline. Daddy, being the only boy, was obviously spoiled rotten as a child. Both his sisters adored him, as did Hetty, as subsequently did my mother Elsa and, of course, eventually me and Jackie. He had a long line of women all competing for his favours. And there's no doubt about it, he was a handsome devil, whom women found irresistible.

Both of Hetty's daughters went into the theatrical world, Pauline became, like Daddy, a theatrical agent, and Lalla, the blonde beauty of the family, became a dancer and one of 'Cochrans Young Ladies'. Among her compatriots were Anna Neagle and Jack Buchanan, with whom she had a mad romance. I obviously inherited some of her characteristics too!

Our flat was constantly full of amusing and vivacious people whom Daddy represented. Comedians, singers, soubrettes, conjurers and ventriloquists. A veritable procession of outgoing personalities congregated there. Daddy often played cards with them until the early hours; he played a mean game of poker which I learned from 'Kibbutzing' over his shoulder.

All of these fascinating people, perhaps to ingratiate themselves with Daddy and get more work, or perhaps because they believed it, would compliment Little Joan on her cute nose, eyes, or personality and usually ended the remark with 'of course you really should go on the stage you know.'

So the seed was planted, although the ground was still fallow.

Daddy was proud of me then, there was no doubt of that. He liked the fact that I was cute, bubbly and captivating, and he agreed with his friends that I did indeed have the makings of proper little actress, although he himself did not advocate the stage as a profession for young girls, having witnessed the

4

heartbreak and rejection so many of them suffered. But it became my secret dream to go on the stage. To be an actress.

I can't pinpoint exactly when I stopped being Daddy's little darling: it could have been when little baby Jackie arrived to take some of the attention away from me. It could have been that with the coming of the London Blitz in the early 40s we were speedily packed off to safer pastures in Brighton, Ilfracombe or Bognor, leaving Daddy alone in London to fend for himself. Oh how my mother worried about him! There was much demand for variety shows and entertainment during the war and he, not a man to twiddle his thumbs in the Sussex countryside, was hard at work organising his many clients.

The war years are a hazy blur of evacuation to new places — boarding with strange people and, horror of horrors, *constant* new schools. Shyness, something I had never suffered from previously, suddenly descended on me along with insecurities and doubts. New children at school whispering and giggling in the corner at the nervous new girl made me feel an outsider. Returning into my fantasy make-believe world of dolls, books, cinema and film magazines. And over all of it the terrible feeling of rejection imagining that if Daddy *really* loved me I wouldn't be away from him.

It was a sporadic existence. When the blitz and the bombings eased up, we would return to London for a few weeks or months. When the air raids started again we were woken in the middle of the night by Mummy and our nanny, bundled into 'siren suits' and down to the basement of the block of flats to fitfully sleep the night away with the sounds of distant exploding bombs and anti-aircraft fire echoing through the dark and smelly air raid shelter.

I was too young to understand how dangerous it really was; of how terrified my poor mother was. With a baby and a small girl to contend with, she was worried sick that anything would happen to us. Her ambivalent feelings of wanting to be with Joe, and yet having to expose her children to peril to do so, must have caused her anguish. So after a short or a long time in London, off we'd go again, to yet another sanctuary, and another new school, and another painful time of trying to make new friends again. And that was the beginning of my gypsy existence.

At the age of thirteen I was awkward, spotty, gawky, shy, boy-hating and introverted.

Convinced I didn't have any charms to capture my father's affection the way I had when I was a toddler, and now with the added horror of a baby brother, Bill, the family's new darling, I decided that there was only one way to regain his affection and make things the way they were, I decided to become a boy! The imminent onset of puberty was a disaster I was convinced couldn't *possibly* happen to me. Girls at school would discuss in hushed tones the horrors of the 'curse' or their 'period'. I searched the library in vain for an explanation of these ambiguities. With no explanation forthcoming from my parents, my vivid imagination could only fear the worst.

I accompanied my father to his favourite football games every Saturday afternoon, freezing to death in my boyish corduroy trousers, jumper and brightly striped Tottenham Hotspurs or Arsenal scarf. Waving my jacket and jumping up in hysterical joy every time somebody scored a goal. Trying, oh, so hard to please.

I really hated football. I couldn't comprehend the fascination of twenty-two unkempt, dirty men kicking a ball around a muddy pitch, whilst thousands of blokes in caps and mufflers cheered till they were hoarse. My loathing of football also extended to other active sports, with the exception of swimming at which I was good. My prowess at netball, lacrosse and tennis was atrocious. But I pretended enormous enthusiasm, and listened with fascination to the Saturday evening football results, hoping to impress my father.

Of course it didn't work. Bill, at two or three, was more fascinating than gawky little me. He pushed his toy cars and trucks happily around on the carpet, watched fondly by my parents, while I glowered at him, stuffed myself frustratedly with sausage rolls, and reaffirmed my vow yet again to become an actress.

I've never really been able to figure out what the word 'Love' means. In spite of two years of analysis and a week-end session at Actualizations, a workshop to explore human potential, my quests for love (I did a film with that title!) although usually successful at the time would leave me two or three years later with a question mark in my mind as to whether or not I had really loved that man as much as I thought I had at the time.

In the time that I spent at RADA, between the ages of fifteen and a half and sixteen and a half, I discovered the opposite sex in all their splendour and fell in love at least 20 times. Since this seemed to work out at a boy per fortnight, one gathers that a great part of the time I should have spent studying was spent in dithering daydreams about my current beloved. Some of the romances lasted as long as three or four months and some were mental one night stands. For this was the flirty fifties and God forbid a nicely brought up half Jewish girl would do anything as taboo as to 'go all the way'. Alas — there were only stolen kisses under the lamp post, furtive feels in the movies, and whispered undying protestations of love in the austere corridors of the Royal Academy.

It was unthinkable for a young girl to sleep with a boy then, and since our knowledge of sexual matters, not to mention birth control, was skimpy, it was an accepted fact between both sexes that you petted and necked, kissed and cuddled but saved the good part until you got married. However, after several months of these breathless and frustrating encounters, I realised that forbidden fruits were becoming more desirable, and had fallen madly and passionately in love with a delicious blond called Barry. He was 22, ancient by my standards, tall and slim, with a biting articulate wit which was very stimulating. He favoured grey flannels, pink or green open necked shirts and loud, but well cut sports jackets. He shared a flat with two other boys, James and Michael, in Ebury Street, and this alone was enough to set the pulses racing, as most of the boys I had been dating were teenagers and still lived at home. The flat at Ebury Street was a Mecca for the swingingest singles from RADA to the London School of Economics. Almost every Saturday a dozen of the most daring would gather to drink, dance and flirt. The boys would bring a bottle of gin or rum, and the girls would contribute themselves in their prettiest dresses, or some of the more avant-garde, like me, their sexiest slacks.

I was popular. David McCallum who was in my class, told me that the first girl he and the other boys in class noticed was me. I was quite conscious of my sex appeal. It was a novelty to be able to attract young men. However, my interest in them bloomed and faded as fast as the summer flowers. When I lost interest in one of them I immediately focused my attentions on another. This little game continued in different fashions for many years. It was a classic case of a young girl with a father complex, looking for affirmation of her desirability by enticing hard to get males.

The ones who flocked after *me* were of no interest, and this pattern continued more or less for years. I have always, with a few exceptions, chosen the 'Love object', been the pursuer, won the heart and ended the game. My span of interest and involvement lengthened as I became more mature, and from the brief mad weekly crushes at RADA, to my seven month first marriage to

Maxwell Reed, and thence to deeper and more involved affairs, they have successively lasted for a longer and longer period of time. My husband Ron Kass and I have now been together for over eight years, something which, at one time, I would have thought an impossibility.

Most of the men and boys I chose were difficult, unattainable, moody, unpredictable, sometimes unable to love or unable to give and that is *always* what made me interested. Not for me to be wooed and won; I was the wooer, and in doing so I was hurt many times.

Barry was probably homosexual, maybe bi-sexual, a fact I must subconsciously have known but refused to acknowledge. He was arrogant and aloof, and I panted after him like a puppy. It must have been a joke for his friends to see this popular and nubile sixteen-year-old trying every trick in her book to get him to fall. By now I was ready to lose my virginity, and I wanted him to be the one to accept it — but unfortunately he either didn't want it, or didn't know how to go about it. We spent hours locked in fiery embraces in his back bedroom at Ebury Street while I waited in fear and trepidation for him to DO IT! To do what I was vague about — my knowledge of sexual *matters* let alone sexual functions was negligible. I had a vague idea that something was put somewhere, but where and how was a giant mystery. And he was no help. His passionate kisses became sadistic bites and his caresses, painful grabs. His delights seemed to consist of hurting me physically as much as he could. His frustrations were probably greater than mine, for at 22 he must have had some experience. But what I touched was soft not hard, and what I felt was pain, sadness and emptiness. and a tremendous feeling of insecurity that I was unable to make him want me enough to perform life's most mystical and magical act.

Our encounters became more frenzied and agonising. He bit my lips so hard they bled. He punched and kicked me and threw me out of bed after abortive attempts at sex. I was covered in bruises from head to foot. But did I stop loving him? Negative. I was too stupid for that. 'It's my fault', I moaned to myself alone in my own bed. 'I'm not attractive enough, not desirable enough, not worthy enough to make him love me.'

Eventually, I decided I must try to forget him. I threw myself into work — studying the classic plays, going to the theatre and reading biographies of the great actors and actresses. I was determined to succeed in my profession and I had already been discovered. A modelling agency, Rosemary Chance, came to RADA to choose two girls for photographic modelling in women's magazines. I was one of the two they chose, and I was able, with the miserly salaries paid to a model, to get better tickets to the theatre and movies to which I went two or three times a week, buy myself some clothes and occasionally even take a taxi

I modelled for the illustrations of love stories in ladies' magazines. I portrayed a terrified teenager in a yellow turtleneck about to be raped by a madman in a haunted house. In another, a heartbroken teenager sobbing into her pillow when she discovers she is pregnant. 'I should be so lucky', I muttered cryptically to the astounded photographer. Although not exactly svelte, I modelled teenage clothes for the pages of *Woman* and *Woman's Own*. There was no such thing really as a teen market in the early 1950s. Jeans and casual gear as they are today, with a mass market geared to the billions, had not yet been discovered, so the clothes I wore in the photos were frumpy and dumpy, and altogether unflattering. I actually did wear jeans and workmen's plaid shirts bought from men's stores in the Edgware Road and Leicester Square. With these I featured giant gypsy gold earrings, from a stall outside Woolworths in Oxford Street, ballet shoes, from Anello & Davide in the Charing Cross Road, and a black polo necked sweater, a hand-me-down from my sophisticated aunt Lalla who bought it in Paris. This was an unusual costume then, and with my exotic maquillage — eyes rimmed with black pencil à la Barbara Goalen, the top model of the day — two-inch thick black eyebrows à la Liz Taylor, everyone's favourite actress, and long straight fringe and a pony tail, I was the focus of attention wherever I went. Leslie Bricusse — then a student at Cambridge — remembers seeing me at a pub in Kings Road and although he didn't know who I was, my image stuck with him.

Picture Post magazine did a photo story on jazz clubs and the first time my picture appeared in print was with my partner and then boyfriend, John Turner, as 'The couple who dress "très Jazz" '. I was unnamed in the photo, as I was also unknown, and it was only my crazy outfit that caused me to be noticed.

Jazz clubs and dancing were my favourite relaxation. Three nights a week, one or two or three girl friends would sit and listen ecstatically to 'Humph', Humphrey Lyttelton's Dixieland Band which played at 100 Oxford Street. Or we went to Wood Green or other outlying suburbs to catch other of our favourites, such as George Melly, Sidney Bechet and Claud Luter, who would come over from France. How exotic! 'Humph' was my favourite and I

9

sat mesmerised for hours as his trumpet played ragtime and jazz from an era that fascinated me — the Twenties — 'When the Saints Go Marching In', 'Jellyroll Blues', 'Hotter than That', and dozens of others. I danced non-stop for endless hours in the steamy cellar at 100 Oxford Street, stopping only for an innocent Coca Cola and a cigarette, and forgetting my complicated love life.

Though my formal education was sketchy as we moved constantly from school to school at the whim of my parents, Hitler and the Blitz, I had still attended dancing and ballet schools regularly every Saturday morning wherever we were. When I danced, Barry was banished to the back of my mind, although through the RADA grape-vine the word came to me that he missed me — was disappointed that I was distant and unavailable and that he had really liked having me around. I was good for his ego because I was so 'decorative'. I gritted my teeth and hung on. I wasn't going to call or come around to assuage his wounded ego and he was too proud to come off his pedestal to ask me. Stalemate.

One fine spring Saturday morning, the phone rang and himself, charm and flattery incorporated, begging, cajoling and teasing, asked me to come over to Ebury Street for Sunday tea. I was elated. I had won — he had called — he cared — he wanted me. I was lovable again!

On Sunday at 3.15 I presented myself at Ebury Street, tastefully attired in the black sweater, black jeans and silver sandals. Three bleary-eyed faces greeted me, Michael, James and Barry, unshaven and still in pyjamas. Empty bottles and overflowing ashtrays were everywhere, and the signs were evident that last night had not been an early one. But I was in heaven.

We chatted and joked and the past few weeks were forgotten and then Barry jokingly suggested I go to bed with Michael. I froze. I had to call his bluff — and I did not feel I had the winning hand. I smiled bravely and said OK why not. He'd thrown the gauntlet. If that's what he wanted me to do, I'd do it and maybe if he watched it would turn him on enough so he might be able to do it too. By this time the precious maidenhood I'd been carrying around for sixteen years was becoming a pain in the neck, and I was dying to become 'experienced'. Several of my girlfriends had recently been de-flowered, and recommended it highly!

Michael looked nervous. He coughed, blushed and looked to the Boss for what he was supposed to do. I was supposed to cry, scream and protest wasn't I? I provocatively sauntered up the stairs turning over my shoulder to murmur sultrily, 'Coming Michael?'

'No, he's bloody not,' said my blond-haired knight in tarnished armour, furiously. 'You bloody little slut, what the hell do you think you're doing, dirty little bitch. .!'

'But Barry *darling*,' I murmured sweetly, 'I want to make you happy. If you want me to go to bed with Michael I'll do it — for you.' I gave him my most sultry and adorable look, the ball was in my court and I was not about to lose the set.

'You're coming with me "Bitch",' he roared and grabbing my arm hustled me up the stairs and into back bedroom number two. How thrilling! It was going to happen at last. I could hardly believe it. He ripped off my jeans, tore off my sweater and threw me on the bed. And we were back to square one. Kissing, biting and hurting for three hours and the gentleman remained unaroused.

We tried. I summoned up every torrid episode I had remembered from *Forever Amber* and various erotic novels to try and stimulate him, but it was hopeless. At last, exhausted, depleted and ashamed we fell asleep.

When we awoke, it was ten o'clock and dark. The house was empty. Michael and James had gone to the pub and we were alone. He kissed me sweetly and told me he loved me and that everything was going to be all right. I was his girl and we were together again, and that was all that mattered. It was April Fools Day!

My career was starting to happen. One day the phone rang and a charming voice introduced himself as Bill Watts, a well-known agent, whose speciality was representing pretty young girls. He had seen my 'rape' pictures in *Woman's Own* and thought that I was a possibility for films.

I met him at his office in Dover Street which was completely covered in photos of young beauties in various stages of undress and bathing suits. He took me to a fancy lunch, and over the shrimp cocktail and chicken vol-au-vent told me that I had 'movie star potential'. 'But I want to be a *serious* actress,' I said seriously. 'Film stars can't act. They are usually discovered behind soda fountains or cosmetic counters. I want to finish my next year at RADA and then do several seasons in rep, and go on the stage. Films are not for me.' I sipped some more white wine and gazed at him challengingly.

My views were heavily coloured by RADA's attitude towards

the movie medium. Frankly they disapproved. Art was only possible in the theatre, and the emphasis was heavily on having the right voice, the right vowels and articulation, the right gestures and the proper classical attitudes. I quote one of my report cards from RADA. . .'with so much in her favour this student is hampered by the weakness of her voice. She seems to lack the confidence to project and make use of the amount of voice she does possess. If she will make up her mind to cast away all fear and self consciousness and speak out she will find her confidence increasing, and the unsure element in her acting will disappear. Otherwise it is "the Films" for her and that would be such a pity.' What irony!

Although I worked hard and diligently, my voice production and projection were constantly criticised by the teachers at RADA and instead of gaining confidence and getting better I became more inhibited. We had endless elocution and enunciation classes. Any dialect was taboo. An Albert Finney or Michael Caine wouldn't have stood a chance to grow as an actor until they learned the right Mayfair accent. We had to speak and act as though we were from the same cookie cutter, and consequently our true personalities and abilities were never really able to unfold. I was trying to talk and behave on stage like someone else: Pamela Brown or Vivien Leigh.

So I was snobbish about 'the Films' and it was only the persuasiveness of Bill Watts, and his insistence that doing a few movie roles would only enhance my ability and not hinder it that made me sign with his agency.

He worked fast. Within a week I was up for the leading role in a film called *Lady Godiva Rides Again* which was about the rise and fall of a beauty queen. I tested at Shepperton with several up and coming starlets, among them Joan Rice and Veronica Hurst. The girl who got the part, Pauline Stroud, was never to be heard from after this film.

The make-up man and hairdresser who coiffed me for Lady Godiva had learned their craft in the dark ages. A thick layer of orange pancake was applied to my cherubic face. 'She's moon-faced,' they said to each other laconically, so dark brown shading was plastered on my cheeks, pale blue eyeshadow on my lids and away with the doe eyes and the Liz Taylor eyebrows. Carmine lipstick completed the look. A cross between a teenage Joan Crawford and Nancy Drew.

No wonder I didn't get the lead. I did, however, win a supporting role as one of the contestants and spent three freezing

12

days in a black, boned bathing suit shivering in Folkestone Town Hall, along with other runners up, among them Jean Marsh and Violet Pretty, who later changed her name to Anne Heywood and went on to bigger and better things (as did Jean, with her portrayal of the maid Rose in *Upstairs Downstairs*).

I thought filming was uncomfortable and boring. Up at five am in the pitch dark, herded around like cattle by a harassed assistant director, freezing to death or boiling under the arc lights and listening to an incomprehensible jargon from the crew: 'Bring the dolly', 'save the baby', 'trim the arc ', 'where the fuck's Chippy', 'Action'. . .little did I realise that this was the lingo I was destined to hear throughout my life.

Soon after, Bill obtained a slightly better role for me as a Greek maid in a forgettable film called *Woman's Angles* starring Lois Maxwell, latterly Miss Moneypenny in the James Bond films. The money, a princely £50, helped me to buy more imitation gold earrings and polo necks, and the publicity helped me become even more of a celebrity at RADA where my amorous adventures were by now legendary!

I now had a double life: aspiring film starlet and dedicated drama student, and the British press were cottoning on to me fast: 'Britain's Best Bet since Jean Simmons' . . . 'She has the come-hither eyes of Ava Gardner, the sultry look of Lauren Bacall, a Jane Russell figure and more sex appeal at her age than any other film actress I've met,' raved *Reveille*, the working man's favourite paper.

But RADA did not approve. 'What's all this filming nonsense?' boomed Sir Kenneth Barnes, the austere and forbidding principal, as he blocked my way one morning with his Hitchcockian build. 'It's nothing serious, Sir,' I ventured timidly, trying to get by his bulk. 'I'm just doing it to make some extra pocket money.' 'Well just don't get carried away by it, my dear,' he said pontifically. 'When all is said and done there is only one thing that matters, and that's the theatah.' 'Right sir,' I agreed and scampered away to cut a class to go to a photo session at the *Daily Mirror*. To tell the truth, RADA was becoming a drag. I was sick of being told my voice was too breathy and my projection was too inhibited. In the plays we performed I was suddenly being given the roles of the 60-year-old aunt or the crazy Scandinavian maid — a form of revenge by the teachers who disliked my voice, I was convinced.

At the studios they told me I was gorgeous and sexy and the actors and the crew flirted with me and made me feel that I was talented and lovely. Bill Watts was my strongest supporter. Of all the agents I have had he is without a doubt the one who not only believed in my ability, but went out on a limb to tell everyone who needed to know how talented I was. It was his gutsy belief in me that got me over my debilitating self-consciousness about my voice and personality and made me realise that I had a lot more to offer than the staff at RADA believed.

I still saw Barry at the Academy. By now his homosexuality was common knowledge even though he was never seen openly with another boy. I still had very strong feelings for him which I couldn't seem to get over but at least my obsession had simmered down and was burning on a low level.

I stopped falling in love with such monotonous regularity and concentrated on myself for a change.

I was dating, intermittently, a boy called John Turner. John was six foot two, with brown wavy hair, kind eyes and the shoulders of a football player. He dressed in plaid shirts, which we bought together in Tottenham Court Road, jeans and a duffle coat. He was a very good actor and an all-round nice guy. We had a good relationship, based on a mutual liking of movies, theatre and music and dancing in the jazz clubs. My parents actually liked him and I did too although Barry was not completely out of my system. . .but I was still a virgin.

I took stock of myself. I never believed the 'Baby Ava Gardner' nonsense that the newspapers were spouting on about. I looked in the mirror and saw a big-eyed, round-faced, slightly spotty young girl, long, thin brownish hair — the bane of my life — at least eight pounds overweight. 'Life is a constant diet,' I groaned, pushing away the potatoes and the cream cakes and reaching for the Lucky Strikes. I drank too much — straight gin usually, smoked too much, in order to look sophisticated, and stayed up too late, either reading avidly until three or four in the morning or dating, so I had dark circles under my eyes. I started a beauty regime from which I have seldom deviated, and went on the first of 300 diets. 'If I'm England's answer to Marilyn Monroe,' I said, as I brushed my hair with a hundred strokes each night, 'I might as well start trying to act the part.' 'And if I get rid of my virginity, that may get rid of my spots too.'

I was enjoying my days at the studio — the camaraderie and rapport, especially that which exists among the members of a film unit. I always gravitated to the crew — their humour and wit appealed to me far more than the pedantic talk of box

14

office grosses and script problems that producers and directors indulge in.

On most of the movies I made on location, *Island in the Sun*, *Sea Wife*, *The Bravados*, *Our Girl Friday*, I would normally be found sharing my box lunches with the hairdresser and the camera crew rather than with the other actors. Although I like actors, I resented the fact that the leading man in a movie usually took it as his prerogative to have an affair with the leading lady, and some became quite offended when their advances were rejected. In 43 films I only became involved with one or two of my fellow actors.

It was time for my first important film role and the beginning of what was to become a series of teenage delinquent and 'good time girl' roles. The part of Lil in *Judgment Deferred*, a low budget thriller, made at Southall studios, was described as 'an exacting and emotional role of a one time beautiful young girl, a convict's daughter, ruined by the colourful and dangerous crowd in which she has sought pleasure — although so young for her emotional role, Joan comes through with flying colours'! Apparently Basil Dearden and Michael Relph felt so too — for soon after completing *Judgment Deferred* I went to Ealing studios, home of the money making comedies starring Alec Guinness, to make a test for Norma, the runaway juvenile delinquent in *I Believe In You*.

Dearden and Relph were a hot team as director and producer and had a string of successful credits, among them *The Blue Lamp* and *Kind Hearts and Coronets*, and whoever got this part was, according to Bill Watts, bound to become a star.

I had made several tests already for other films but they were all unsuccessful for me, usually due to my youth or my sultry looks — English roses were still in. One with Dirk Bogarde was especially exciting. I wore a pink baby doll night gown and slithered around on a vast satin double bed with him, doing lots of cinematic kissing and necking. I thought he was attractive and fun, but far too grown up for me. I was still involved with John Turner. It had lasted several months. Although we spent the night together when circumstances permitted, he was too much of a gentleman to take advantage of my by now encumbering virginity. And after the ghastly experiences with Barry I was not about to try and seduce him — so we hugged and kissed and kept it light.

My picture appeared on the front page of *Reveille* — my first cover! I was thrilled, more so when I was recognised while making a quick tour of the jewellery counter at Woolworths looking for more plastic bangles to add to my collection. Even though I was becoming known, and in demand, I was making not much more than £20 a week and a girl doesn't shop at Dior on that kind of money.

Although we were 'well off', Daddy wasn't exactly lavish with the lolly. Mummy had to save out of the housekeeping to buy herself little extras and although she was always well dressed and jewelled, I know how persuasive she had to be with my father to get the dresses and the hats and bags she wanted. I vowed at an early age that my desires for material things would never depend on the whims of a man. It was extremely important to me to become financially independent as soon as possible. In fact, throughout my entire life, through three marriages and affairs with rich men, I have always bought all my own clothes, furs and most of my jewellery, and paid most of my own bills.

Summer vacation started. One of my closest girl friends at RADA, Jackie, became pregnant and had the most horrific abortion at the hands of a Ladbroke Grove butcher. John went back to his parents in Nottingham for the holidays, and I made a third test for *I Believe In You*. One of the producers was hot and heavy for me and I got the message loud and clear that if I was 'nice' to him, the part would be mine. Since I was not about to be 'nice' even to those I was madly in love with, the thought of the sweaty embraces of this (to me) elderly gent was quite appalling. He was somewhere between 35 and 45 with long greasy hair, a florid complexion and a strong tendency to sweat profusely, especially when he came near me. I declined with as much grace as I could muster while he drove me home in his Jaguar after the test, and gloomily realised that I had probably blown the part — if not the producer! For the first time the realities of the casting couch started to materialise — the favours of pretty young things were barter, to be used to help them get up the ladder of fame and fortune, and if I was not to take advantage of these opportunities there were plenty of other girls who would be only too happy to oblige.

I had to make a decision, and I made it, and have NEVER gone against that original decision. I would not be 'nice to', 'sleep with' or even kiss anyone for a job or a part no matter how tempting the role that was offered.

When Buddy Adler, who was head of Twentieth Century Fox, to whom I was under contract, asked me in his own home if I would like to be the biggest star on the lot, I said 'Yes of course.' 'All you have to do,' and he smiled suavely as he manoeuvred me across the lacquered dance floor of his Beverly Hills mansion, 'is be nice to me, and the plum parts at the studio will be yours.' 'What do you mean exactly by "be nice" Mr Adler?' a worldly and sophisticated 22-year-old Joan asked warily. 'Listen, honey,' he held me closer in the dance and whispered in my ear. 'You're a beautiful gal and I'm not exactly an ugly old man — in fact a lot of ladies find me very attractive!' He smiled conspiratorially. I looked at him. Over six foot, tanned, silver hair, and at least old enough to be my father. 'We'll see each other a couple of times a week, you can still have your own life and I'll have mine, of course.' He glanced over to his attractive blonde wife Anita Louise, 'And you'll have your pick of the scripts.'

'Mr Adler,' I moved away frostily. 'I came here with my agent, Jay Kanter, why don't we discuss the deal with him?' He looked surprised and then he laughed. 'Honey, you have quite a sense of humour.' 'You bet your ass I have,' I muttered to myself, as I went to regale Jay with this sweet story, 'and my sense of humour is about all you'll ever get from me.'

But at seventeen I wasn't quite as sure of myself and I was convinced that by my coolness to the producer I would not get to play Norma. I left for a short holiday in Cannes with my sister Jackie, and my Aunt Lalla and threw myself into getting tanned and terrific in a bikini. Sidney Bechet and Claude Luter were playing in Juan Les Pins and I was able to continue my favourite sport — dancing. When the telegram arrived. 'Dear Joan, thought you would like to know you have got the part signed Basil Dearden.' I was ecstatic — this was a major film at a major studio and the chance to play with some fine actors: Celia Johnson, Cecil Parker, Harry Fowler and Laurence Harvey. Bill Watts called me, 'Come home, all is forgiven,' he joked — 'You start shooting in two weeks.'

The costumes I wore in *I Believe in You* were sordid and sleazy. Anthony Mendleson, the costumier, believed in realism, so we toured the second-hand clothing shops of the East End until we finally found the appropriate clothes. I was convinced I would pick up a rare venereal disease from trying on these outfits, some of which still bore the distinctive odours of their original owners, but the final effect was splendidly delinquent. For my opening scene I wore a brown sateen dress with a low neck and short puffy sleeves — it was ten years old and had probably been worn by its owner for a great deal of that time. It went to the dry cleaners three times before we got rid of the smell. My long hair was

17

covered in olive oil to make it lank and greasy and flopped sadly on my shoulders. I had vermilion lipstick, rhinestone earrings and down-at-the-heel ankle-strap shoes. I looked like a pathetic little cockney tart, and Dearden and Relph were very pleased.

I posed for innumerable publicity pictures — in bikinis — in shortie nighties — in bras and suspender belts — in shorts and the ubiquitous black polo neck. I now had a new item in my wardrobe from Juan les Pins — flat sandals with leather thongs that laced to the knees — a stunning look but impossible to dance in, as the laces kept dropping and twice I fell flat on my face in front of the adorable Humph! I was a minor celebrity — I opened fêtes, attended garden parties and went to premieres, all for the great God — publicity!

The first day we shot my most difficult scene. Cecil Parker, as a Truant Officer, finds me hiding in his apartment having escaped from reform school. I had to cry hysterically and I did, over and over and over again. At the end of the day I had cried for 60 different takes. Sometimes the tears were real and sometimes the make-up artist, dear old Mr Wilson, blew crystals in my eyes. Basil Dearden seemed happy with my performance, but he was somewhat austere and since I had always had enormous difficulty in communicating with older men, my shyness and nervousness and desire to excel in this film made me a bumbling and respectful slave to him. I could never call him Basil as the others did. He was, throughout the eight weeks shooting, 'Mr Dearden'.

Celia Johnson was a gifted, sensitive actress whose most memorable film performance was in Noel Coward's *Brief Encounter* with Trevor Howard. She was extremely kind and thoughtful towards me, helpful and patient. She played my Probation Officer and our scenes together were really enjoyable.

And then there was Larry, Laurence Harvey, or to give him his full Lithuanian name, Larurshka Skikne. He was flamboyant, eccentric, gifted, extrovert; he smoked endlessly; drank white wine incessantly; drove dashing cars; wore elegant and expensive suits; told fabulously witty, naughty stories; and I became instantly smitten. He epitomised a life style to which I knew I could become accustomed: the rich, fast life of the Ivy, the Caprice, international travel, sophisticated parties, and scintillating conversation. He took me under his wing. 'I'm going to educate you little girl,' he told me, sipping a vintage claret at La Rue, while a tinkling piano in the background played Gershwin medleys. Elegant women in black strapless cocktail dresses flirted delicately with suave, lounge-suited men, and red-coated waiters hovered discreetly. 'To have the only things in life that really matter' — that was Larry's policy. And so he did. He tried to teach me how to dress, and to make the most of my physical appearance. He tried to educate me about wine and the best of French cuisine but he did not try to teach me about life's greatest mystery. He had a zest for living that was unparalleled and yet underneath was a deep sadness that perhaps he was not all the man he should have been.

I didn't know it but he was living with Hermione Baddeley at the time. When he asked me to a party at 'Toties', I innocently said 'Yes'. Immediately we arrived she approached saying, 'So this is the one you're seeing, Larry, is it? This is the "the new Jean Simmons".' She gave me a sarcastic look up and down not missing a detail, her red curls bobbing, a cigarette hanging from carmine lips. 'Let me tell you my dear, Jean has absolutely nothing to worry about — you don't have her looks — you don't have her talent — and you certainly don't have half the things the newspapers have been saying you have.' I burst into tears and rushed to the front door to escape her tirade. 'That's right, leave,' she cried. 'No guts, that's the trouble with you young ones today — no guts at all!'

Larry caught up with me in Park Lane and tried to smooth things over. 'Don't worry darling, she's drunk — she doesn't mean it — I really want you two to be friends.' 'Oh, Larry,' I sobbed, 'I'm so humiliated — please take me home.' He plonked me in a cab, gave the driver a pound and me a paternal kiss on the forehead, told me he loved me and went back to the party.

I went home and cried myself to sleep. My fragile ego had again been crumpled. If a woman as talented and professional as Hermione Baddeley thought I was untalented and unattractive, maybe I really was. I was quick to believe the worst about myself — especially if it was from someone I respected. Highly sensitive to criticism, I seemed to spend my life trying to do everything to please everybody. Consequently not only did I not please myself, but I was so busy being what the other person wanted me to be that I almost assumed another identity. This was especially true of my more neurotic boy friends. When I was with Barry (whom I still occasionally saw — masochist me) I became a non-person — a slave — my moods matched his. If he wanted to be quiet, I was quiet as a mouse. If he wanted to tell funny stories and be rowdy I did too — anything to make him care. But Barry was seldom in my thoughts these days as I plunged into the exciting life of a rising film actress.

19

2

Gemini Misunderstood

The J. Arthur Rank organisation were the most powerful and prolific film makers of the 1950s and 1960s. For several years they had put young actors and actresses under contract for between twenty and fifty pounds a week and 'groomed' them for stardom. This 'grooming' was somewhat like going back to drama school but with great emphasis on externals, such as charm, posture, elegance and animation. A 'charm school' had been formed but was now disbanded, and dozens of eager young thespians had received the dubious benefits of what that had offered. Among them were Honor Blackman, Susan Shaw, Petula Clark, Patricia Roc, Kieron Moore and Maxwell Reed.

Maxwell Reed was my childhood fantasy hero. From the time I first saw him smouldering on a Sicilian island with Patricia Roc in *The Brothers* to the night that Larry Harvey introduced us at La Rue, I had had a tremendous schoolgirl crush on him. I also adored Montgomery Clift, Gene Kelly and Richard Widmark, but Max epitomised all my adolescent fantasies. He looked divine gazing out of the cover of *Picturegoer* in 1949, black brooding eyes, thick wavy black hair, lips cruel, thick and wet in anticipation of Margaret Lockwood or Phyllis Calvert. 'You'll probably marry him one day' said my closest school chum, Diana, confidently. 'He's so gorgeous, almost as handsome as Gregory Peck.'

'Oh, he's much better than Greg Peck,' I said, as I lovingly Sellotaped his smouldering countenance to the inside of my desk. 'But I'm never going to get married you dope, I'm going to be a famous successful actress and have lots of lovers.'

Diana looked disapproving so I changed the subject, but my fascination with Maxwell Reed never waned. When I looked up at him that autumn night in La Rue my heart literally leaped into my mouth. There he was in a white-on-white shirt, white tie with the biggest 'Windsor knot', navy blue pin stripe suit with the widest shoulders and the narrowest peg top trousers — and polished winkle-picker shoes.

A schoolgirl's dream come true, and he smiled at me so sexily that I blushed from head to my toe. He had an American accent, which was odd for a man from South London, and he bought me a whisky and coke and chatted about Hollywood from where he had just returned after starring in a Universal swashbuckler with Ann Blyth.

I was heavily impressed. This was the real thing — a real live handsome famous film star, and he was flirting with *me*! I felt inadequate and badly dressed. I was earning thirty pounds a week on *I Believe in You* and was starting to invest some of it in a suitable wardrobe, but my sense of style was still underdeveloped in spite of Larry's tutoring, and I was wearing a matronly green and gold brocade dress with puffed sleeves and a Peter Pan collar, black patent high heeled shoes and some imitation pearl earrings. This was hardly what Ava Gardner would have worn, but dressing well takes time, energy and a sense of style which would take a few years to develop. Max seemed to like what he saw anyway, and after he ditched the girl he was with, he came and joined us for drinks. He and Larry had recently made a movie together — and were good buddies.

I had an early call at Ealing and since I didn't drive and couldn't afford a hire car I would have to be up at 4.30 to get to the studio by 6.30, but this did not detract from my enjoyment of this thrilling evening. I smoked half a packet of Lucky Strikes, drank many whiskies and coke and tried to be witty, scintillating and sophisticated. I didn't want him to know I was only seventeen as I thought a thirty-three-year-old man would have no interest in a girl of that age — and especially a virgin to boot. How naive I was!

At 7.30 the next morning the phone rang in the make-up department and a sultry American accent came on the line. 'Hi Baby,' he drawled, 'howsit going?' We chatted for a few minutes and then he asked me out. I knew it would cause trouble at home if he came to pick me up. Going out with Larry who was only in his twenties had driven my parents mad at first, until they realised what a gentleman he was and could be trusted with their precious daughter, but a man in his thirties — a man with a reputation as a swinger, womaniser (and, as I found out later, a pimp), this my mother could never have accepted. I arranged to meet him the following Sunday outside Bayswater tube station.

I was in an agony of indecision for the next two days as to what to wear — casual or formal? Jeans or brocade dress? My choices were limited but going out with such a man of the world I felt I had to at least complement him.

I finally chose out of safety my 'uniform' of the day. . .a tight, black gabardine skirt with slits up the side, a sleeveless and very low necked tight black sweater, cinched in by a wide black patent leather belt that accentuated my 22-inch waist, black stockings and ~~bound to see us together and report back to Daddy who seemed to~~ three bangles instead of my usual ten and my smallest gold gypsy earrings — completed what I thought of as a sophisticated look. My toilette took three hours. I was terribly nervous, almost as nervous as I was before the first day's filming of *I Believe In You.*

Would I be interesting enough to hold his attention for the evening? Would he think I was too immature and be bored by my conversation? Where were we going to go? If we went to any restaurant or club in the West End or Soho someone would be bound to see us together and report back to Daddy who seemed to have spies everywhere.

I was so nervous I smoked eight Lucky Strikes just while applying make-up and my hands were shaking so much I could hardly get my eyeliner on. My mother bade me a fond and approving 'Goodnight have a good time darling'. I had told her I was going to a party with Larry and then to a club so for her not to worry. Larry was seeing 'Totie' that evening so I doubted that he would phone. All I had to worry about were my looks, my personality, my figure and my conversation, all of which I was convinced were way under par.

I took the tube from Baker Street to Bayswater Station, a major mistake, as I got leered and leched at all the way in my provocative outfit and arrived at my destination in a frenzy of nerves and fifteen minutes early.

He arrived twenty minutes late, by which time I was convinced he would never appear and I would have to go and drown my sorrows in gin at a nearby pub, owned by my best friend Beryl's father.

I peeked in my compact for the 300th time and lo and behold a gigantic sleek powder blue American Buick drew up to the kerb and there he was!

'Get in Baby,' he drawled, not bothering to get out and open the door. I had become so used to Larry's impeccable manners that I was slightly taken aback for a second, but I jumped in obediently and we drove off into the London traffic.

He was casually dressed in a black open-necked shirt and trousers but seemed friendly and glad to see me. We smoked Luckies and drove through Hyde Park. I had never been in an American car before and was interested in its gadgety interior. Larry drove an elegant old Bentley and the other boys I had dated either had no cars or drove battered MGs or Triumphs. 'Bill would really love this car,' I trilled, referring to my seven-year-old brother. 'He's mad for cars.' I realised how boring that must have sounded and cast desperately around for some wittier dialogue. He gave me a sleepy-eyed Robert Mitchum look, 'Oh yeah, we must give the kid a ride one day.' How considerate, I thought, film stars are human beings after all. There was some more silence and I smoked furiously whilst thinking of a suitable subject. A tongue-tied, seventeen-year-old virgin, I thought bitterly, he must be so bored.

We had been driving for about twenty minutes and I paid no attention to where we were going, but suddenly realised that we had just been driving round Hyde Park all the time. 'Where are we going?' I ventured to say. He shot me another Mitchum look. 'You'll see, Baby , it'll be a surprise.'

I sat back expectantly. I liked surprises and he probably knew some exciting clubs and dives. In the 1950s in London, many clubs were situated in unusual places: lofts, cellars, in apartment buildings and in houses, so when we drew up outside an old Georgian house in Hanover Square, I did not find this strange. 'What's this place?' I said gaily. 'The Country Club — Baby, come on up.' We walked up four flights of stairs past empty office suites and at the top came to a door which he unlocked with a key.

I was slightly puzzled because there were no sounds of conversation or music, but when the door opened it all became clear.

Up yet another flight of stairs, these now carpeted in thick crimson carpet, and we entered what was obviously somebody's apartment, and when I took a good look through my starry eyes, I realised it was Max's. Instant panic gripped me — this was very tricky. This was no Barry who couldn't make it — this was not polite, gentlemanly John Turner who would never take advantage of my innocence, or urbane, sophisticated Larry Harvey to whom sexual matters were unimportant. We hadn't even had dinner and Max had brought me to his flat already. I tried to hide my nerves by examining some of the interesting pieces of furniture and objects scattered around. The flat was decorated in Medieval-Spanish-Hollywood style. There was a lot of crimson velvet and

23

gold braid, purple silk lampshades on six-masted schooner lamps, some carved wood throne-like chairs and three or four Impressionist oil paintings. Oh, there was also, I saw out of the corner of my eye, a sort of sofa bed against the far wall which appeared to be covered in a zebra-skin rug and three thousand velvet cushions.

'I'm going to have a bath,' said Maxwell Reed casually, as if this was a perfectly ordinary thing to do on your first date. 'Do you want a whisky and coke?' I nodded numbly. I needed a drink desperately and his having a bath would give me a chance to think about the situation, which seemed to be fraught with dangerous possibilities. He was obviously going to try and seduce me. The flat was an absolute love nest. Subdued lighting, sexy paintings, everything seemed designed to set the scene for an orgy — and I didn't know this man.

All my mother's dire prophecies came flooding into my mind, 'Men only want ONE THING.' She had drummed that into me since I was twelve . . . when I had asked her what the word 'fuck' meant. I had seen it written on railway carriage walls and toilets. I had gone to the Public Library and looked it up in every dictionary I could find but there was no such word apparently. We were walking down Oxford Street one Saturday morning when I asked the question and my mother threw a mini-fit, grabbed me against the wall of Dolcis' shoe shop and hissed at me vehemently, 'Don't you ever say that word — that's a terrible word. I told your father that if he ever said that word I would divorce him.' So that was the end of finding out what the word 'fuck' meant literally. And although I naturally found out a few years later what it *meant*, it seemed now that I could be on the verge of finding out what it was like figuratively.

Maxwell interrupted my thoughts as he pressed into my hand an immense Spanish goblet full to the brim with my favourite scotch and coke and into the other a slim book in a brown cover. 'Make yourself at home, Baby, and have a read while I have a bath,' he said, sitting me down in a purple velvet chair. 'I won't be long' — he disappeared and left me to my thoughts. I took a huge swallow of the drink which tasted slightly different than the usual scotch and coke mix, but different brands of whisky had different tastes and I didn't worry about it too much. I had other things to think about.

I opened the book and gasped. It was an illustrated volume of extremely explicit and detailed drawings of men and women having sex. I had never seen anything like this before and my mind boggled at some of the different and peculiar positions they were in. I finished the drink, and started to feel very strange indeed, and then nothing — total oblivion — I was out.

I came to, to find Max and me entwined on the sofa. I was feeling violently ill and could barely keep from vomiting. 'I'm going to be sick,' I gasped. 'There I'll get the bucket again,' he said, and pushed my head into a cleaning woman's old tin pail.

'Again!!!' I thought through the waves of nausea. 'Again — have I been sick before then?' I threw up endlessly it seemed and lay back drained on the zebra skin.

I realised that I had finally 'done it' and that I had not even been conscious — only the pain and the blood were evidence. Max turned on the television set but it was dark — 'Telly's finished for the night,' he said, passing me a Lucky Strike. 'What do you mean — what time is it?' I said. If the TV had closed down for the night that meant it was after 11 pm and I had been here for over three hours. Doing What? Oh God, I can't remember!

I passed out again and came to with him trying to push a strange soft object into my mouth. 'I can't! Stop it!' I tried to say — the nausea rising uncontrollably — 'Please, please, don't — I'm going to be sick again.' I staggered weakly away from the bed and the debris and tried to find the bathroom.

My favourite black sweater was ripped and lying on the floor, next to a crumpled heap of clothes. My stockings were torn and the clasp had been ripped off my bra. He turned and smiled at me lazily when I returned and patted the couch. 'Come here Kid,' he said, 'and lie down, I think we both got a little more than we expected.'

'What did you expect?' I moaned as I fell exhausted on to the couch.

'Well, I gave you a bit of a Mickey Finn to make you feel sexy,' he smiled, inhaling deeply. I listened horrified. 'Larry told me you were a virgin but I didn't really believe him. . .gorgeous little seventeen-year-old birds like you don't stay virgins for long in this business Baby. Did you like it?' he turned to me and my pallid and tear-streaked face. I looked at him dumbly. I hurt — it was horrible — degrading and demeaning — and that *thing* he wanted me to put in my mouth — my stomach turned over and I reached for the bucket again. It was even worse than my mother had led me to expect. Were there actually women who *liked* doing this sort of thing. — and women who got paid for it? It was all too much for me in my weakened state and I drifted off into a fitful sleep.

25

I felt him start touching me and then entering me and I felt nothing — not even pain. I felt foul and used and exhausted and I slept on while he continued to — — what??? — well no wonder 'fuck' was considered a dirty word.

I came to again to find him making me drink some strong coffee.

'Come on Kid,' he urged, 'gotta get you home to Mummy and Daddy. Are you working tomorrow?' I nodded numbly — I had a 6.00 call.

'It's after three' he said. 'Come on girl, up at'em.' I panicked. My parents would wait up for me even though they pretended to be asleep, as soon as the clock struck two and I wasn't home, Mummy would be pacing the floor.

He helped me into my torn and tattered finery. The stockings were a write-off so I didn't even bother to put them back on. My face was a disaster. I stared at it in horror in my compact mirror — mascara-stained cheeks, caked foundation and smeared lipstick. I lurched into the bathroom and washed everything off with soap and water and then shakily applied some lipstick and tried to comb my hair. I couldn't think about what had happened. I still felt incredibly ill and I was getting nervous thinking about Mummy and Daddy's reactions.

He helped me on with my coat and took my arm to guide me down the endless flights of stairs. We said very little. He kept giving me his laconic Robert Mitchum look as he drove me home to Harley House which was luckily only about seven minutes drive from Hanover Square at that hour.

'Stop before you come to the entrance,' I squeaked nervously as we approached the grim Victorian outlines of the flats where we lived. 'I'll get out here.' He leaned over me to open the door. 'Will I see you again, Baby?' he said, putting his hand under my skirt. 'Of course,' I gulped, nervously pushing his hand away. 'I'll give you a bell in a couple of days,' he said, then kissed me perfunctorily on the cheek and zoomed off into the deserted streets.

I staggered into Harley House. I heard the voices raised and the phone ringing even before I put my key in the door.

We had lived in this huge basement flat for several years. It looked out onto busy Marylebone Road and got very little daylight, but it was big and spacious enough for three kids and was also just behind Regents Park. I opened the heavy oak door and my mother rushed forward and grabbed my arm. . . .'Your father's furious with you!' she hissed. 'Where have you been? I've called everyone, and *why* are you home so late?' I looked at the grandfather clock in the hall. It was indeed now half past three and I would have to be up in an hour to take the train to Ealing. 'I've been to a party with Larry,' I said feebly trying to muster up some power in my voice.

'Your mother called Laurence Harvey,' said my father coming out of the bedroom and tying the knot in his red and blue striped dressing gown. 'He said he had not seen you tonight, and did not know where you were — so where the hell have you been?'

When my father shouted at me like that my stomach went cold and I got a weak feeling in the back of my knees. He truly scared me to death when he was so angry. He had never actually hit any of us, or used any physical violence at all, but his temper was so strong and his anger so fierce that he often threatened to 'beat the daylights out of you' and although he actually never did, it was a threat that we kids thought could come true if we behaved badly enough. I think now that it would have been better if he had occasionally hit us — because it couldn't have hurt us that badly — it was the constant threat that he *might* that was so terrifying.

'Larry was terribly worried,' said Mummy, trying to smooth things over as usual. 'He called some of the people at the studio to see if you were with them, but they didn't know where you were either.' 'So where were you?' said Daddy, 'You'd better tell us, or you'll be here all night.'

I looked at the clock and for one wild moment felt like shrieking at them, 'I've been drugged and raped and abused by a thirty-three-year-old degenerate film star so you can both go to hell!'

But my courage was waning. Instead I tried histrionics and hysterics, which sometimes worked. I needed to lie down and have a bath before I left in 45 minutes for the two hour trip to the studio and time was running out. 'I went to Beryl's father's pub,' I sobbed in my mother's arms. 'And we had a few drinks and went over to Wood Green jazz club. We met some friends from RADA and went back to their flat to play some records. I was having so much fun I didn't realise the time.' My shoulders were racked with sobs as my mother rocked me gently. My crying had become real. I was very, very upset. As the realisation of what had happened dawned on me I felt abused and dirty.

This garbled explanation seemed to satisfy my father. He barked a few more terse sentences about 'disowning me ' and went back into the bedroom. Mummy walked back to my room with me. I badly wanted to tell her what had happened. I needed comfort and advice — I needed to be mothered in fact — but I could never trust my mother completely because she sometimes repeated what I said or did either to my father or one of her girl friends. Besides, if I told her, she would be absolutely horrified, and convinced yet again that 'Men only want one thing' and would forbid me to ever see Max again. I needed time to think.

I kissed her goodnight and ran the bath. I scrubbed my body thoroughly, washed my hair, cleaned my teeth for ten minutes, put on jeans, sweater and duffle coat and, after making a strong cup of instant coffee, slipped out of the front door again and into the dark and silent streets of Marylebone Road. I walked swiftly for five minutes to Baker Street. In the 1950s a girl could walk around London streets in the dark and not be concerned with muggers or rapists. Having been raped once that evening already, the odds were against it.

I sat in the railway carriage and looked at my face in the mirror. I tried to analyse if I had changed. A workman in paint-stained overalls was looking at me. 'I wonder if he can tell,' I thought to myself, 'that I'm not a virgin.' My face looked the same — there was no change — the circles under the eyes were darker but that was lack of sleep. I looked young and vulnerable. But I felt I had ended a chapter of my life. I didn't feel like a girl any more.

There was no such thing as 'the Pill' in England yet. I needed to talk to a woman to find out what I had to do. I spoke to Ursula Howells, an actress in *I Believe in You*, about my experience. She was highly sympathetic and concerned — especially about my becoming pregnant. Horrors! that hadn't occurred to me. But since it seemed there was nothing I could do about it now, like Scarlett in *Gone With the Wind* I would have to 'think about that tomorrow'.

I worked hard all day. At the end of the day I went to wardrobe where they outfitted me in a delicious gold brocade dress worn by Audrey Hepburn in her first film and the publicity boys took me to Ciro's Club where *Photoplay* magazine were holding their annual Christmas party, although it was still only autumn. Many stars were there, among them Anthony Steel who had that summer followed my sister, Jackie, and myself all through the streets of Cannes, Dinah Sheridan, Kenneth More, and Kay Kendall to name but a few. I had gone out with Steel a couple of times and he seemed quite nice but drank too much. Besides I had thought that I didn't really like older men.

Max was turning out to be an exception, however. He had called me at the studio in the afternoon and asked if I was free for dinner that night. After the party I went to the Caprice, London's most exclusive theatrical restaurant, and met him. Why did I go and meet him with the ghastly events of last night still fresh in my mind? I was probably flattered that he still wanted to see me after having 'had his way with me' as my mother would have put it. And I wanted to prove to myself that I was not just an object — a thing to be used and discarded at a man's whim. I was frightened at the possibility of being rejected by him after he had seduced me. The only way to win was to play the game, and try to pretend that last night had not really happened.

I also apportioned much of the blame to myself. I shouldn't have dated him in the first place. When I saw I was in his flat I should have gotten the hell out of there. I could twist this incident in my mind to such an extent that it could all become my fault totally, but most of all I was still curious about him as a person, since our conversation last night had been negligible.

That day the studio had given me a special coiffure and I thought I looked grown up and glamorous. We made an arresting couple and I was made aware of that fact. He was witty that evening, telling jokes and anecdotes about his life in the Merchant Navy, his days with the Rank Organisation and his recent trip to Hollywood. I was fascinated to hear first hand about Hollywood, as there had been some talk of me going there to do a movie with Bob Hope — Bill Watts was keeping me informed as to the progress of this project. Unfortunately it didn't happen as the producers thought I was too young to play opposite Bob, but I did appear with him and Bing Crosby several years later in the last of 'the Road' pictures, *The Road to Hong Kong*.

Max had a good sense of humour — a trait which has always appealed to me strongly and I was in fits of laughter all night. The previous night was not mentioned and, apart from some discomfort, it was almost as though it hadn't happened. Another part of my fantasy life. He took me home and acted in a very gentlemanly way as he kissed me goodnight. I think he was feeling some self recriminations about what he had done but we avoided the subject.

During the next month we saw each other constantly. I became very, very involved — in fact, I fell in love, but he was exceedingly moody. We had days of lighthearted fun — boating, going to movies and theatres and dancing all night — and then for three or four days he would be in a black mood — surly and vile, snarling, cruel, sadistic and sarcastic. It was hard for me to understand these sudden changes of mood, but I put up with them as well as I could, as I had strong guilt feelings about his having 'deflowered

29

me'. And also because my childhood dream was coming true — I was dating famous, handsome, favourite movie star, Maxwell Reed. As far as sex went in our relatonship, I gritted my teeth and tolerated it. In fact I found it really boring without a flicker of pleasure.

In the days before *Cosmopolitan* magazine told you how to have the most thrilling sexual adventures — before Masters and Johnson published their theories on the female orgasm and sexual freedom — before the sexual revolution of the 60s — sex was something a girl just did not discuss or think about too much. I realise now that Max was not a considerate lover. And since there were certain things he liked to do which, after that first night, simply revolted me — I tolerated the love making because I thought I was in love with him, and because I genuinely thought that this was the way things were *supposed* to be. It wasn't until several years later that I started to get any real pleasure from sex. Luckily for me the couch on which we usually made love faced the TV set, which was usually on, so I was able to concentrate on something else. It was ironic that at this time I was being hailed as 'Britain's Best Bet for Stardom' and the sexiest thing in a bathing suit that the usually dreary British papers had ever seen. I was constantly doing publicity photographs — which appeared in papers and magazines and the emphasis on all these stills was always on my sex appeal. Little did those who saw them realise that this 'Pocket Sized Ava' or 'Rival to Jane Russell' was a frightened, frigid little girl underneath the smouldering exterior.

Max started to write a film to star the two of us, about pirates and princesses in the South Seas. I was excited. I was still shooting *I Believe In You*, still going to jazz clubs, visiting RADA to see my friends and observe the plays, doing interviews and publicity and seeing Max two or three times a week. I was very, very busy, with little time to think.

I have always been able to do two or three times the amount of activities the average person can do. I have enormous energy and wake up practically every day wanting to take life by the balls! And this was a frantic and exciting period for me. J. Arthur Rank were getting interested in signing me to a seven-year, exclusive contract. They had seen the rushes of *I Believe In You* and obviously liked what they saw. Bill Watts was negotiating with them. Hollywood had made a couple of nibbles — I was getting hot.

When the rumour got back to my parents that I had been seeing

Maxwell Reed, they were livid. But Max assured them that he was only educating me in the problems of being a star, that he was my mentor and not my lover, and that our relationship was totally platonic. Luckily they believed him. He was as convincing a liar as I had ever seen.

After several months he started to talk to me about moving in with him. I was thrilled at the idea — his apartment was cosy and fun and I was fed up with the rules and regulations I had to conform to at home. Daddy was very strict and I had to be home at one o'clock every night or there had to be a good reason why. But it still seemed premature. Although Max had told me he loved me, in the back of my mind I knew there was something vitally wrong with the relationship.

He started to suffer bad back pains, sometimes after lovemaking and he would be doubled up in agony. Naturally, he blamed me for causing this but we didn't really know the cause. He had started talking to me about marriage seriously now, since living together didn't seem possible, but I was still resistant and unsure.

One day he was in such severe pain that his brother, Clive, called a doctor right away. The doctor examined him and sent him immediately to the hospital. The next day when I phoned the doctor he told me Max had a slipped disc and would probably have to be operated on. It was upsetting for both of us — but expecially for Max — for after the operation he found he had a total loss of feeling in his lower body. The whole area had become completely numb.

The doctors assured him it was only temporary, that the nerves had been severed during the operation but that in a few months they would heal, but it put him into the blackest and foulest of moods and he consistently accused me of causing his injury. This was totally unfair because I never instigated lovemaking and in fact went to lengths to avoid it. But it was no good — I was the villain and the cause of the whole problem.

My guilt was immense, however. As he ranted and raved, screamed and berated me because he had not made a film for several months, because he was short of cash — and for every possible thing that went wrong, I was the scapegoat.

He definitely wanted to marry me even more now, but I felt dubious as to the likely longevity of our marriage. I was still only seventeen and extremely immature mentally and emotionally in spite of my physical appearance. My emotions veered between ecstasy and misery with very little in between. There is a very fine

31

line between love and hate, and I was treading it.

Because of his disability Max could now only get aroused by being exceedingly sadistic and cruel to me. Since I was frightened of him I went along with the beatings and the perversions he thought up. He insisted I pose for some nude photographs which he thought might turn him on. My pity for him was intense — and my guilt — but the more he hurt me physically, the more excited he became. I tolerated it because I hoped it would only be temporary and that when he regained his feelings he would stop. He kept telling me how much he desired me and how difficult it was for him and how I must understand his pain and I, poor fool, went along with it.

My contract with the J. Arthur Rank organisation was signed. I was the first actress Rank had put under contract for over a year and they went to town on a build-up for me. Every day I did some sort of publicity, and every other day the papers had something to say about me, good, bad or sarcastic.

Rank's contract was probably based a lot on my personal reviews for *I Believe In You*. Although some of the critics were lukewarm towards the movie, most of them had high praise for my potential. Jympson Harmon, one of the top critics, wrote in his review, 'Joan Collins makes a tremendous impression as the wayward girl. She has a dark luscious kind of beauty which puts her in the Jane Russell class, but Joan already seems to be an actress of greater ability. On the showing of this first big film part, she looks like the most impressive recruit to British films for many a moon.' And *News Of The World* raved, 'A dozen of my darkest red roses to Joan Collins. Fire and spirit in her acting and that odd combination of allure and mystery that spells eventual world stardom.'

This was heady stuff for a teenager. Max had started kidding me about how, with my looks and youth, he and his friends could make a fortune if I would become a high-class courtesan. I thought it quite funny at the time, as they were constantly cracking jokes about sex. In fact, sex and women made up 90 per cent of the subject matter of conversation between Max and friends, and were usually discussed in a derogatory fashion. I knew they had no respect at all for women and were the epitome of what my mother had always described — the men who want only 'one thing' — but I tried to use my sense of humour and not let it affect me. Since neither of us was acting in a film, we decided to appear together at the Q Theatre in *The Seventh Veil*, in the roles made famous on the screen by James Mason and Ann Todd. Max played the part of the sadisticly cruel piano teacher. He played it well and with so much authenticity that in one of the scenes where he is terrorising me, he threw me across the stage with such violence and ferocity that I was black and blue for three days. The audience loved the sado-masochism obviously, because we immediately started rehearsing yet another similar story of a 'young frightened girl, intimidated but mesmerised by an attractive sadistic older man' — absolutely the story of *our* relationship. This one was called *Jassy* — freely adapted from the film of the same name with Margaret Lockwood and yes, of course, James Mason!

I loved working in the theatre and was only regretful that these engagements lasted only one week. My reviews were excellent, and I started looking for a suitable property to do in the West End.

Max went to my parents to ask for my hand in marriage. Although my father had had a suspicion of this, I think he was surprised that it was actually happening. The four of us sat self consciously in the living room of our Harley House flat. Dinner was over. The television sound had been turned down. Max and I perched on the green velvet Knowle sofa sipping tea from Mummy's best pink china.

When he wanted to, Max could charm the birds out of the trees. My mother was already won over, I could tell, but Daddy was a harder nut to crack. He disapproved of Max's flashy West End image, he disapproved of the age difference, he disapproved *totally* of everything the man represented and would absolutely not allow me to get married at such a tender age to such an unsuitable person. 'Well, then,' I said, finally asserting myself in their conversation. 'If you won't let me marry him I'll go and live with him.'

My parents stared at me in alarm. 'You must be out of your Chinese mind,' my father said. 'What would people think? Can you imagine what our friends would say. It would be the talk of the West End. You absolutely *will not* live together, I will not allow it!'

'You can't stop me,' I said defiantly. 'We love each other, Joe,' said Max smoothly. 'And we want to be together, what can we do?'

Both my parents looked bemused. I think Mummy was secretly thrilled by the romance of it all, but didn't dare come around until my father did first.

'All right,' said Daddy, puffing vehemently on a Player's. 'All

33

right, but I'll tell you something — and mean it,' he looked at me
and I got that funny feeling in the back of my knees again. 'This
marriage had better last, because if it doesn't,' he stared at me
hard, 'I never want to speak to you or see you again.' I looked at
Mummy. She looked away. I looked at the walls and mantelpiece
and sideboard of the room. They were covered with photographs
of me — in bathing suits and ball gowns, with my brother, Bill,
and sister, Jackie. Was he serious, my father, about disowning me
if my marriage failed?

'That's all. That's it,' said my father and he leaned over and
turned up the sound on the TV. 'Make us another cup of tea, Elsa,'
and the subject was closed.

Max and I left as soon as possible and went to the Mandrake
Club where we celebrated our engagement with Pimms Number 1.
I was outwardly happy — I was going to get away from home and
have some freedom. But my mind was a turmoil of doubts.

One of Max's favourite sayings was 'Hate is Akin To Love'. It
seemed a bit weird to me but maybe it helped explain my
ambivalent feeling towards him. He was not very good for my
ego. Although he thought I was beautiful, he was consistently
belittling my conversation, my acting ability and my personality.
He advised me often to 'Cash in on all you have going for you
now as by the time you're twenty-three you'll be old and washed
up.' Twenty-three was apparently the cut-off point for Max and
his cronies to be attracted to a girl. Anyone older than that was
'an old scrubber'.

We married the day after my birthday, at Caxton Hall, in a blaze
of publicity. I had spent most of the previous week sobbing myself
to sleep at night. The thought of getting married terrified me. I
didn't now want to leave the safety and security of the cosy flat
where I had spent so much of my childhood. I was frightened of
my father and frightened of Max. I lost eight pounds, and in my
white and gold wedding dress, my waist was tiny. I heard some
women in the crowd outside Caxton Hall say I was too skinny! I'd
achieved something I had been trying to do for years without
succeeding. Misery must be good for the figure.

We drove to Cannes for our honeymoon in the Buick. I always
became drowsy on long car trips and kept falling asleep. Max
pinched and yelled at me to 'wake up'! I tried to keep my eyes
open by looking at the pictures and the articles that had appeared
about us on our wedding day. How happy we seemed. How
grown-up and assured I looked, as if I married a film star every

year. I read with interest a particular story that was printed in the
Daily Mirror.

'I shall do no cooking or cleaning!' the headline stated boldly,
shocked that a woman should be so untraditional as to not get
kicks from wearing a frilly apron and cooking tasty meals for her
husband. 'Her ideas of marriage are honestly unconventional,'
cooed the article. 'She doesn't want to have children for 7 or 8
years at least — and she wants to keep on working all the time.'
These were revolutionary ideas for the fifties. Women felt guilty if
they did not adore housework and want to have a house full of
kids. My sights were set a little higher. Even if I had chosen to
marry I did not feel I had to conform to the usual patterns a young
wife was supposed to follow.

Our honeymoon was a nightmare. Max was extraordinarily
jealous of me where other men were concerned. However, the
wealthier a man was, the less jealous he would become and he
often suggested that I could make a bit of money by 'being
nice to that chap'. When a couple of young photographers came to
take photos of me on the beach, Max afterwards took me back to
our cramped hut on the Carlton Beach and slapped my face so
hard I felt my teeth would fall out.

'You belong to me now,' he screamed so loudly that I knew the
ladies sipping afternoon tea on the Carlton Terrace could
probably hear. 'So don't be looking at other men — ever — unless
they're the ones *I* choose!' The veins stood out on his neck and his
eyes bulged in a frenzy. He truly looked like a madman. I pressed
myself against the wall of the hut. In my tiny pink checked bikini I
felt vulnerable and terrified. I took a good look at the man I
married. His hair was dyed black and permed. I should know —
he had taught me to do it in the sink at his flat. His eyebrows and
eyelashes were heavily mascaraed. Today he was not wearing
make-up as we were on the beach, but he often did in daily life. He
wore a ridiculous pair of minute white shorts, black thong sandals
that laced up to mid-calf, and three large gold medallions hanging
around his neck. He got more wolf whistles in the South of France
than I did.

'Thank God I'm going to start work next week,' I thought
fervently. Rank, having now put me under contract for £50 a
week, had loaned me out to Columbia to play in Boccaccio's
Decameron Nights to be made in Madrid and Segovia. It would be
my first American film, and I was full of enthusiasm.

Max decided to stay in Cannes and enjoy himself for another

week. He had met a millionaire who impressed him and vice versa, so he was happy. And when he was happy he was nice to me, and then I was happy. But I was not happy in sunny Spain. The picture starred Joan Fontaine and Louis Jourdan, and consisted of three or four episodes of Boccaccio's stories. I played Joan Fontaine's handmaiden in one segment and in another had tender love scenes with Louis Jourdan, an attractive Frenchman. This role was much smaller than my role in *I Believe In You.* But Rank had insisted I do the film, otherwise they would release me from my contract. There were not many roles for sexy-looking teenagers and Rank was getting a good loan out price for me, too, none of which I saw, of course. I just got my £50 a week. The director, Hugo Fregonese, was cold and treated us casually. Segovia was smelly and dirty and the hotel where we stayed a veritable doss house.

I missed Max at first but when he arrived a week later we started fighting again. I became petulant, bad tempered, and unpopular, and was not sorry to return to London and start working on another movie.

Cosh Boy was the story of a group of youths who spent their time getting their kicks by robbing and beating up people — rather like today's muggers. I played Renee, the innocent young girlfriend of James Kenney. We had an explicit love scene in the garden of a deserted house, which by today's standards was tame enough to be in a Disney film. After the seduction I become pregnant and try to commit suicide. It was a shop girl's melodrama and the public loved it. I enjoyed working with Jimmy and all the other young actors. The director, Lewis Gilbert, was adorable to me, and good to work with. And Max finally got a job and left for Jersey to make *Toilers Of the Sea* for Raoul Walsh. It was just the sort of pirate potboiler he loved and he was playing the 'heavy' against Rock Hudson, which of course was right up his alley.

Bill Watts asked if I wanted to do another play at the Q Theatre. the play was *The Skin of Our Teeth* by Thornton Wilder, one of the great American classics. And the part I was wanted for was Sabina, the ageless vamp, which had originally been played by Vivien Leigh. I was flattered and excited. Finally I was going to play a classic role in a great play. Maybe my RADA training hadn't been wasted after all.

The Q Theatre specialised in revivals and although a small, intimate theatre, it nevertheless put on excellent plays and it was considered a coup to play there. Although he was too young for the role of a 60-year-old man, Antrobus, Max put on a ton of make up, greyed his tinted black hair and played the part quite well. When he stopped posturing and posing and using a phony American accent he was a fairly good actor. We had just finished a film together for Rank *The Square Ring*, again directed by Basil Dearden. I played a cameo role as Max's girlfriend, and he wasted much time accusing me of upstaging him. Since I was still so inexperienced in film acting I had no idea how to do a lot of things, let alone upstage anyone, I became uneasy during our scenes together for fear I was displeasing him.

The reviews for *The Skin of Our Teeth* were excellent and I enjoyed it more than any film I had made so far. I wanted to do more theatre, but first I had to make a strong dramatic film for Rank called *Turn The Key Softly*. This was the tale of one day in the lives of three women just released from prison. It was an authentic and harrowing film, so authentic, in fact, that the opening scenes of Yvonne Mitchell, Kathleen Harrison and me being released from prison were actually shot in Holloway Women's Prison.

I played a young prostitute, in the clink for shoplifting, who wants to keep on the straight and narrow, but is tempted by the bright lights and glamour of the West End. We shot on actual locations around London in the dead of winter. It was bitterly cold and I was fitted out in a tight black satin skirt, slit to the thigh, black stockings and ankle strap shoes, a flimsy low-cut lurex sweater and a yellow short-sleeved jacket. I was blue with cold for most of the time and started thinking pensively of sun-kissed California from where Bill Watts was getting regular calls about my availability.

Rank was still giving me a tremendous publicity build-up. I became known as 'Britain's Bad Girl' and had hardly any time for myself. At night, exhausted from shooting, I would return to our flat in Hanover Square and attempt to cook dinner and do the housework before I flopped exhausted into bed. For, contrary to my brave statements in the *Daily Mirror*, Max was a true chauvinist and expected his hot dinners every night — no matter what! My mother had not educated me in the culinary arts because as a child I had so many projects going after school that she was loath to take me away from them. Besides my voracious reading (at least seven or eight books a week) I spent a great deal of time writing to film stars for their autographed photos, or cutting and pasting pictures of stars into great scrapbooks.

Cooking was too boring to contend with and besides, I thought I would never need to do it. But Max liked his meat and potatoes so it was he who taught me the rudiments of cooking. But if it didn't turn out to his satisfaction he would throw the whole plate of food across the room, and I would be down on my hands and knees picking up peas and bits of steak for hours.

There was a mirror above the kitchen sink and I would look at my bedraggled reflection doing the washing up and compare it to the provocative and alluring face which was adorning magazines and newspapers. They seemed like two different people. My marriage was a fiasco. I lived in fear of his moods and rages, and yet I didn't have the courage to get out. When I wasn't working I rushed to voice lessons, acting lessons and self-improvement lessons . . . anything to get out of the house.

After I finished *Turn The Key Softly* I had several meetings with an Italian film director, Renato Castellani. He was to make a film of *Romeo and Juliet* and the Rank Organisation decided that I would be a perfect Juliet!! This did not please either Signor Castellani or myself. I did not think I was the Juliet type — I had always preferred parts with more muscle, such as Sabina in *The Skin of Our Teeth*, or Cleopatra. I did not see myself as an innocent fourteen-year-old virgin, which was how Castellani wanted the part played — but the studio was adamant. He must test me . . . and test me he did. At least two or three times.

The final test at Pinewood I did with Laurence Harvey, who was signed to play Romeo. We were still friendly and I was very fond of him and he of me, but even he agreed that I was too sophisticated-looking for their version of Juliet. Signor Castellani came to me before the last test and gave me his ultimatum. 'You will havva the nose job,' he said in his heavily accented English. 'I will havva the what?' I said incredulously. 'Julietta she hassa the Roman nose — you havva the nose it goes up — is not aristocratic — you go the good plastic surgeon — he makka the Roman nose — you be Julietta!'

'Oh NO — You've got to be kidding,' I wailed, and broke into hysterical tears and laughter. A nose job to get a part? No way. Besides, I liked my nose . . . hadn't one of the papers said that the three prettiest noses in Britain belonged to Vivien Leigh, Jean Simmons and Joan Collins. I drew the line. Bill Watts was summoned and, amidst much Italian screaming and yelling and my hysterics and total refusal to get the plastic nose, Rank reluctantly backed down and an unknown actress was signed for Juliet.

Although I'd been under contract for some months, Rank still didn't have much idea what to do with me, so when Noel Langley and George Minter approached them about a loan out to star in Langley's own novel *Our Girl Friday*, they allowed me to do it. It was an absolutely gorgeous part. The script was hilarious and the three actors who were in it were important stars. I played Sadie, a wilful, beautiful spoiled brat on a holiday cruise with her parents when their ship is wrecked and she and the three men manage to reach a deserted island where they live for many months.

Kenneth More played Pat Plunket, the ship's colourful Irish stoker with a fondness for liquor and an eye for the ladies. Kenneth had recently had a huge success in *Genevieve* and had become a big star. George Cole played Carrol, a cynical journalist who hated Sadie, and Robertson Hare — one of the greatest farce actors in England — played Professor Gibble, a prim and proper old economics professor.

This motley group assemble on the island, realise that it's uninhabited and are appalled — one girl on a desert island with three men! A situation fraught with peril for them all, but with great amusement for the audience, of course. We shot on the island of Majorca. I was given the opportunity to look desirable and wholesome for a change and to wear some revealing outfits. The film was a minor hit in England and then in America where the title was changed to *The Adventures of Sadie* and my performance started to seriously interest the heads of several studios — among them Darryl Zanuck, the head of production at Fox.

Edward Leggevie, an executive at Fox in London, asked if I would be interested in the idea of going to Hollywood under contract to Fox. Would I!!!!! My heart leaped at the idea. I was getting so sick of doing endless tests for parts that I didn't get — for the snide remarks the press were starting to lay on me . . . 'Let's have an end to the Puppy Fat Stars,' said Logan Courtney. 'She strains to look like Marilyn Monroe,' said Donald Zec (a total lie). Too much publicity and not enough performances — although I seemed to be working non-stop — and maybe if we went to Hollywood, Max could find some work too and stop being such a moody pain in the ass. By this time the marriage was so intolerable that I would do *anything* to get away from London. The location in Majorca was wonderful. I felt free for the first time ever. But I needed more freedom. I called on the support of my loyal and trustworthy Bill Watts. He promised to find me a play to go on tour.

The Praying Mantis was a new play and not a particularly good one, but I didn't care. I had to get away. The Rank Organisation gave me a bonus of £900 — a fortune to me. I was still making £100 a week and making numerous personal appearances in cheap and cheerful clothes. In *The Praying Mantis* I played a young Empress in Byzantine times who, after making love to her young men, sent them away to be executed. Hence the title, from the insect of the same name!

The director, Esme Percy, was a touch grand. He had been a well-known character actor, but now was over sixty and possibly bitter over the passing of the years. He told me condescendingly I looked like 'an expensive toy', a compliment not guaranteed to bring out the best of one's acting talents.

We played for a week at the Q Theatre to lukewarm reviews and houses, and then went on tour for three weeks to Brighton, Wimbledon and Folkestone. I completely adored it. For the first time I felt I was achieving what I had originally set out to do . . . to become a theatre actress and not a starlet. I loved the rapport and jokes between the actors. I loved the old draughty, smelly dressing rooms, with the musty mothball smells of a thousand ancient costumes and stale greasepaint. Our troupe would sit for hours after the show, in seedy pubs and in our even seedier digs, talking about our lives and aspirations — gossiping, drinking, playing cards and being ourselves. I felt I was accepted for what I was: a young girl trying to grow up with faults, weaknesses and insecurities about herself, but also I had humour and guts and was intelligent. I didn't have to act the sexy starlet with Fanny, Jimmy and Ian, and we were all one happy family. Although the play did badly it did not deter me from doing another, and on returning to London, I immediately started rehearsals for *Claudia and David*, a sequel to *Claudia*, a gay and tender romantic American comedy about a slightly scatty child-bride and her husband.

Max was travelling to and from Rome to try to get work at the time, and on one of his trips back he suggested we go to our favourite restaurant-cum-nightclub — Les Ambassadeurs.

Les Ambassadeurs was divine. All the visiting American actors and producers and citizens made it their home from home. The club itself was in an elegant old Georgian house in Hamilton Terrace. The furnishings were subdued and impeccable, the food excellent, and the music, although slightly tame for my jazz-oriented taste, was gay and danceable.

I sat drinking Pimms, and thinking about *Claudia and David*, while Max was chatting to an elderly Arabian gentleman on the banquette next to him. I ignored them. Max had a habit of gravitating towards rich, elderly men who usually lusted after me. They talked for a long time, animatedly.

I was busy watching Linda Christian and Edmond Purdom doing the cha-cha when Max pulled my arm and introduced me to the gentleman. 'This is Sheik Abdul Ben Kafir,' he said. I nodded coldly to this aged roué, who smiled excitedly and looked me up and down. I was wearing a low-cut white chiffon blouse, a green velvet skirt, and was starting to get a vague idea of what this was all about from the look on Abdul's face.

'Excuse me, Sheik,' said Max smoothly. 'Back in a minute. Going to take little Joanie for a trot around the dance floor.' He pulled me to the floor and to the strains of 'From This Moment On' we danced. 'Ten thousand pounds,' said Max, his face aglow with pride. 'He'll pay you ten thousand pounds for *one night!!* — and I can even watch!!!!!!'

'I'm sorry, Max,' I said as coldly as I could, fear gripping the pit of my stomach. 'Are you *seriously* suggesting I go to bed with that old fart for money?'

'You bloody little berk,' he snarled, whirling me to the far end of the floor. 'Ten Grand! Tax Free!!! Do you realise what we can do with that sort of money? We can go to Hollywood. We can maybe even buy a cottage in the country. You better start cashing in on what you've got girl — doing plays at the Q for ten quid a week is *not* going to make us rich in our old age.'

I started to protest but he was very insistent and held me tighter and tighter. I felt tears welling up and forced myself not to cry. 'One night, Baby — that's all. One night with Abdul and we can say "Fuck You" to all of 'em.'

I looked at Abdul nodding and smiling over his champagne, his pendulous jowls wobbling. I looked at my handsome, *loathsome* husband and burst into tears, 'Never!' I screamed, turning the heads of Linda and Edmond who were dancing right behind us. 'I will never ever, ever do that.' I couldn't control myself and rushed from the club. I grabbed a cab and went home. And home was my parents' flat. That was the final straw. I couldn't take it for another minute. I didn't care if my father disowned me for not making the marriage work. I didn't care if Max made good his oft repeated threat to 'have some of the *boys* carve your pretty little face up with a razor if you ever leave me' — nothing mattered any more except saving my self-respect and my sanity.

3

A Funny Thing Happened on The Way to Hollywood

We tried a brief reconciliation but it was hopeless. Not only did I not love him any more: I disliked him intensely. His ailment never improved and his sexual tendencies became increasingly sadistic and perverted. My parents were glad to have me home again and I moved back happily into the familiar back bedroom.

The meetings between my agent and the Fox representatives hotted up and negotiations began to buy my contract outright from Rank. Meanwhile, I left for Rome to play wicked Princess Nellifer in a lavish Biblical epic *Land of the Pharaohs.* It was my first big American film, with an international cast headed by Jack Hawkins. Directed by Howard Hawks, one of the most famous of the oldtime Hollywood directors, it was written by an imposing duo of men — William Faulkner and Harry Kurnitz. Although they slaved away writing and rewriting daily, it was in spite of their efforts a very hokey script with some impossible dialogue.

I was lucky indeed to get this break and I knew it. I plunged feverishly into an endless series of photo tests, costume fittings, hair and make-up tests. I must look Egyptian, exotic, and evil, and a multitude of excitable costumiers, blase hairdressers and enthusiastic make-up men strove to turn a gauche teenager into a sultry, bitch goddess. My hair seemed to be the despair of the brittle, hawk-eyed American hairdresser. Long, thin and stringy it conformed not at all to the 'luxuriant cascading abundant tresses' attributed to the Princess in the script. After countless encounters with possibly every piece of false hair in Rome, the hairdresser, by now my least favourite person in the world, was constantly lamenting my lack of locks.

'We'll just have to call you old pin-head,' she sneered jovially, stabbing my skull once more with her 3-inch steel hair pins, and finally found a wig she and I both liked. It was waist length and contained the life savings of the hair of twelve Italian nuns. It was

42

so heavy that when I moved my head it was as if in slow motion. To keep it stuck to my scalp we used 47 bobby pins, 92 sharp hair pins and half a bottle of toupee glue.

When, as often happens today, *Land of the Pharaohs* is shown on the late show and I get lavish praise for my appearance, I smile when I think of the agony I endured at the hands of the hairdresser. Not to mention the complex I had for years because of the 'old pin-head' line. Although I have a small head it is not deformed, as I was led to believe, but in my naivety I thought I was a bit of a freak in the skull department.

Rome was exciting. '*La Dolce Vita*' was in full swing. Down the Via Veneto strolled well-known American actors escaping their heavy taxes by taking 18 months out of the States. Gorgeous raven haired starlets sat sipping cappuccino at the sidewalk cafes, waiting to be discovered. Everyone was alive and gay. It was summer and I was in love.

Sydney Chaplin was the second son of Charlie Chaplin. He was very tall, very dark and quite handsome, with black curly hair flecked with grey, and amused brown eyes. He had an outrageous and scurrilous wit. He was so hilarious that I could literally weep with laughter.

Every day we started laughing and didn't stop until the early hours of the morning, when we would stagger out of Victor's Club, the Number One, or whichever disco or club we hit upon that night, and giggle all the way back to the sedate Hotel de La Ville where most of the international cast stayed during the filming of *Land of the Pharaohs*.

There had been an absence of laughter and gaiety in the latter months of my life with Maxwell Reed. Sydney was like a glass of lemonade in the desert. He filled a tremendous need in my life — to have fun; to enjoy one's flaming youth and to be a non-conformist as far as the 'Establishment' went. I didn't deliberately set out to shock people, but Syd gave not a damn about what the world thought of him. Since I was a chameleon where men are concerned, I too adopted temporarily his 'Screw you' attitude towards his fellow man.

After two weeks of staying up 'til dawn and listening to Sydney enthrall a room with his crazy monologues and outrageous jokes, we finally laughed our way into bed — where we proceeded to become, if possible, even *more* hysterical. Someone said to me once, after literally chasing me around my living room for half an hour with me evading this humorist's clutches 'til, weak with laughter, I managed to usher him to the door, 'Well, I may not be much of a lover but I'm a "Funny Fuck"!' Although this was not strictly true of Syd, nevertheless our love making often ended in my breaking up and him doing a comedy routine. *Nothing* was to be taken seriously and after a year of torment with Max that was O.K. by me.

His favourite expression was 'Mother-Fucker' — usually shortened to 'Mother', and his vocabulary was so sprinkled with four-letter words that it was always slightly surprising to do a scene with him and hear normal dialogue come out of his mouth. Sometimes when we played scenes together I would have to dig my nails into the palms of my hands to stop myself from giggling. To Syd, life was one great big ball. He loved to drink, to dance, to gamble and to play. He didn't take acting seriously. It was just a way to make some bread. I had thought that he would have been quite wealthy, since his father was surely a multi-millionaire, but that was not the case. He had a small allowance but not enough to lead the crazy playboy existence he desired. He owned two expensive sports cars, a red Ferrari and a blue Alfa Romeo, and he lived out of two alligator suitcases.

We would drive back from the beach at Ostia or Fregene in the early hours at 125 miles an hour, the convertible top down, the warm wind whipping my hair wildly, and the trees above us melting into a ceiling of green leaves. And laughing all the way. It was a miracle we were never killed. We gave a new meaning to the word reckless. Unfortunately, the drinking was taking its toll of my figure.

The part of Princess Nellifer necessitated many changes of wardrobe, each one more exotic than the last. The seamstresses at Scalera Studios were hard at it, sewing hundreds of yards of gold lame, silver brocade, chiffon, silk, and gold braid into elaborate costumes that I would wear when I became the Egyptian Queen, but my opening outfit was somewhat simpler. I wore a gold mesh bra and a long purple brocade skirt which sat low on my hips. Over this was a velvet cloak, for when I was presented as a gift to the Pharaoh, I was wrapped in it.

However, my naked navel presented a problem. It was the mid-fifties and censorship was severe. If the Hays Office thought a scene or a costume too risque it was cut, and thousands of dollars went down the drain.

My outfit was as authentic as the Italian costumier could make it, but my navel was a no-no as far as the censor was concerned. 'Cover it up,' said Howard Hawks testily when I presented myself to him for final approval on this costume. 'Find a way to cover it up. The censor thinks navels are obscene,' he snorted despairingly, and went back to his scene. The designer, Mayo, an excitable Latin, shrugged, 'Il censore e *matto* — complete mente *matto* — ma'cosa fachiamo adesso?'

'How about a band-aid,' I joked. 'Or some plasticine inside it. We'll get some plasticine and dye it to match my stomach, and then I'll be navel-less, just like a big doll!'

They looked at me pityingly — English humour does not appeal to Italians. 'Ahah! ' suddenly shrieked Mayo, jumping up and down excitedly. 'Mettiamo una butoni in sua piccola bucca!' My Italian was scratchy but roughly translated this meant, 'Let's put a button in her little hole!' They scurried to their treasure chests and pulled out dozens of buttons — silver, gold and finally a beautiful ruby. Mayo tried in to insert it while I squirmed uncomfortably. It was my sensitive spot. 'Bella!' said Mayo proudly. 'Molto Bella! Cara — you think so too?'

I looked in the mirror at the little ruby twinkling brightly in the middle of my stomach and burst into uncontrollable laughter, and with that the ruby exploded out of its place and disappeared under a sewing machine. 'Che Cosa?' said Mayo angrily. 'We must put the sticky stuff — we stuff it in hard and it stay there. Bellissima — un effeta Bellissimo.' I endured a pound of Johnson's liquid adhesive poured into my navel, and there the ruby stayed. . . proud and glistening, defying the censor. I thought it looked infinitely more obscene and erotic with the shiny stone drawing attention to what was meant to be unobtrusive, but everyone seemed satisfied, and shooting commenced.

However, several weeks in Sydney's company, scoffing fettucini and lasagne at Alfredo's, and il Piccolo Mondo and drinking quantities of red wine and green creme de menthe had added about eight pounds to my already voluptuous figure, and when it came time to do a retake of this scene I was embarrassed. Zaphtyg was an understatement. I knew Howard Hawks hated plump ladies (he had discovered, or sponsored Lauren Bacall, Lizbeth Scott and Angie Dickinson, none of them exactly blimps), I endeavoured to hold my stomach in tightly during the scene, but each time I squeezed in my muscles, out would plop the dreaded red stone!

Howard Hawks was going crazy.

'For God's Sakes — get some airplane glue. Get anything to keep the damned thing in place.' And then accusingly to me:

45

'You've gained weight. I told you last week in the rushes you looked *fat*. Have you been dieting?'

'All I've eaten for two days is three hard-boiled eggs,' I lied feverishly, thinking of the vast amount of Spaghetti Bolognaise and Zabaglione I had consumed at Alfredo's last night.

'Well you better cut it down to "two" hard-boiled eggs,' he said crustily. 'Princess Nellifer should not look as though she is four months pregnant.' He stormed off and I felt properly chastened. He was right. Here I was playing the best role of my career and I was goofing off. Too many late nights and too much pasta and wine do not a love affair with the camera make. I vowed to discipline myself.

I was playing the role of a lifetime — being directed by one of the world's greatest movie directors, playing with some of the finest actors around, and I was acting and behaving like a stupid schoolgirl, trying to cut classes and go to the beach. I was wrong and I knew it. I quit drinking, banished the idea of 'pasta' from my mind, and was in bed at 10 o'clock each night with a copy of *Land of the Pharaohs* in front of me.

But it was not easy with Syd. When I stayed in the hotel and went to bed early he went out with his gang anyway, and since I loved him I wanted to be where the action was — and that was with him. To keep his interest and desire for me I felt I had to mould myself to his way of life.

Sydney, too, had put on a few pounds, and as the time drew near to start our love scenes together we both made a concerted effort to cut calories and get in shape. His costumes were even more 'kitsch' than mine. He wore a small beige felt skull-cap which was cunningly cut out to reveal his ears — not his best feature — a long loin cloth of ornate fabric, and a vast neckpiece of gold and ebony. Curious pointed slippers and two large gold slave bracelets on his upper arms, which due to the amount of eating we were indulging in made the flesh squash out above and below in a most unattractive fashion. I was wearing a pink chiffon gown, low cut and heavily embroidered with crystals, and on my upper arm a tight silver and ruby bracelet around which the flesh also bulged. Thank God I wasn't wearing the ruby in my navel too.

When Sydney and I met at 8.30 am on the sound stage at Scalera Studios we took one look at each other and burst out laughing. 'Is this how Theda Bara started?' I said gaily. 'More like Ma and Pa Kettle meet the mother-fucking Pharaoh,' said Syd, tripping over his pointed sandals, and getting entangled in his maxi-skirt. 'Quiet, now hold it down,' called the assistant director, and we started blocking the scene when Trenah (Syd) declares his love for Princess Nellifer.

Actors have two dreaded nightmares. One is to appear on stage and forget one's dialogue — the other is to be unable to speak the dialogue because of an uncontrollable urge to laugh. The latter nightmare happened to Sydney and me that day. It was truly ghastly because however hard we forced ourselves not to, one or other of us would at one point or another in the scene start to collapse. The angrier Howard Hawks became the more we heaved. I was actually terrified and upset after this occurred four or five times, but it didn't help. One look at Syd's earnest face, with his ears sticking out of the weird hat and I was corpsed. I would try not to break up completely, but he saw the strain in my face and that would set him off. It was an hysterical bad dream. It was also catching. Half the crew were starting to smile, but it was when we caught sight of the overly serious and cross faces of Howard and the more sombre crew members that we broke up again and again.

Eventually Howard stopped shooting and bawled Sydney and I out vehemently. He sent us home to get some rest and lectured us sternly to stop behaving like children. He brought us down to earth with a big bang.

This time I really decided to pull myself together — lose the excess pounds and take my work more seriously. I realised I was 'losing face' and that my behaviour was becoming terribly unprofessional.

I had tried to file for a divorce in London before leaving for Rome but you could not file unless the marriage had existed for three years or more. All I had was an unofficial separation from Max, who was also in Rome at the time working on *Helen of Troy*, another historical soap opera.

I was sunbathing on the beach at Fregene one day when I felt a shadow looming over me. I looked up and there he was. Tanned, dyed black hair and small white shorts, and an ominous look on his face. 'I want to talk to you.' I was surrounded by friends who tried to get rid of him but he was insistent. 'You better come and talk to me now or I'll make a scene right here,' he said menacingly. I reluctantly followed him to the beach bar. 'Do you remember the photographs I took of you,' he said casually, offering me a cigarette.

I did remember them. It is not an uncommon occurrence for

husbands to take nude photos of their wives. A lot of our friends did, and although he had coaxed me into posing for them, with assurances that he would never show them to a soul, I had not been thrilled at the time. The pictures were fairly tame as far as I remembered. I wore the bottom half of a bikini and was posed bored and sulky on the zebra-skin sofa. Tame stuff by today's standards. 'So what about them? ' I said brazening it out. 'I've got a good offer from one of the Italian magazines to buy them from me. They'll pay me a lot of money and I need it.' He smiled his Mitchum smile. I looked at him numbly. He surely had to be the lowest form of human life. How could I have ever married such a vile creep? Just looking at him filled me with revulsion.

'So what do you want from me?' I said.

'All the rings I gave you when we were married,' he said smoothly. 'Wedding, engagement and the topaz.'

'You're welcome to them,' I said icily. 'I'll have someone bring them to your hotel.'

'And the cheque,' he said blocking me as I tried to get back to the beach. 'Don't forget to sign it.'

I couldn't believe he was serious. In the past month he had sent several crazy letters to me professing his love, and in one of them he had enclosed a blank cheque from my personal account and asked me to sign it.

'You know I don't have much money,' I protested. 'There's only a couple of hundred pounds in my account, that's all.'

'The cheque and the rings at my hotel tomorrow night, or the magazine gets the pictures. Ciao, kid,' and he sauntered off to the bar. I was furious. The man had no ethics at all. He was a street fighter. Maybe I should become one too. I told my mother who was staying with me. She had grown to hate Max as much as I, as I had told her more of the horrors I had been through. We discussed our strategy with Eddie Fowlie, a friend, who had also been on *Our Girl Friday*. He agreed to take the rings and the blank cheque to Max at the Residence Palace Hotel the next night.

I didn't have much choice. The money wasn't important and the rings had no sentimental value, but it would have been disaster for my career had those nude photos appeared in print. Rumours had been circulating that nude photos of Marilyn Monroe had been printed some time ago on a girlie calendar.

The world was puritanical and quick to condemn any public figures whose morals were less than faultless. I was nervous that if a whiff of this possible scandal reached the ears of Twentieth Century-Fox, who were in final negotiations with Rank to buy me, my career could be finished before it had barely started.

Mummy and I sat in a nearby cafe nervously drinking cappuccino and brandy while Eddie went to get the photos. He returned triumphantly with a large sealed manilla envelope. I opened the envelope and out fell twelve glossy publicity pin-up pictures from Rank!

'That fucking bastard!' I was so furious I didn't even censor my language in front of my mother 'Of all the low-down, filthy lying tricks. He's still got the goddamned pictures.' Mummy and Eddie looked at each other helplessly. 'I'm going to go and punch him out,' said Eddie. But my mother laid a restraining hand on him. 'No, let me talk to him first.' She ran to the phone. I knocked back a brandy, and wondered what I'd done to deserve this.

When Mummy came back she was trembling with fury. 'He said the photographs are in London and in a safety deposit box,' her voice was shaking. I was proud of her, she didn't assert herself too often and it couldn't have been easy but there she was, a tigress protecting her cub.

'I called him all the names under the sun, but he said he wants to keep them to remember you by.'

'Oh, charming,' I said bitterly. 'He can show them to all his dirty old Arabian millionaires and tell them what they've missed.'

'Anyway,' said Mummy, He's promised *ME* that he will not sell them to any publications, so I suppose we'll just have to take his word for it.'

'His *word* — Ha!' I threw down another brandy. 'He doesn't know the meaning of honour and ethics.' Mummy patted my hand comfortingly.

'Never mind darling, I'm sure we've heard the last of him this time.' I hoped she was right but I had a nasty suspicion that my last chapter on Maxwell Reed had yet to be written.

'Three hundred and fifty dollars a week,' announced John Shepbridge, his eyes glowing with excitement. 'What do you think of that, Joanie? That is terrific for the first year.' 'Not much,' I said diffidently. I sat across from 'Goulash', as he was affectionately known, sitting behind his highly-polished walnut desk in his Mayfair house at 16 South Audley Street. The house, coincidentally, next door to South Street, where I would eventually live with Ron. The weak London sun seeped through the tiny, Georgian latticed windows and reflected off the silver and porcelain objects which were scattered tastefully around his office-cum-living room. We were meeting to discuss my deal with

Fox. Rank had accepted the fifteen thousand pounds that Fox had offered to buy me out of my contract and Goulash, who was a senior executive of the Famous Artists Agency, was now negotiating my salary terms.

My dream was about to be finalised: to go to Hollywood on an exclusive seven-year-contract with Twentieth Century-Fox. It was an offer not to be sneezed at, but I was sneezing. The reason for my lack of enthusiasm was at this minute in Paris, probably languishing in some bistro or boite, consuming quantities of coq-au-vin and vodka.

John Shepbridge looked at me, a flicker of annoyance crossing his face.

Three hundred and fifty dollars a week is not that much money, Goulash. *YOU* know that and I know that. Now if Fox is willing to pay Rank so much money to sign me, I'm quite sure they will be willing to pay me more as a contract player. I was thinking of, say, twelve hundred and fifty a week.'

I had read in a magazine that 1,250 dollars a week was a reasonable salary for a young contract player, and if one settled for less than that the studios thought of you more as a feature or bit player and it was harder to obtain leading roles. Although I would have sold my eyelashes to get to Hollywood, I had ambivalent feelings at the moment because of my love affair with Sydney.

'You're crazy,' said Goulash angrily, his Hungarian blood rising to the occasion. 'They will never go for that. Never. Never. You're totally *unknown* in the States. Why should they pay you three times as much as they usually do? — Crazy — Crazy,' he stomped around his desk angrily mumbling to himself.

'What am I going to tell Charlie?' he said. 'He's been talking you up to Darryl for three months now. It's because of him you're getting this deal. He's going to be furious.'

Charlie was Charles K. Feldman, top executive agent at Famous Artists and a wheeler-dealer to be reckoned with. I knew that because of his influence with Darryl Zanuck, head of production at Fox, who trusted Feldman's enthusiasm for me, I was being offered this contract, and I also shrewdly realised that the chances of my getting the better roles at Fox and not being just another two-bit contract player would be enhanced by getting a large weekly salary rather than what was virtually a pittance. (Studio grips got more than $350 a week.) It was a calculated gamble and if I lost I could always go back Syd in Paris, or to Rome where I had been getting movie offers.

'I'm very appreciative of all that you and Charlie have done for me,' I said formally. 'But it's my life and my decision. I want 1,250 a week and if I don't get it — forget it.' I got up to leave. 'Darling, Goulash — I'm leaving for Paris tonight. I'll be at the Hotel Tremoille. Let me know what happens.' I kissed him goodbye and he raised his eyebrows in a gesture of resignation.

'Crazy little girl,' he said. 'You can always find a good fuck, but a good contract is a once-in-a-lifetime thing. I hope you're not blowing your career, Joanie.'

'I'm not,' I said confidently. 'In the immortal words of Joan Crawford, "You can't cuddle up to a career at night" — Ciao, Goulash.' I walked into South Audley Street feeling grown-up and confident. I was still a teenager but I knew what I wanted — and I was *not* going to sell myself short any more.

As soon as I arrived in Paris, Sydney and I took off in the Ferrari with his friend, Adolph Green, for a trip to Vevey, Switzerland, to visit Charlie Chaplin. Adolph was squashed in the tiny back seat and we had a hair-raisingly hilarious trip over the snowy, winding mountain roads. I was excitedly looking forward to meeting Syd's family and especially the legendary Charlie.

The house was set in a secluded area, just outside the tiny picturesque village af Vevey, which looked like every post-card of Switzerland. It was an imposing two-storey mansion, with an apparently endless series of rooms. The rooms were necessary because there seemed to be an endless array of children and nannies, maids, gardeners and cooks. Although the senior Chaplin had a reputation of being penurious, his lifestyle was lavish. Beyond the rolling green lawns and flower beds was a beautiful lake where all the kids and Charlie and his lovely black-haired, madonna-like wife, Oona, swam and sunbathed. I liked being around this happy family atmosphere and, although Charlie reminded me somewhat of my father, very much the Patriarch, strict and authoritarian, he was also warm and human, funny and, strangely, extremely shy.

Although over sixty, Charlie was still busy siring babies. They ranged in age from Charlie Jr, who was about thirty, to the newest baby of only a few months old. I admired Oona for her lovely maternal calmness and, playing with the babies, I felt for the very first time a slight flicker of maternal instinct. 'What a crazy idea,' I said to myself, dismissing it instantly and putting down baby, who was in the process of covering his entire face with nourishing Swiss chocolate. 'I've got years to go before I even think about having kids — got my whole life ahead yet. Kids!!! Ugh!!!! Quel horreur!' (I'd started picking up a bit of French.)

Sydney and I stayed with his family for three days, and another side of his personality revealed itself. He was much more subdued around Charlie, not nearly as bawdy, and didn't want any 'romantic interludes' in the same house as his father.

'But why?' I whispered. His room is miles away.' 'I don't know, for Christ's sake,' he whispered angrily. 'I just feel funny about it — can't you understand that?' 'I guess so,' I said, imagining my reactions in the same situation. 'But since they know we have the same room, do you think they imagine we're playing gin rummy all night? And from the number of kids they have I bet *they* don't play cards too often.'

I was slightly piqued. Even though I understood, I took it as a rejection, and after months with Max I did not take kindly to rejection. A pang of jealousy shot through me as I remembered Syd regaling me with stories about him, his brother and his ex-stepmother Paulette Goddard. Charlie and Syd were about thirteen and fourteen years old, Paulette not more than a dozen years older. In the morning they would often jump into Paulette's silken covered bed with her and share her toast and coffee whilst she read her mail, talked on the phone and generally enjoyed herself. She would tease and caress the adolescent boys almost relentlessly, and they, in the manner of young male animals everywhere would respond to her charms — although never to consummation, Sydney assured me.

Since these sexy practices had gone on in Charlie Chaplin's house — and with Charlie's ex-wife, I couldn't quite understand this great unwillingness on Syd's part to sully the Swiss sheets now. Maybe he couldn't make a joke out of it and consequently felt trapped. Or maybe he was a genuine prude — people who swore the most often were.

We drove back to Paris. It was a carefree time. Staying up all night at Jimmy's night club or L'Elephant blanc, or our favourite restaurant Moustache. The owner, a huge man with a fine hairy upper lip was a friend of Syd's, and we spent wonderfully convivial evenings there. I took long walks through Paris and along the Seine while Syd played golf. I loved exploring the sophisticated left bank boutiques and tiny cluttered antique shops. We played Sinatra records and cards all day, pinball machines in over-heated cafes all afternoon, drinking Beaujolais and falling about with laughter, night-clubbed all night — and I felt good.

A Funny Thing Happened on The Way to Hollywood

When Goulash called to tell me not only that Fox had accepted my terms, but that they wanted me in California almost immediately, I was thrilled but dismayed.

Syd and I sat in a tiny restaurant in Montmartre. The candlelight flickered on the red checked tablecloth and the air was thick with the smell of Gauloises and garlic. I was leaving the next day for London to pack and depart for the States. Syd tried to comfort me as I sobbed into my wine. We loved each other. We would be together soon, he tried to assure me. As soon as he knew about a job that he was waiting for, he would join me in Los Angeles. Not to worry, it would all work out in the end.

I felt bereft in London, but I was surrounded by family and friends, and photographers coming over to take my picture, and dressmakers bringing new finery so I was caught up in a whirl of activity and excitement. Finally, amidst tears, laughter and sadness I said goodbye. I hugged my little brother, Bill, whom I felt I hardly knew, kissed my fifteen-year-old sister, Jackie — we had just finally started to become close and now I was leaving — a big hug for Daddy (who knew when I would see him again?) and, finally, my darling mother whom I was beginning to understand and love more and more. She was trying desperately hard not to cry — and so was I. We were surrounded by reporters and photographers trying to get a human interest photo-story on 'Britain's Bad Girl Goes To Hollywood'.

Every two or three minutes we heard the sound of a plane taking off. I clutched my brand new, ankle-length mink coat tightly around me and tried to be brave. 'I'll write you every week,' I said, my voice breaking. 'And I'll come and visit as often as I can — It's only nine thousand miles, after all.' Nine thousand miles seemed like a million in the days before Transatlantic jets but I had to say something. The flight was called and I was off, leaving everyone I knew and loved — leaving cold, austerity-ridden England; the Sunday papers; the English country lanes; the pubs; the Jazz clubs. My whole life was being left behind and I was going to a strange new country. To a totally different environment. To meet and work with people I didn't know and to start a new life in Hollywood.

4

Rich Men's Sons

'They're going to love you in Hollywood,' Goulash had told me confidently. 'They love English girls. You'll be a smash.' I thought ruefully about his words as I sat in my orange and yellow hotel room in Beverly Hills for the seventh consecutive night alone and looked at an unusual person on television called Liberace. The days were so full I didn't have time to think. Fox was a hive of activity and I was running from wardrobe department to hairdressing to the stills gallery for a never-ending succession of photographs and interviews. I met every producer and casting director on the lot and didn't remember any of their names. I sat in the bustling, hustling commissary at lunchtime eating a new delicacy called 'tuna fish salad' and observed wide-eyed the comings and goings of the stars.

Fox had a huge list of contract players, all of whom were either working in the many films that were in production, or were on the lot doing what I was doing, and at the same time, getting their faces in front of the directors and producers who were preparing projects. They included Susan Hayward, Sheree North, Debra Paget, Jeff Hunter, Barbara Rush, Robert Wagner, Gene Tierney, Joanne Woodward, Clifton Webb and many more. I hopefully looked each day for Fox's top star, Marilyn Monroe, but she preferred to lunch in the seclusion of her dressing room.

Although Fox were making many movies, their box office returns for the past couple of years had been poor. Zanuck was not in as much control as he had been when the studio was making such blockbusters as *Gentleman's Agreement*, *A Letter To Three Wives* and *All About Eve* and, although they had made the first cinemascope film a few years before, *The Robe*, things were not zingy at the box office. Their films with Marilym Monroe, queen of the lot and America's number one pin-up, usually made a profit, but of late Miss Monroe had been giving them certain

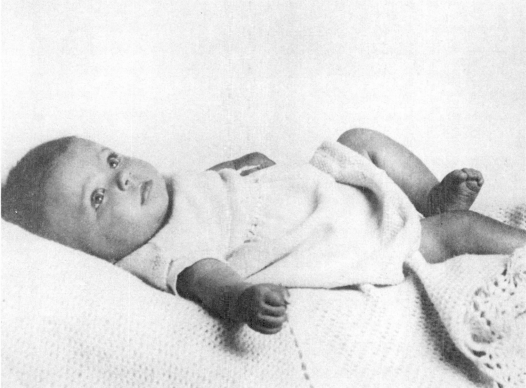

TOP: Mother, Father and Uncle Lew, now Lord Grade. I arrived seven hours later. No wonder she looks anxious. BOTTOM: Voila! 'I wonder what the world holds in store for me?'

TOP LEFT: Daddy earning our daily bread . . . TOP RIGHT: Mummy and Daddy taking the air — Dad in his Fred Astaire outfit. CENTRE LEFT: Hetty with my father — another beautiful baby! Note Hetty's emancipated attitude. CENTRE RIGHT: Pauline, Lalla and Joe: three well-behaved Edwardian children. BOTTOM: Grandma Henrietta Collins on tour in South Africa in the early 1900's.

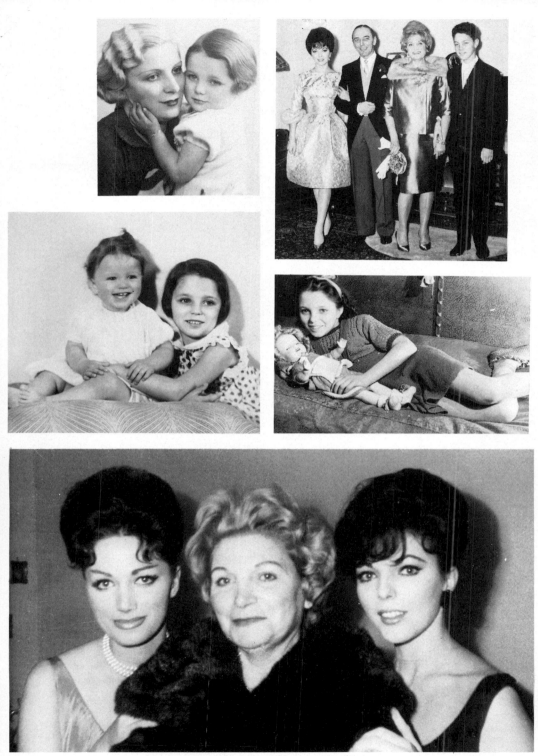

TOP LEFT: Mother love. TOP RIGHT: Joan hangs on to Daddy; Bill hangs on to Mummy. CENTRE LEFT: Sisterly affection. CENTRE RIGHT: Dolly love. BOTTOM: Elsa and her daughters. Two months before her death.

TOP LEFT: Baby bathing beauty — a bikini was considered *very* daring at the time. TOP RIGHT: My first rape scene — in the first British 'X' film, *Cosh Boy*, 1953. BOTTOM LEFT: The 'come hither' look that led to my discovery. BOTTOM RIGHT: The 'Coffee Bar Jezebel!'

CORNEL LUCAS

TOP LEFT: Maxwell Reed, my schoolgirl crush — the picture that started it all. TOP RIGHT: Wedding reception — eating out of his hand. BOTTOM LEFT: But they didn't live happily ever after. BOTTOM RIGHT: On the set of *The Square Ring*, 1953. Who's wearing the most mascara?

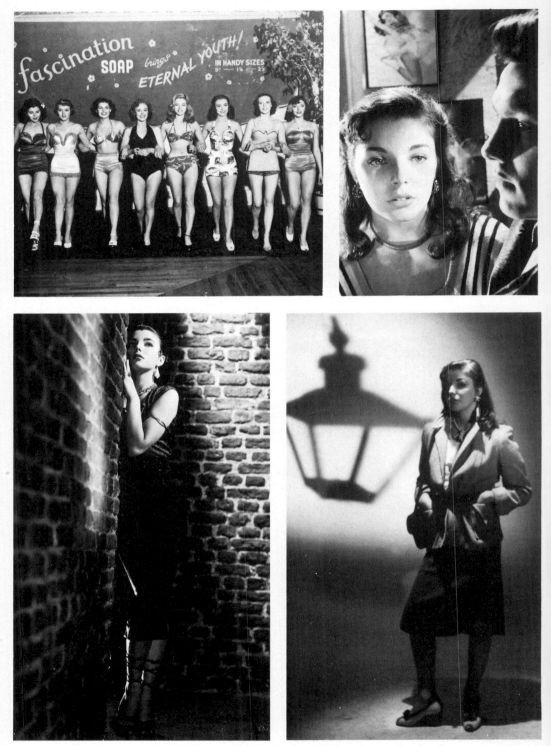

TOP LEFT: Stepping out to stardom in *Lady Godiva Rides Again*. In the line-up are Diana Dors and Anne Heywood. TOP RIGHT: First big break — *I Believe in You* with Laurence Harvey. BOTTOM LEFT: 'Britain's Bad Girl'. BOTTOM RIGHT: Thrilled with my career as a rising film star!

TOP LEFT: 'Santa Claus is coming to town' . . . and some of my other numerous publicity shots.

Rank signs me and announces me as 'Britain's answer to Ava Gardner'! I didn't feel she had to worry.

problems by refusing to make such epics as *The Lady In Pink Tights*, and had been spending time on suspension. Fox was starting to groom two girls, Jayne Mansfield and Sheree North, to take her place. They didn't take sass from anyone — not even Marilyn.

Goulash's words seemed anything but prophetic as I sat miserably alone night after night. The phone rang with invitations to dinner from men I had heard of but did not know. Nick Hilton — Bob Neal — Greg Bautzer — but I was faithful to Sydney and waited hopefully for him to arrive.

The vastness and variety of Los Angeles astounded me. The place went on for ever. Fashionable Beverly Hills — Gracious Bel Air — Swinging, youthful Westwood — Seedy Hollywood — and the endless suburban fringes — with quaint names like Pomona. Orange County, West Covina, Redlands, Santa Ana, Anahein — it seemed bigger than *England!* Each area had a character of its own and after I got a car I explored each of them diligently. I had never seen so many drug stores and gas stations in my life — but they all looked alike.

The only people I knew socially were the make-up man from *Land of the Pharaohs*, and my agents and, although they were very kind, and I went to dinner at their houses, I had not yet found any friends of my own. The social structure of Hollywood and Beverly Hills was based on dozens of varied cliques. Some people belonged to one clique and some overlapped and belonged to several. Three or four or five hundred people made up the social centre of Hollywood then, and I didn't know one of them.

I was cast in *The Virgin Queen*, a highly coloured and fictionalised account of Good Queen Bess's supposed romance with Sir Walter Raleigh. The redoubtable and legendary Bette Davis played Queen Elizabeth. This was the second time around for her, as she had had a huge success in *Elizabeth and Essex* some years back with Errol Flynn. Richard Todd played Raleigh and I played Elizabeth's innocent lady in waiting, in love with Raleigh and pregnant by him, much to Good Queen Bess's chagrin. Again I seemed to be playing a wayward girl, but instead of the sleazy costumes of *Cosh Boy* and *I Believe In You*, I was exquisitely dressed in beautiful Elizabethan hoop skirts and farthingales.

Painstaking effort and attention to detail went into the design and construction of these costumes. The wardrobe department at Fox was humming day and night with dozens of seamstresses, tailors, milliners and dressmakers making each creation a vision of perfection. I don't think even in the highest fashion houses of

Paris that there has ever been so much time and attention to detail lavished on clothing as there was at the major film studios during their heyday. Each costume was a work of art. One dress was completely embroidered in thousands of tiny seed pearls over rare Belgian lace. Each pearl was sewn on by hand, The inside seams and workmanship were as carefully done as the visible parts. For some outfits I would have six or seven complete fittings and stood for hours while every seam was measured to an exact eighth of an inch — God help me if I put on a pound or two at lunch. The waist seams would be snipped and unpicked painstakingly and the dress would be re-fitted all over again. After I endured this agony a couple of times, I bought a weighing machine and started watching my weight like a hawk. I was impatient at fittings and would yawn, stretch, scratch, fidget to the despair of these dedicated costumiers.

Bette Davis awed me, and I avoided her off the set whenever possible. I had been warned she did not take kindly to young, pretty actresses, and since she had a scathing wit and was not known for mincing words I thought it best to keep a low profile around her. I was still insecure about my work. Reviews from the British films constantly emphasised my looks and sex appeal, and this seemed the only aspect of me that the magazine writers and reporters were interested in talking about. My measurements, my love life, and what I ate for breakfast were of far more interest to them than my brain, my approach to my craft, and what I thought of the State of the Union.

I had been warned by the vast publicity department that I should not talk about anything controversial (politics, religion, capital punishment, etc) and there was a morals clause in my contract which guaranteed that if I did anything to invoke the wrath of the Daughters of the American Revolution, the members of the John Birch Society or any other of the dozens of anti-anything organisations that proliferated in America at that time I would be in trouble. America was in a time of prosperity but living in the aftermath of the Joe McCarthy hearings, and everyone attempted to be good, clean, upstanding, patriotic and loyal to America, with no whiff of communist leanings or subversive activities to sully their records.

Sydney finally arrived, and we rented a small, hygienic furnished apartment on Beverly Glen Boulevard, just four minutes from Fox, and set up house together. This was considered daring, living together openly, especially since I was still married, so we tried to keep it as quiet as possible, especially from the

Snoop Sisters, the gossip columnists Hedda Hopper and Louella Parsons.

I worked hard on *The Virgin Queen*. On my days off I would have to learn horseback riding, for me a frightening affair as horses petrified me. There were also the constant fittings, lunches and photo sessions, which went on endlessly.

It couldn't have been easy for Syd. He was living with a girl who not only was paying the rent, but also was busily working all the time. He was not, and there didn't seem to be much on the horizon for him so he threw himself into golf, cards and television. . .the man would get square eyes.

He'd changed. Maybe it was being away from his beloved Europe and his cronies. America did not suit him. There were no cosy corner cafes to pass the time of day sipping coffee and telling bawdy stories. No friendly neighbourhood bistros full of hearty. red-faced, black-bereted men knocking back absinthe and playing the pin-ball machines. No Ferrari. No night clubs to sit in until five in the morning, with the action still going strong. Add to this no work, and no wonder a sullen despondency suddenly settled on my handsome, usually laughing, usually happy lover.

All day, if he wasn't at the golf or tennis or bridge clubs, he was glued to the Box. 'Milton Berle', 'I Love Lucy', 'Dragnet', Ed Sullivan' . . . he watched them all. . .*AND* the soap operas, even the children's programmes. TV bored me stiff. It had been useful to watch in London as an alternative to Max's unromantic interludes, but I would much rather go to a movie and be enveloped in wide screen, colour and cinemascope than concentrate on a flickering black and white screen.

Life was an adventure, and although I was still shy and reticent with people I didn't know, I wanted to start experiencing it to the hilt.

Sydney was part of Gene Kelly's group. They were among the more stimulating and intellectual people in Hollywood, and included Harry Kurnitz, one of the writers on *Land of The Pharaohs*, one of the most amusing men who ever lived, Stanley Donen, Adolph Green and Betty Comden — playwrights who had had many smash musical successes on Broadway and were now writing musicals at MGM — Oscar Levant, a great wit and a great pianist, and Betsy Blair, Gene's wife, an actress and a very bright lady indeed. All of these people intimidated the hell out of me and although they all couldn't have been nicer I felt like an outsider.

I was still in my teens. It was only three years since I had made my first film in England and now I was part of a Hollywood group that I felt inferior to. They played volleyball which, on the rare occasions when I attempted to play, ended up with me spraining a finger or breaking a nail. And charades, which they all played with skill and expertise. Nevertheless, I loved hanging out at Gene's Cape Cod style house on Rodeo Drive, and observed and absorbed all I could. I wanted to expand my knowledge, which I felt was limited, having left the last of my many schools at fifteen. I wanted to learn. To experience more of the world of art, literature and music, and to be able to converse easily and knowledgeably with this, to me, highly civilised group. I was conscious of my lack of higher education. I wanted to belong and yet I felt like a little girl whose nose was pressed against the candy store window — a babe in the Hollywoods.

One Saturday night at the Kellys' I noticed a rather nondescript blonde girl sitting on the sofa near the bar. Nobody was paying any attention to her so I wandered over and started a conversation. It was unusual for me to find someone shyer than myself. She wore a white knitted silky dress, rather low cut and sleeveless, no bra which was frightfully daring in the mid-fifties. Her short blonde hair was combed carelessly. She had little make up on her pretty face. It was hard to realise that this was Miss Marilyn Monroe in the flesh! She appeared to be at the party without a date, but her mentor, Milton Greene, was lurking in the background somewhere.

She seemed glad that someone was talking to her and we discussed astrology and found out that we were both born under the sign of Gemini — 'the terrible twins'. She admired my hair which I wore long and straight with bangs, to the despair of the hairdressing department at Fox who were always trying to persuade me to cut it into a fashionable bubble cut. It was fascinating to talk to the world-famous Monroe — legendary sex symbol and idol of millions. She appeared just an ordinary shy girl with many complexes and a fear of people. She left the party early and I wondered if we would ever bump into each other on the Fox lot. But Marilyn was well-protected and insulated from the outside world at the studio and I never did see her again.

She had been supposed to star at Fox in a film about the Stanford White/Harry K. Thaw/Evelyn Nesbit triangle, one of the great scandals of the turn of the century, but she had refused to do it. Probably wisely since Evelyn Nesbit was supposed to be seventeen or eighteen years old and Marilyn, although marvellous-looking, was around thirty. The studio was going ahead with the movie which was to be called *The Girl In The Red Velvet Swing* and there was much rivalry on the lot as to who would get the plum role of Evelyn Nesbit.

Terry Moore, Debra Paget and several others were tested, and as soon as I completed *The Virgin Queen* I too was called to make a test. I didn't hold out much hope of getting the part because it was essential that the girl be American and I still had a strong British accent. I worked on an American accent studiously before the test and waited for the result which was not long in coming. I read the announcement in *The Hollywood Reporter* 'Collins to play Nesbit.' I was jubilant. To play the leading female role in what was to be one of Fox's most extravagant productions was an achievement for an English girl who had been under contract less than four months.

I was plunged into frantic preparations. Evelyn had started in the chorus at the Floradora Theatre so there were two lavish production numbers to learn and, although I had taken dancing classes since childhood, keeping up with professionals doing strenuous numbers like the Cakewalk was exhausting. We rehearsed the dances in the morning, and after a quick lunch break I would be over to wardrobe to fit some of the 27 costumes I was to wear. Then work for two hours on my accent with Jeff Hunter, a contract actor who had been assigned for some curious reason to be my vocal coach. It was hard to get rid of my clipped British delivery, and I realised that if the accent was going to be authentic at all I would have to adopt it for everyday life too. I instilled in myself a sort of mid-Atlantic drawl, which usually reverted back to clipped English whenever I returned to England. The word I was never able to master, however, was 'girl'. The 'rl' sound was impossible for me to say with the right drawl. So Jeff and I went through the script substituting whenever possible synonyms for any word ending in rl. . .not an easy task.

Richard Fleischer, a young director who had had recent successes at Fox was directing, and Ray Milland and Farley Granger were to play Stanford White the architect, and Harry K. Thaw the dissolute playboy respectively. If I thought I had been busy publicity-wise before, it was nothing to what happened now. The publicity department had instructions to fill the newspapers and magazines with stories and photos on me. After all, I was still relatively unknown, and Fox wanted to be sure my name was familiar to the American public before *Swing* was released. Now I didn't even have lunch hours to myself. Fox insisted that articles and photos of me were in all the major fan magazines.

In print I came out sounding like a cross between Margaret Rutherford and Linda Christian. 'She thinks America is cool, crazy and jolly good.' Enthusiastically bannered. . .*Photoplay* and *Modern Screen* — 'The Lady Is Dangerous', shrieked *Motion Picture*. Various epithets were attached to me: 'Bundle from Britain' — 'Electric and Elusive' — 'Cool, Cool Collins' — 'A Bohemian At Heart' — 'Global Glamour Girl' and my particular favourite from the Italian magazine *Oggi*: 'The Pouting Panther'!

I was maligned, scorned, criticised, lied about and my fairly normal mode of living was considered scandalous and disgraceful. All of a sudden I found myself with a reputation as a raving sex-pot, swinger, and home wrecker, whom Beverly Hills wives were supposed to live in fear of in case I cast my green 'orbs' in the direction of their men. Ninety-nine per cent of this was total fabrication. I was outspoken, yes; never a diplomat, I have always found it easier to tell the truth than beat around the bush, but the outrageous stories that proliferated about me surprised even the publicity department. For some reason I got an instant reputation as a free-living, free-loving rebel and it was hard for me to handle.

The electric, elusive bundle from Britain, Hollywood's gain and England's loss bounced into the tiny apartment after work one evening and excitedly started getting dressed for the first press screening of *The Virgin Queen*.

'The bathroom's all yours now,' I yelled to Syd who was lying on the orange living room couch engrossed in 'The Mouseketeers'. 'Aw honey, I'm really beat. I don't think I can make it,' he called, not raising his eyes from Annette Funnicello's ears. 'Beat. Beat from what?' I angrily surveyed myself in the bedroom mirror as I towel-dryed my hair.

He was always 'beat' lately. He played golf from noon 'til five, hung out and drank with the guys, and played poker all night — for stakes he could ill afford. The life and soul of every party we went to, at home he went into a morose depression. Whatever happened to the jokes and the laughter when we were alone together? 'Oh Sydney must be so much *fun* to be with all the time,' trilled a blonde starlet as we combed our locks together in the powder room of a Bel Air house, as he was at the bar wowing them with his gags. 'Sure,' I thought bitterly. 'Only if he has an audience of more than one.'

Recently we had adopted a new friend, as bitingly humorous and witty as Sydney but in a slightly more reserved way. Having him around guaranteed that there was never a dull moment, and for the past few weeks the three of us had been inseparable. His name was Arthur Loew, Jr, and he was the scion of one of the royal families of the motion picture industry. His grandfather Marcus Loew had founded Metro-Goldwyn-Mayer studios and his maternal grandfather, Adolph Zukor, was one of the oldest, most respected and most successful industry figures. Arthur dabbled in writing and producing features at MGM, but his heart was not truly in it and he was considered to be a rich playboy, squiring beautiful starlets to premieres and parties and living the good life.

I liked him a lot, and so did Sydney, so when Syd suggested that I go to the screening with Arthur my anger was slightly mollified. Recently I had confided in Arthur some of Syd's and my problems, and he had been a sympathetic and intelligent listener.

After the screening we went to dinner at a LaCienega steakhouse, and there on the red leather brass-buttoned banquette, drinking whisky sours and chain-smoking Chesterfields I started to feel an empathy with Arthur. He was extremely sensitive, an attribute he covered up with his flippant jokes and casual attitudes. He well understood Sydney's dilemma: that of a young out-of-work actor being practically supported by an even younger fast-rising actress, and the insurmountable problems we faced.

Sydney and I had never been strong on the communicative level. Deep feelings and profound philosophising were not verbalised between us. We never even argued. Our relationship, which had been great fun at the beginning had disintegrated badly because of a lack of communication. If I found eight pairs of slacks and ten sweaters and dozens of old socks on a chair for weeks, the pile growing and growing, I would not bother to make waves by mentioning it, even if it irritated me, so a chasm had developed. I tried to make him hustle to get jobs, but he was admittedly bone-lazy and would not go out of his way to grasp opportunities. In a town where opportunities must be grabbed as soon as they appear, this left him sitting by the phone waiting for it to ring. A deadly situation for any actor.

Arthur and I talked on and on. I felt I hadn't really *talked* to anyone for months. I had listened and gossiped and giggled and small talked, but it was an unusual experience to be having a deep conversation about feelings and emotions. Arthur was in analysis and had been for a few years. Although not yet thirty, and wealthy, he had suffered during his life. His parents had been divorced several times each and, although close to his mother, Mickey Loew, his great affinity was with his uncle Gerald, who lived in Arizona. 'One day I'll give up all this producing bull-shit and have a farm in Arizona and raise cattle,' he announced prophetically. 'How boring,' I thought to myself. 'What fun,' I said.

We fell in love. — or did we fall in 'like'? It seems to me that in the halcyon days of extreme youth saying 'I love you' was akin to saying 'Pass the Salt.' The feelings I had for Syd for nearly a year were gradually over a period of weeks transferred to Arthur. Sydney left for Portland, Oregon, to make a western with Jeff Chandler, and after visiting him there for a few days I told him the truth and we parted without bitterness.

I am a strong advocate of monogamy — sequentially, that is. I think it is hard. . .very hard to stay desperately and madly in love for any length of time. Be it three months, three years or fifteen years. Eventually a time will come when the thrill is gone and if there is not something infinitely stronger than romantic sexual attraction, the relationship will flounder. Only with experience can one realise at the onset if a relationship has a true basis of compatibility which can surmount the vagaries of a fickle heart.

With Arthur's encouragement I threw myself into thrice-weekly analysis to try and find out what and why and who the hell I was. At the same time I was trying to fulfil myself as an actress and was caught up in the merry-go-round of being made into a 'star'. I started to hate the word star. It denoted being untouchable. Stars are perfect. They are revered and worshipped. They must always look and act and dress as if they are not mortal. Watching the careers of Elizabeth Taylor and Brigitte Bardot, I have felt pity and sympathy for women who cannot even go to the corner drug store without causing a riot; whose every move is tabloid fodder. Who can live a normal life with the harness of stardom around their neck? To have the constant pressure of having to live up to the box office returns of your last picture. To have every line and wrinkle in your face eagerly awaited by avid gossip-columnists. To be surrounded by yes-men and pressures that a 'civilian' would find hard to understand, is unhealthy and poisonous to the mind and spirit.

It takes a very strong character indeed to become a star. . .remain a star. . . .and, be a real person. Paul Newman is one of the few people I know who is unaffected by his more than twenty years of stardom. But there are dozens who, believing in their invulnerability and their publicity, have fallen from the grace of the public to become bitter, sad and pathetic people — seeking solace in drink, drugs or frantic sexual activity.

I realised in analysis that that was not my goal. Above the title — below the title — it wasn't important. I wanted to work, I wanted to *live*, and I wanted to enjoy my life and my work without obligations to a public whose fickleness stars lived in fear of.

I took a small apartment on Olive Drive just off the Sunset Strip, conveniently located for Ciro's and the Mocambo nightclub and near Arthur Loew's house on Miller Drive. I worked practically every day on *Swing* and every Saturday morning, so there was not time to play. I was determined to give a good performance as Evelyn, but I found that a great deal more emphasis than I wanted was being attached to my physical appearance. Granted, Evelyn was the original 'Gibson Girl' and one of the great beauties from an age in which great beauties abounded, but I felt the constant scrutiny of a corps of make-up men, hairdressers, costumiers, lighting directors, cameramen and even the director, Richard Fleischer, were beginning to inhibit me.

I was supposed to look exquisite in every frame of the film which entailed being combed, sprayed, kiss-curled, powdered and lip-glossed before and after every single take. If I moved too violently and a stray lock would fall out of place I would hear 'Cut' and the wrecking crew would leap to my person. If my smile became too broad there would be the dreaded word again, 'Cut. Joan, don't smile so wide, you're showing your gums,' or 'the light's reflecting off her teeth.' 'Joanie, a little less *grin*, sweetheart — you look like you're catching flies with that smirk.' If I did not hit my mark *exactly*, the key light would be a millimetre off, meaning my face would not be totally perfectly lit. 'Cut, let's go again.' I was frightened to breathe too hard in case they complained about my chest moving too much.

Added to this were the costumes which although breathtakingly gorgeous to look at, were agony to wear. I wore an authentic corset which laced my waist into the fashionable hour-glass figure of the 1900s. On top of this went several lace petticoats with millions of ruffles, a camisole and then one of the 27 gowns, all of which had more tiny bones in them than a kipper! The collars had little bones or stays in them so that if I moved my head at too much of an angle I would get stabbed in the throat. On my head sat an enormous black wig, beautiful but heavy, secured with 97 hairpins and stuck to my forehead and the side of my face with glue. Sometimes on top of this hair would rest a gigantic hat —

covered in cock feathers, or an abundance of flowers on trailing ribbons, and this was secured to the wig with several lethal hat pins. To dress and arrange the wig alone took an hour and a half each morning — and then another 45 minutes for make-up and body make-up, which was applied to every inch of skin the camera might possibly glimpse. Add to this the extremely hot lights, and the presence of the REAL Evelyn Nesbit Thaw on the set, watching me like a hawk, and I was understandably nervous.

Mrs Thaw was a lady in her 70s and any vestige of the great beauty she had once possessed was long gone, except for the luxuriant grey hair. I scrutinised her features to find some residual of her looks but to no avail. She was fond of the gin bottle, and ate violet-scented cashews to disguise the smell. They didn't. Closer than a foot from her face and I became dizzy from the fumes. She constantly told me how much I reminded her of herself when she was a young girl and the toast of New York, and showed me fabulous paintings and photographs of herself from that era. I found this utterly depressing. . .To have been one of the world's great beauties and to finish a penniless, garrulous old woman was an ironic twist of fate. To be born physically perfect is akin to being born rich, and gradually becoming poorer with age. I felt thankful that I did not think myself particularly beautiful and would, perhaps, with maturity be able to develop the inner me rather than the exterior which was currently being so over-emphasised.

On days when I was not on call I threw on old jeans and a shirt, leaving off make-up completely and, in fact, barely bothering to brush my hair and went to the supermarket — a place I loved. The studio was not thrilled to see their rising glamour girl looking like a fugitive from Bucks County and the awesome Hedda Hopper severely censured me in print for 'looking like she combs her hair with an egg beater'. Dick Fleischer, coming across me lolling with a group of girlfriends in the commissary one day threw up his hands in mock horror exclaiming, 'My God, I didn't recognise you. You look so ugly!' This caused me in my over-sensitive state to cry. I seemed to be going from the sublime to the ridiculous. I got the reputation of being a rebel, a swinger and a non-conformist, in a day when it was un-chic to be so.

Anyone whose mode of dress was in any way unkempt was suspect. Brando and James Dean were the foremost exponents of the new 'couldn't give a damn attitude'. Both were greatly admired on one hand, but by the so-called Establishment they were also despised.

Jimmy Dean was a fascinating young man who had become a giant star with his first movie *East of Eden*. He played to perfection the brooding troubled boy in competition with his more favoured brother, and questing for the truth about his relationship with his mother. The youth of the fifties immediately adopted him as their symbol and his star ascended rapidly. He made *Rebel Without a Cause* which was written by Arthur's cousin, Stewart Stern, and immediately after that was completed, starred in the mammoth production of *Giant*.

It was during the filming of *Giant* that I first met him. It was a brief meeting at a small dinner party in the Valley. I was particularly mesmerised by his eyes, which were a deep piercing blue and could change instantly from a look of sullen brooding to an expression of extreme mischievousness. He was quite short for a film actor and had longish, blond wavy hair. He seemed enormously shy and held the hand of his girlfriend, a gorgeous Swiss starlet under contract to Paramount called Ursula Andress. She had a fabulous body and the shortest haircut I had ever seen, and they made a striking couple, both in white tee shirts and levis.

We saw him sometimes at the home of Oscar Levant, a witty brooding man known for his succinct and biting humour. On one occasion Oscar remarked after viewing me in a rather low cut blouse, 'I have now seen every part of Joan's anatomy except her forehead!' This was because I always wore bangs that almost covered my eyes.

Jimmy and Oscar, although tremendous opposites, got along famously. Each relished the other's unusualness. Arthur and I would drop by the Levants' after dinner and sit until the early hours talking and laughing, and Jimmy would often be present.

A group of us had dinner one night at Don the Beachcomber's, a Polynesian restaurant in Hollywood, noted for its incredibly strong rum-based drinks. After three or four Navy Grogs I was feeling delightfully daring, so when Jimmy asked who would like a drive in his brand new red Porsche I cheerfully volunteered. Arthur, who usually indulged most of my whims with good grace, pulled me aside and told me not to drive with Jimmy. 'He drives like a maniac,' he said earnestly. 'And after four of those "Zombies", or whatever the hell it was we've been drinking, it's too dangerous.' 'Oh don't be such a stick in the mud,' I giggled. 'Come on, Jimmy. Let's race them to Oscar's house.' we jumped into his shiny new Porsche, the interior was cramped and it smelled of new leather, but it was indeed a beauty. Jimmy threw the gears into first and with the gear box protesting violently we screeched into the Hollywood Boulevard traffic. During the ten minutes it took us to get to Beverly Hills I sobered up rapidly. He certainly did drive fast, recklessly, but with the summer wind blowing through the open windows and the radio blaring classical music, it was exhilarating, but scary.

'Don't you think we should slow down,' I said nervously, as we sped down the Strip at about 70 miles an hour, dodging in and out of the after dinner traffic. He gave me one of his mischievous, brooding looks. 'Chicken?' he asked. 'What, me — oh no. I'd just like to live to be 21.' I gulped nervously, hoping a cop car would miraculously appear. 'The thing about these cars is that they're fail-safe,' he said, expertly overtaking a bleached blonde in a Cadillac and oozing in just a car's-length behind a slow moving Ford. 'These cars are made like tanks. They have the best engine and the best transmission, they're totally safe,' he talked on about the merit of his baby until we screeched to a stop in front of the Levants'. 'Well, thanks a lot Jimmy,' I said descending on trembling legs. 'If I ever need a quick ride to the airport I'll call on you.' 'Do that,' he lit up a cigarette and smiled at me sleepily, amused by my timorousness. 'Let's go see Oscar.' I followed him into the house, making a mental note never to get in a moving vehicle with him again. When Arthur arrived 15 minutes later I told him he was right about Jimmy's driving. 'He's going to kill himself one of these days if he continues to drive like that!'

A couple of months later I was in New York at the Plaza and doing promotion for *Virgin Queen*. The doorbell rang insistently and woke me up. It was only 8.00, far too early. I grumpily trundled to the door. 'It's me, Arthur,' said a strained voice. I opened up. Ashen-faced, he handed me the *New York Times* and then went and sat heavily on the sofa. I read unbelievingly: 'James Dean dies in automobile accident.' He was killed in the red Porsche. He was 24.

Arthur and I walked into Chasens, one of my favourite restaurants. It was Friday night — no work tomorrow and I could go on a two-day eating binge. I was looking forward to having shrimp cocktail and steak Diane, and the terrific hashed in cream potatoes Chasens is renowned for. Maybe even a soufflé for dessert. A headline caught my eye on the front page of the *Los Angeles Times*, stacked neatly on the steps outside the restaurant. 'Actor sues actress for $1,250 support per month,' screamed the banner.

'Oh darling, buy the paper. I wonder who that is,' I chirped.

We sat in our booth and I scanned the paper. My face stared out at me smiling from column two.

'Oh my God!!!' I howled to the surprise of the head waiter, who was smiling and taking our order for drinks. He raised his eyebrows fractionally, ignoring the outburst.

'Christ, that rotten bastard has gone and sued me. What am I going to *do*???' I wailed. Arthur grabbed the paper and read the article out loud.

'Actor Maxwell Reed announced from London today that he was suing his wife, actress Joan Collins, for $1,250 dollars per month. "I know this is unusual," said Reed, "but I have not worked in over a year and am practically destitute. My wife has been in Hollywood for the past nine months. She is making a lot of money and I think she owes me something".' The article continued but we didn't bother to read any more.

We looked at each other. He smiled and patted my hand.

'Poor Babee,' he said playfully. 'Didn't your mummy tell you that all men are rotten?' When things got rough Arthur joked, and I was not in the mood for jokes. Being sued for alimony is a fairly common occurrence for men — but I had never heard of a woman being sued before.

My parents had been sending me various stories that had been appearing in the English press about Max. They were all based on the same snivelling premise.

'I found her. I made her a success. I loved her. She left me . . . to go to Hollywood. Now I can't get a job.' One particularly revolting story featured a picture of Max trying to look humble in a $45 cashmere sweater and heavily mascaraed eyebrows, clutching a large photo of me to his breast, and complaining about his love for me and his poverty . . . and he was wondering why no one would employ him! It was nauseating, but I was so busy, I had no time to think of divorce plans and, like Scarlett O'Hara, 'I'd think about that tomorrow.'

Nothing, however, could put me off food and we ate heartily, whilst discussing strategy. At the end of the evening my face felt very hot, and hive-like bumps had broken out over my back and shoulders. Peculiar, I thought, probably nerves — and dismissed it from my mind.

I started shooting what I considered to be my first 'grown-up' role. In other films I had played girls — wayward, spoiled, delinquent, or sexy. Nevertheless they were juvenile-type parts. But the part

67

of Crystal in *The Opposite Sex*, a remake of *The Women* was definitely not a girl. She was all woman. . .and more!

The Women had been a big success in the 1930s, with Joan Crawford as Crystal. The cast had included Norma Shearer, Paulette Goddard, Joan Fontaine and Rosalind Russell.

MGM, who had borrowed me from Fox for this part, was getting an equally prestigious cast for the latest version. June Allyson, the darling of the Metro lot; Ann Sheridan, 'The Oomph Girl'; Ann Miller, Dolores Gray and Carolyn Jones, and many others were set for this up-to-date version of ladies in the jungle warfare of sex, men, husband-snatching, gossip, backbiting and bitchery. Crystal was the biggest bitch of them all. . .and loved it. She was a showgirl who has an affair with June Allyson's husband, and flaunts it to the world.

Although the part was not that large it was flashy and juicy, and I had some good scenes. June confronts me in my dressing room and accuses me of the affair. I nonchalantly continue with removing my brief stage costume and changing into street clothes while she addresses me and progressively becomes more angry. June was a tiny lady, about five foot two in heels. She was famous for her cute blonde bob and her 'Peter Pan' collars. She was petite, delicate and ladylike so I was not concerned about the fact that she had to slap my face after the following dialogue:

June: 'By the way, if you're dressing for Steven I wouldn't wear that. He doesn't like clothes quite so obvious.'

Crystal: 'When Steven doesn't like what I wear I take it off!'. . .and she hauled off and belted me. And little June, with her tiny hands, had a punch like Rocky Marciano! I felt as if a steam roller had hit me. Something fell from my face and hit the floor with a loud clatter — my teeth — Oh God, no. Please don't let her have knocked out my *TEETH*! My head was ringing as the slaps had connected to my ears, and I couldn't hear a thing. Stars danced before my eyes and I staggered to a chair and collapsed.

'Cut — Cut, for Christ's sake Cut!' screamed director David Miller.

'What the *HELL's* going on here?' June burst into tears and collapsed into another chair. Make-up men and dressers rushed to the set with smelling salts and succour.

I put my hands tentatively to my mouth. Thank God, a full set of teeth still, but what flew off me? The wardrobe lady solved the mystery, retrieving the long rhinestone earrings, which the strength of June's slap had sent spinning. But any more shooting was out of the question. On each of my cheeks was forming the perfect imprint of a tiny hand! Branded, if not for life, for two or three days, as it took that long for the welts to go down. June was desperately sorry and it took longer to calm her down than it did me. Luckily when they saw the scene on rushes it was unnecessary to re-shoot the slap — it had complete authenticity!

I had a number of problems on *The Opposite Sex*. A long bathtub scene entailed Crystal sitting in an ornate marble bathtub, covered in bubbles, talking on the telephone to her boyfriend, and having a conversation with Dolores Gray and a little girl. David Miller believed in endless rehearsals, and we rehearsed for two days, with me immersed in bubbles. Since bubbles do not last very long the prop men had to keep adding to the water a mixture of dishwashing liquid, Lux soap flakes and detergent.

At the end of the first day my nether regions were pink and puffy. At the end of the second day they were sore and swollen. On the third day, when we finally started to shoot I was a mass of tender raw flesh. It was agony to sit down and when the detergent-filled water touched my body I felt as though I was Joan of Arc being burned at the stake. The misery on my face was evident. Something had to be done. The studio doctor was called to give me pain-killing injections, and the prop department evolved an ingenious contraption to prevent my delicate blistered body from touching the water. To the onlooker viewing the scene, one saw a glamorous creature chatting cattily on the phone, luscious bubbles cascading around her body. Underneath the bubbles, however, was a sheet of strong plywood with a hole cut in it to fit my body and the bubbles were on top of the plywood. Underneath the plywood I was encased in vaseline and bandages, and on top of this an attractive pair of men's longjohns from the gentlemen's wardrobe department. Over this was a large rubber sheet in case any sneaky bubbles managed to slither through the armour. I sat on several cushions and all in all, was feeling no pain and relishing the comparative comfort of these appliances.

Then a young man burst onto the set in the middle of a scene.

'Joan Collins?' he asked accusingly.

'Errr yes — I think so,' I said nervously, signalling to the assistant director to remove this madman before he did me some injury.

'Cut — Cut,' yelled David. 'What the Hell's going on around here. Who is this jerk?'

'Sign here, please,' said the jerk, handing me a summons from my dependable husband. I read it unbelievingly while three assistant directors gave the smirking successful 'process-server' the bum's rush. (Years later Max's lawyer proudly declared in the national newspapers that it was he personally who had served me the subpoena.) Maxwell Reed was taking me to court and insisting that I pay him the $1,250 a month he had demanded for support. It was an injunction from a Los Angeles Court judge. I had to do something. And fast.

Fred Leopold was an attorney who specialised in divorce cases and he later became Mayor of Beverly Hills. He advised me to pay up. I had a seven-year contract starting at $1,250 a week for the first year, and escalating to $5,000 for the seventh year. He told me that if I did not make a deal with Max now that he might wait two or three years and get even more money from me in the future. I was furious. It was unfair. His allegation that he had 'discovered' me and sent me to Hollywood was totally false. I thought I had escaped his vindictiveness but I still sometimes awoke in the middle of the night with the terrifying nightmare again: 'One day you'll think you're safe, Baby. But one night you'll walk around a dark corner and one of the "boys" will come and carve that pretty little face of yours up until no one will ever want to look at you again.'

I woke in a cold sweat. It was chilling and not beyond the realm of possibility that he would do this ghastly thing to me. God knows he knew enough petty criminal types around London. And now he had come here, to Los Angeles. To try to find work . . . . and to get money from me.

I moved into Arthur's house on Miller Drive. Fred Leopold advised me strongly against it but I was scared, and I needed someone close by when I woke up with the nightmare.

The divorce cost me over $10,000. I had to get an advance in salary from Fox for I did not have that kind of money even though I did not live lavishly. Leopold had persuaded Max to accept a lump sum of $4,250 — after convincing him and his lawyers that I was not as wealthy as they expected. I also gave him all the money in our joint bank account in London. . .about $1,400, and I had over $4,000 in legal fees to pay — his and mine. The judge in Los Angeles Superior Court seemed amazed at this settlement and cross-examined me on the stand for 10 minutes as to why I was paying this supposedly-healthy, reasonably-young man such a grand sum. I prayed that the divorce would be granted and that I would be finished with Maxwell Reed for ever. He granted it. I walked out of the courtroom a free woman — older — wiser — poorer and with a growing distrust and hostility toward men.

My mother's words were always in the back of my mind. 'Men only want one thing. Men will use a girl like a piece of Kleenex, then throw her away when they are tired of her.'

Although part of me realised these phrases were ridiculous and biased, another part of me said: 'She's right. She's right. Look at how badly my father treated her. Look at how Barry abused you — *and* Max, and now even Arthur.'

I looked at Arthur, sprawled out on the comfortable sofa of his ranch-style house high in the Hollywood Hills. He was as bad as the others. He had me. I lived with him. I bought all my own clothes and furs (although he had given me a few pieces of jewellery). I paid for my airfare when I went to London. I was young — beautiful — desired by many men. . .successful. Why should he have all of this for nothing. He was young, rich and good-looking. Tall, blond, thin — an aquiline nose and a terrific sense of humour. I liked him. We had fun together. I wasn't 'in love' because ours was not a passionate relationship, but I felt great affection for him. Maybe I should marry him.

He had recently finished producing a film starring Paul Newman called *The Rack*. Newman was talking to Arthur now. The two of them lolled on the sofa drinking beer and telling jokes like schoolboys. The house was full of people, as it was most nights. Arthur ran an open house and there were always eight or ten people for dinner. I was leaving for London in a week to start another film. The gossip columnists had started hinting that we were on the verge of matrimony — well, why not? It seemed like a good idea at the time.

After all the guests departed I broached the subject.

'Do you think we ought to date other people while I'm gone?' I said casually pouring two cognacs into large snifters and handing him one. He looked at me quizzically, 'Who have you got in mind, Richard Burton?' Burton was to be my co-star in *Sea Wife*.

'Burton's married,' I said flatly. 'No, I mean three months is a long time to be apart.'

'But I'm going to visit you in Jamaica,' he interrupted.

'I know that,' I said trying to get to the point. 'How do you feel about me going out with other men, then?'

'I'd rather you didn't,' he said flatly, drinking the cognac and preparing to end the conversation.

'Well, then what are you going to do about it, Arthur? If you don't want me to date other guys then we ought to get engaged or something.'

71

'Engaged!' he looked flabbergasted. 'You've only been divorced five minutes. You've been saying for a year that you don't EVER want to get married again, so why do you want to get engaged, for Christ's sake?'

'Don't you want to?' I said calmly, lighting a Pall Mall and blowing furious smoke rings.

'It isn't that I don't want to, Babee,' he slumped beside me and entwined his long bony fingers in mine. 'I just don't know if I can be faithful to you for that length of time.'

I looked at him with growing consternation. 'You mean you want to fuck around?'

'Spoken like the Queen of England,' he said dryly. 'No, my dear, I don't *want* to fuck around, as you so beautifully put it, but if, in the twelve weeks of our separation, a lady should appear who should — how shall I say — arouse my libido, I might. . .just might find the temptation alluring enough to — well — yes fuck around,' he drained his glass and looked at me, his boyish face challenging. 'It doesn't mean I don't love you, Babee. '

'Yeah, what's a fuck between friends,' I said sarcastically, pulling my fingers away from his. 'Don't you have any *control?*'

'I'll tell you what,' he pulled my rigid body towards him and put his arms around my shoulders. 'Let's play it by ear. If we can be faithful to each other during the time you're away then I think we should get engaged when you come back. You funny old-fashioned thing, you,' he pulled me towards him and I moved my face quickly so that his lips connected with my ear.

'OK,' I jumped up and ground my cigarette out violently. 'That's a terrific idea, Arthur. You try to be faithful to me, and I,' I looked him straight in the eye. 'I will *try* to be faithful to you. And now I'm going to bed.' I walked upstairs, seething with rage. How dare he put me on trial. Who did he think he *was?* Another phrase of my father's flitted through my thoughts: 'Why buy the cake when you can have a slice for free?'

I felt degraded, full of pain. I determined to try and hurt him.

Fox were about to film *Sea Wife and Biscuit.* It was a best-selling novel about a nun wrecked on a desert island with three men! I had already made *Our Girl Friday* which also had a girl on an island with three men, but for me to play a nun was not only the biggest acting challenge I had yet faced but also to many people one of the greatest pieces of miscasting since Lana Turner played a vestal virgin.

Roberto Rossellini, the volatile and talented Italian film

director, famous not only for having directed the touchingly beautiful *Open City*, but also for his volcanic affair and subsequent marriage to Ingrid Bergman, had chosen me as his 'Face of Innocence', after seeing one reel of *The Girl In The Red Velvet Swing*. He obviously realised that behind the wigs costumes and plastic facade I presented in that film that there was a naive and vulnerable young girl. And Italians do have perception! Rossellini was a stubborn, opinionated genius, who had total autonomy over all his productions. This was to be his first American film and he was determined to do it his way.

Fox was agreeable to practically everything he wanted except for one thing. They absolutely would not allow Richard Burton who played 'Biscuit' to kiss 'Sea Wife' the nun. Rossellini thought this was an essential part of the story, as it is in the novel.

Although Fox was making another nun film, with sexual overtones, around the same time, *Heaven Knows Mr Allison*, with Deborah Kerr and Robert Mitchum, nonetheless they were strongly opposed to there being any *hint* of sex between Burton and myself on the screen. For one thing, they would never ever get a seal of approval from the censor, and for another, every Catholic women's group in America would be up in arms, probably boycotting *all* their movies. So they were understandably worried about Signor Rossellini's pre-occupation with the kissing scene.

That was the least of my worries, as I arrived in London to face a barrage of press, splitting their sides with laughter at the thought of 'Britain's Bad Girl' playing a nun.

'Sister Sizzle' giggled Donald Zec in the *Daily Mirror*.

'Is *this* the face of Innocence?' jeered the *Daily Sketch*, under a two-column picture of me with a ruby in my belly button and a come-hither look in my eye. All the old labels were pulled out: 'Torrid Baggage' — 'Coffee Bar Jezebel' — and the press had a field day with this excruciatingly funny piece of Show Biz news. The more I tried to be serious and mature in the countless interviews I gave, the more the press sent me up. It was hurtful, because I really did believe that I was right for Sea Wife. Without make-up and with my hair cropped short and unstyled I did have a trusting, innocent look, and I resented the attitude that most people were taking towards me.

Arthur had christened the picture before I left for California: 'I fucked a Nun!' and the sacrilegious side of this was quite funny.

I spent the two weeks of pre-production in London immersing myself in every book on Catholicism I could get my hands on.

And visiting a group of nuns in a small convent in Chelsea. I spent many hours with them, observing their attitudes, manners and bearing. They were a delightful group of women and girls, with a wonderful inner glow and beauty that emanated from their whole beings. Some of them even had wicked and wild senses of humour, and many of my preconceived notions of nuns as 'holier-than-thou goodie-goodies' were shattered. They were real, warm, vibrant human beings who were happier and more at peace with themselves than most of the people I knew.

We made the usual make-up and costume tests, and with my scrubbed face, short no-style hair and nun's habit, it looked very much as if Rossellini's intuition had been right and I did have the 'face of innocence'.

Meanwhile, there were two scripts to study. One, the Fox-approved script, without any intimations of sex and love between Biscuit and Sea Wife, and the other, Rossellini's infinitely more interesting story of a young novice nun, who had not yet taken her final vows, finding her emotions deeply disturbed by an extended period of time on a deserted island with an attractive and compassionate man. And in the latter script the two do indeed have a 'romantic involvement', which necessitated some torrid love scenes.

Rossellini had left for location scouting in Jamaica after our initial brief meeting and film test in London. There he remained with script number two which he was now adamant was the only one he would shoot.

When the cast and crew arrived in Jamaica we found Signor Rossellini incommunicado in his suite at the Jamaica Inn. We set up camp and waited for the first day's shooting to commence. We had been hearing rumbles of major rows on the phone between the Fox Brass back in LA and Rossellini. The assistant directors kept on saying we would be shooting tomorrow or the day after, but several days went by with nothing happening, and everyone sat around swimming, drinking rum punches and playing poker, having a relaxing holiday in the sun. . .all expenses paid.

Four days later a call sheet was pushed under the door of my suit. 'Title of Production: "Sea Wife" — 1st Day's Shooting — Exterior Shipwreck — Director, Bob McNaughton.'

'Bob McNaughton!!!! Who the hell was *he*?'

I rushed next door to the Burtons' suite to find out what was going on. Richard was sitting with his pretty Welsh wife, Sybil, drinking tea and playing Scrabble. He seemed not at all perturbed by my agitation and confirmed what I, and the rest of the crew,

had feared. Fox would not back down on their script. Roberto
Rossellini would not back down on his version. It was a total
impasse. Rossellini was fired and instead of spending the time and
money to import another director from London or America, Fox
was putting the reins in the hands of a director, Bob McNaughton,
who was on the unit list as 'Production Manager'!

A production manager was going to direct *Sea Wife*! I was
horrified. I had been looking forward to being directed in this role
by the fabulously talented Rossellini, whose ability to get
magnificent performances from his cast, and to bring magic to the
screen was legendary. What a bummer! What chance did I stand
now of being sensational. Although I was fairly confident in my
ability to play the role, I knew that I needed the extra impetus that
only a really good director can give to an actor to make my
performance come believably alive. And what of Bob
McNaughton? The poor guy would have so many problems with
just the mechanics and technicalities of everyday filming, I felt
sure there would be little time to give me the support and help I
needed.

He turned out to be a nice, stolid, middle-aged Englishman,
eminently more suited to dealing with the million and one major
and minor details of managing a production than 'directing' one.
The picture thus became just another 'run-of-the-mill' programme
filler. Burton didn't give a damn about it. This was the last of his
multiple picture deals with Fox and he didn't particularly like the
script or his role. He had a 'take-the-money-and-run' attitude
towards it, which I found quite depressing. Already a millionaire,
he had cleverly set up all sorts of tax havens and was one of the
very first actors to take up residence in Switzerland. Although a
successful film actor, his true love was still the theatre, and he was
longing to get back to New York where he was due to do a play.

Burton was about thirty-three years old, with thick, light
brown hair, intense strong features and eyes of a piercingly
hypnotic greenish-blue. His voice was magnificent — deep,
resonant — a voice made to declaim *Hamlet* and indeed all of
Shakespeare's plays. His skin left a lot to be desired, however.
Due to years near the coal mines of Wales his back and shoulders
were deeply pitted and rutted with pimples, blackheads and what
looked like small craters.

I had admired him for years, and as a schoolgirl had stood
outside the Queens Theatre on Shaftesbury Avenue to get his
autograph after seeing his performances in Jean Anouilh's *Ring
Round The Moon*. I had watched him, mesmerised by his voice

and talent, from high up in the 'Gods', and thought him so devastatingly handsome and talented that I immediately wrote off for an autographed photo, which duly arrived personally signed: 'Thank you for your letter. Best wishes, Richard Burton.' This treasured memento went into the autograph book along with other trusty favourites. And now, here I was acting opposite this paragon of theatrical proficiency.

His reputation as a lady's man had also preceded him. Although married, rumours of his affairs were discussed knowingly and openly and he lost no time in making known his intentions towards me. A few days after filming had commenced we took a swim together during the lunch hour to a small diving raft a few hundred yards from shore. I wore a bikini, no make-up and short-short hair, and presented a wholesome and well-scrubbed look. I lay on my back on the raft, eyes closed, panting after the swim and feeling the hot Jamaican sun absorbing the salt water from my skin. I was feeling happy. I was enjoying the film and Bob McNaughton was nice, not a terrific director, but not bad either. The crew was fun, mostly English, and I had been spending a lot of time with them playing poker and giggling at their typical English humour. Arthur had written me several letters, professing undying love and adoration and 'fidelity', and missing me madly, and I was in the sun all the time, which pleased me as I was an avid sun-worshipper and got deeply tanned. I was working on the tan when I felt fingers gently stroking my wet hair.

'Did anyone ever tell you you look pretty with short hair?' he said, casually moving his hand down lower.

'Yes,' I said, firmly removing the roving hand and squinting up at the gorgeous greenish eyes, now a foot from mine.

'Mr Rossellini thought I looked adorable with short hair. And so does Arthur, my BOY FRIEND.' Hint — Hint. That should stop him.

'Ah, yes, of course, you go out with the heir to the Loew millions, don't you?' he said, amused and not at all deterred by my evasive tactics.

'Yes. He's very JEALOUS.' I peeked through my wet lashes to see if he had taken the implication.

'My dear, what the eye does not see the heart does not grieve for,' he breathed and pressed his salty lips to my firmly closed ones. I gritted my teeth and let him kiss me. There is nothing more off-putting to a man than to kiss a girl who is a block of stone.

'Why don't you relax,' he whispered, his hand fiddling with the ties on my bikini top. 'None of the crew can see us.'

'I am relaxed,' I said gaily. 'Relaxed, and lying in the sun and thinking about *ARTHUR!*'

He laughed and lay back on the raft next to me. I turned and looked at him. He certainly was attractive. . .if you ignored the spots. But Mrs Burton was languishing in her suite at the hotel, and I was not about to get involved with a married Don Juan.

He looked at me and we both smiled.

'I'll get you yet, Miss Collins,' he said lightly and then proceeded to tell me vivid details about his seductions and conquests of of the actresses he had worked with — on stage and screen!

'How fascinating,' I breathed during this lengthy saga of lust and intrigue on sets and in dressing rooms and elegant boudoirs.

'They *ALWAYS* succumbed to you finally?'

'Always,' he said triumphantly. 'Even if,' looking meaningful, 'they were not receptive at the outset'.

'Well, it should be interesting to see what happens now,' I said noticing that the third assistant was signalling to us frantically from the beach.

'You have eight more weeks on location with me, but I never have liked being part of a collection.' I dove into the warm Caribbean ocean and swam rapidly back to where the crew were assembling for the next set up. He followed, joking and talking until we got to shore. It was amusing. The great Richard Burton, not only a womaniser but a scalp collector to boot! It would give me the greatest of pleasure to NOT be another one on his belt.

I was in the mood for some romantic involvement, however. Even though I missed Arthur a lot, I was still bitter about his doubts of faithfulness while we were apart. If that were the case, then I was determined to be the first to fall.

Jamaica at night was incredibly romantic. The Inn at Ocho Rios was right on the beach, and the seemingly endless full bright moon, shimmering on the white-gold sand, and the gently waving palm trees and the sound of steel bands playing in the lounge of the hotel, echoing in the background was a honeymooner's paradise. Many years later, when I married Ron Kass, we went back to Jamaica and to Ocho Rios for our wedding and honey-moon.

Although I was not a honeymooner I gazed enviously at those

who were, and spent my evenings either alone in my room or walking on the beach, or playing cards with the crew, and finally, it was the young focus-puller on the camera crew whom I chose to make my evenings less lonely. He was twenty-six, with thick curly blond hair, an angelic boyish face and a dark tan, which was well in evidence most of the time as his working clothes on location consisted of a red bathing suit and tennis shoes. Our eyes would meet fifty times a day as he would pull the tape from the camera to my nose to measure the correct focus. Since I was the only young girl on the picture, quite a few of the crew were locking eyes with mine after the first week or so, but as soon as he and I paired off they stopped. Other location romances also blossomed throughout the unit via the numerous visitors to the romantic island.

DCOL became one of the catch phrases of the location. 'Doesn't Count On Location!' Like shipboard romances, which take fire throughout the voyage and fade quickly at the end of the trip, location love affairs have the same character. It is not at all unusual for six or seven fairly serious romances to develop on any location. Husbands and wives of actors, actresses and crew who go on location to far away and exotic places can never be quite sure that their beloved has not indulged in a little extra-curricular activity when the cameras stop grinding after the day's shooting. As far as my relationship was concerned it was an infatuation fed by the dreamy, sensual atmosphere of the island, and fired by my desire to get back at Arthur.

This boy was, up until this point in my life, the most exciting lover I had experienced. Maybe it was the fact that there was very little to do at night on the island — no TV or radio, no phones, movies, or theatres — not distractions and making love suddenly became my favourite occupation for the duration of the film.

This alliance did not particularly thrill Mr Burton, whose ego was piqued by the fact that I had rejected him in favour of a lowly member of the camera crew. But after trying to persuade me again, to sample his wares, he found other ladies to console himself with. Some were quite attractive and some were, to put it bluntly — dogs! I glimpsed an almost toothless and rather elderly Jamaican maid leaving his quarters early one morning with a satisfied gleam in her eye. When I questioned him about her later in the day he freely admitted he had dallied with her. We were lying side-by-side on our stomachs in the warm sand waiting for the crew to set up.

'Richard, I do believe you would screw a snake if you had the chance,' I laughed unbelievingly.

'Only if it was wearing a skirt, Darling ' he countered smoothly. 'It would have to be a female snake.'

I still wrote to Arthur and he to me. According to his letters he was a paragon of fidelity and spent all of his evenings either watching TV or going to dinner with his friends Stewart Stern, Paul Newman or George Englund. I didn't believe him, because I felt it unlikely that he would write and boast to me of his affairs if he was having them. I was not giving him descriptions of my liaison so why should he? He had brought this on by telling me he didn't think he could control his promiscuity, so why should I feel any remorse? Nevertheless, as the time drew closer to Arthur's impending visit pangs of guilt assailed me and I wondered if I could handle the situation.

He arrived in a blaze of hilarity and jokes the last week of shooting in Jamaica. The first night we had dinner with a group from the film and Arthur was so wildly funny and entertaining, he had everyone, including me, in stitches all night.

During the week he visited we spent very little time alone and had not time to talk about anything pertaining to our future. The focus puller was aware of the situation, and apart from the smouldering looks we exchanged above the camera tape we were being cool.

'Where's Joan,' said Bob McNaughton one day.

'She's laying Loew,' said the unit wit, and everyone collapsed with laughter.

We were coming to the culmination of the film, which necessitated some difficult and emotional scenes for me. I was involved and concentrated on my role. The weather turned rainy and everyone was getting edgy. They wanted to finish the picture and get the hell off this island and back to England. Eight weeks is a long time to be away from home, and the halcyon first weeks of the location had worn off for the crew and the actors. They wanted their fish and chips for lunch and their *Daily Mirror*, their football on the 'Telly' and their warm beer in the pubs. Bored already with the rum punches and the rice and jumbo shrimp — Englishmen belong to England — they wanted out, so anxious faces scanned the sky each morning for the dreaded drops of rain that might delay our departure.

Eventually we finished, and I bade a tearful goodbye to Arthur in our suite at the Inn. I was going to London for several more weeks of shooting and post-production, and he back to Los

Angeles the following day. I was genuinely miserable on the plane to London. I loved him even if it was not as passionate and exciting as I had finally discovered. But we had not communicated anything of our private thoughts and feelings during the week we had been together. No talk of marriage — fidelity — engagements — no deep communication at all. It was just one big laugh all the way and I felt sad for us.

Although it was summertime, England was predictably cold, wet and rainy. I moved gladly in again to the back bedroom at Harley House, luxuriating in my mother's spoiling and attention. On the days when I wasn't shooting she would bring me scrambled eggs and tea in bed in the morning and we would chat and gossip and become closer than we had at any time during my childhood. I felt like a child again, in the familiar surroundings. Although Jackie had taken my room when I went to Hollywood eighteen months previously, my mother had put back many of my possessions since Jackie was now in Los Angeles.

All my old scrapbooks of movie stars were there, and I spent hours looking at all the magazine pictures I had so painstakingly stuck in so long ago. What was ironic was that so many of the stars I had admired I had now worked with or met. There was Maxwell Reed, glowering sexily, as usual — UGH! I shuddered and quickly turned the page. . . .if they only knew! There was Richard Burton, young and innocent in *The Last Days of Dolwyn*, his first film — not so young and innocent now, I thought. There was chirpy, cockney schoolboy, Anthony Newley, in *Oliver Twist* and *Vice Versa* and *The Huggets* who, unbeknownst to me then, I would marry a few years later. And there were others I had finally met: Elizabeth Taylor — Gene Kelly — Humphrey Bogart — Monty Clift — all staring and smiling out from my make-believe paper world. It seemed so long ago and yet it was only a few years. So much had happened already — what would happen to me next? I sighed and thought whimsically that my life was becoming a soap opera.

Arthur had written me immediately.

'Dear Sweetie Poops, otherwise known as dear Fatty Tissue (a reference to my constant complaints about my figure).

'I wish I were able to tell you and show you how much I really love you but somehow when we are together I have great trouble in letting my hair down and seem to be flip all the time rather than warm. It seems during my stay in Jamaica that my main task was to be funny and entertain the crew rather than be close to you.

Anyway, from now on I am really going to try and *force* myself to show you how I feel toward you. . . .'

He went on in this vein and I felt pity for him that he was unable to show his love, and sadness for me too, that I chose to love someone who had to *force* himself to show his feelings.

I saw the camera assistant all the time at the studio. We were working at Elstree in the huge water-filled tank that was on stage, shooting the shipwreck scenes and the night scenes on the raft. It was cold, draughty and uncomfortable, and every evening after work we would adjourn to the pub across the road and drink gin and orange, warm beer and eat sausages. It was convivial. When I didn't have an early call he and I would have a bite to eat and sometimes I would stay on a houseboat on the Thames where he lived but without his red bathing suit and his tan, and the warm tropical nights, I found myself less and less intrigued and made more excuses to stay home nights with Mummy and Daddy. Although Jackie was in Hollywood, my eleven-year-old brother, Bill, was there and I suddenly found I really liked family life. Because I was now a sophisticated divorcee and over twenty-one, my father was far more lenient with me and I was more or less free to come and go as I pleased. For the first time *EVER* practically, I had no one to answer to.

'Where have you been?'

'Who with?'

'What time will you be home?'

I had space of my own and I think my parents were so glad to have me back that I could have stayed out all night and they wouldn't have cared.

I borrowed a friend's flat in Eaton Terrace and stayed there sometimes alone, reading, studying my script and thinking about my life. I didn't think I liked this life of a 'star' too much — and I didn't really want to marry Arthur either. I decided to take each day as it came — let the chips fall where they may. The one thing I really loved was working, *that* I craved.

I had a few weeks off after *Sea Wife* and then was to leave, again for the West Indies, to shoot *Island In The Sun*. Arthur was put out by the fact that I was off on location again after nearly three months of being apart. But I had no choice. I was under contract to Fox and they had the right to do with me what they wanted for 40 weeks of the year. Besides, *Island In The Sun* was a best selling book by Alec Waugh, with a highly topical theme. Darryl Zanuck himself was going to personally produce it and had chosen an exciting cast for this story of tension between blacks and whites in the West Indies.

There were fourteen stars, among them James Mason, Joan Fontaine, Harry Belafonte, Dorothy Dandridge, Stephen Boyd, and Michael Rennie, and it promised to be a highly explosive and controversial film. It would be the first American film to show love scenes between blacks and whites, and already the censor was getting nervous.

I flew back to Los Angeles for a few weeks. My sister Jackie was living in my apartment on Olive Drive and having a terrific time. Arthur and I continued our almost sibling like relationship. I picked up several awards for being Most Promising Actress, or Starlet, or Performer from various theatre owners, exhibitors and magazines, all of which prompted me to comment ruefully: 'I'm afraid I'll be a has been, before I finish being promising,' and then I was back on the plane and on the way to Barbados in the British West Indies.

There was a great similarity between the locations of *Sea Wife* and *Island In The Sun*. The same hot tropical days and romantic nights. But *Island In The Sun* is still talked about as being the most enjoyable location ever among the British film units. It has become almost legendary. We had an enormous crew, including a second unit. Over 100 technical men and women converged on the tiny island. Robert Rossen, the American director, working again after years of being on McCarthy's blacklist and most known for the award winning *All The King's Men*, was a hard taskmaster and expected total support and obedience from his actors and crew.

We did not have a tight schedule and because of the sun, we finished work by four o'clock every day. The rest of the time we did as we pleased. I have always liked to play games, and an endless series of card and party games started up: charades, Monopoly, Scrabble (which Burton had taught me) and, of course, poker — Gin and Liar's Poker Dice. It was a never ending party, with every night ending with everyone taking a dip in the warm Caribbean, after dozens of Planter's Punches and dancing ourselves to death to the music of the Steel Bands, by which I was besotted. Although we all drank a lot and stayed up late, none of us felt tired or had a hangover. Cast and crew alike were operating at peak proficiency. The crew were like my brothers, and I loved them all, so when the day of departure finally arrived the production manager had to come and literally yank me out of the ocean where I was taking a last nostalgic swim, having stayed up all night to do so.

I was sad on the way back to New York on the plane. I felt bereft. Never again, I thought, would I be in an atmosphere of such warmth, trust and friendliness. It was back to bitchy, back-biting Hollywood, where I had to kow-tow to Hedda and Louella and the studio heads — watch my dress, my manners and morals, and be aware that the newspapers were avid for snide gossip about me. There had been much speculation about my marriage to Arthur Loew. The relationship had lasted for nearly 15 months, but I was cooled off now on the idea of marriage to him and although we still saw each other we decided to date others.

I wanted more than a semi-platonic relationship, and after Jamaica, I realised that sex was quite important to me. In the 1950s it was still considered shocking for a woman to admit she liked sex and thought it natural however.

Jayne Mansfield tried to change that. Arriving under contract to Fox around the same time that I did, she plunged in where Marilyn Monroe left off. . .but more so. An unbelievable figure — 40-18-36. The studio publicity blurbed: 'Long platinum hair, baby blue eyes and a talent for gathering publicity out of the most mundane things.' She starred in several forgettable films but became the American working man's number one sexual turn-on.

Fox had the brilliant idea of co-starring her and me in a film together. It was a serious and seamy John Steinbeck novel called *The Wayward Bus*, and for this true slice of Americana in the raw, they cleverly imported a young French director from Paris. For the role of the sluttish, nagging alcoholic wife who runs the tacky diner where the bus makes pit stops, they chose me. I was pleased. Another chance to perform and not just be the wallpaper. The studios were happy with my performances in *Sea Wife* and *Island In The Sun* and were giving me a meaty character role which showed their confidence in me had grown.

I was aged for the role of the drunken wife. Bags and circles were applied under my eyes, my hair, still short from *Sea Wife*, was a snarled and tangled mess, and I played most of the film in a stained dressing gown. It was wonderful to be able to work on a character totally unlike myself. All of my personal characteristics, from accent (mid-Western) to walk had to be changed. In *Sea Wife* I had been able to use a lot of myself that was never revealed in films before — the innocence, vulnerability, and naivete — which was part of my own make-up, but this role was a character

83

role and I was surprised Fox had not given it to Joanne Woodward, their resident young character actress. Surprised, but glad for me, I threw myself into the movie with tremendous enthusiasm.

Unfortunately, the director, Victor Vicas was so unfamiliar with the American way of life that it was difficult for him to bring any of Steinbeck's realistic and grimly sordid story to life. And the film was reviewed unfavourably and bombed at the box office. I, however, got a lot of favourable comments and some excellent reviews, and I hoped that this would bring me meatier roles and not just 'pretty-pretty' ones. Some people seemed amazed that I could act: 'But you were GOOD!' they would say, the surprise thinly disguised in their voices. Or 'I didn't know you could act!!!'

I gritted my teeth and smiled politely. I was gaining more confidence in my ability. What a pity I had to constantly prove it again and again and again. This has continued for years. I am always having surprised people — directors, actors or crew — come up to me on the set and tell me how talented I am, as though they never expected it. It is galling, but it is a fact of my life that maybe I shall have to live with for ever.

After 44 films, 7 plays and over 25 television shows, I am still treated by many people like a brainless flip starlet whose only talent is to go nightclubbing and have affairs, and who has made a career built only on attractiveness and sex appeal. I know, since my career has continued solidly for over twenty years, that this view of me couldn't possibly be true. I am not employed *today* just because of my looks, but because there are perceptive people in the industry who realise my aptitude. There are any number of young actresses who flowered and bloomed in the flush of stardom for a few years and then went into total obscurity, unable to get a job. There are very, very few so-called beauties or glamour girls who have sustained a career for over two decades. This is a business of survival in the end, and to survive you have to be good. You don't get charity-jobs.

I also have been penalised and criticised for wanting to enjoy my personal life fully. If I want to go to parties or nightclubs and have fun, who is to say I am a worse actress or person than Miss X, who stays home nights with a boiled egg and a copy of Stanislavsky, and is perhaps not highly rated in the looks department? It has always been easier to be considered a serious actress if you are not good-looking. Beauty is definitely an asset at the beginning of a career. I know it was basically my looks that got me to Hollywood, but after a few years they are no longer an asset and in fact, a hindrance in an advancing career. It took a long time for Elizabeth Taylor to be recognised as a fine actress, although I have seen her give a dozen excellent performances. There is still too much connotation of 'the girl behind the cosmetics counter' syndrome for people to accept a beautiful woman and a good actress in the same package.

However, I was not about to go to seed and fall apart physically just to prove I could act, and in fact, I won't do that today. I enjoy being good-looking and dressing well, and it amuses me to find out that some people are resentful of the fact that I look as I do today.

'How do you *do* it?' they ask bitchily, trying to look behind my ears for some tell-tale scars, or :'What are you doing to yourself, you've got some magic secret for staying young — tell me what it is'.

The truth is there's no secret. I believe in enjoying the life you have as much as possible, in living without envy, frustration and bitterness towards others — and in trying to be happy and worry-free. (Not an easy goal in my life.)

I would like to say that there was some magical prophetic man or woman in my life who became my mentor and helped and guided me through the difficulties of my career. Unfortunately, they did not appear, or if they did, I was unreceptive. I went through the jungle alone. Not for me a Carlo Ponti, Roger Vadim or Dino de Laurentis to help guide me. Not even a trusty agent or manager has gone the distance, with the exception of my first agent, Bill Watts, now alas, passed on.

In my life the one person who has helped me as *ME* the most, is my husband Ron Kass. Although, like most married couples, we have our differences — sometime verbalised violently — Ron, in the eight and a half years we have been together, has done more for me, for my confidence, my ego, my ability and to make me financially stable than any other person I have known.

With three films under my belt in less than a year, I took off for Acapulco for a short rest. Arthur and I had come to a final parting of the ways on New Year's Eve.

We were dancing at the Charles Lederer's bi-annual New Year's Eve party. The music was soft and romantic, but we were not. We were having yet another peevish row, quietly, so that the imposing array of guests from show business could not overhear our heated discussion. But they could not fail to hear the following dazzling dialogue:

85

Arthur: 'You are a fucking bore.'

Me: 'and you are a boring fuck.' And that was the end of that.

I stayed in Acapulco for four weeks, tanning until I almost looked Mexican, and becoming an expert water skier. My first sportive enjoyment.

I started dating Nick Hilton, a well-known playboy, first husband of Liz Taylor and the son of Conrad Hilton of the huge hotel chain. Nick was good looking in a dissolute and rakish way. Dark-haired, dark eyed and well built, he enjoyed a reputation as one of Hollywood's swingingest playboys. Although he had an office, and was supposed to be some sort of assistant to his father in the hotel business, he preferred to spend his time with girls, at the race track and nightclubbing. I was not in the mood for serious involvement and neither was he and we dated on and off for several months.

Nick was a sexual athlete and enjoyed trying to break his previous records. There was a joke in Hollywood that between the three Hiltons, Nick, his brother and father, they had a yard of cock! Although not strictly true, Nick loved this story and told it often. Sometimes he had a little scoreboard next to his bed and would make a mark for each consummation! A devout Catholic, he also kept a rosary on the bedside table, which featured an amazing array of pill bottles in all shapes and sizes — girlie magazines — pornographic books — bottles of coca cola — a crucifix — and a gun. He enjoyed filling the gun with blanks and firing it repeatedly in the middle of the night to the terror of his neighbours on Doheny Drive, who would call the police in a frenzy of fear.

Although only in his early thirties, he had seen and done it all. Had been everywhere, could get practically any girl he wanted and was completely jaded. He had a Southern drawl and was racially bigoted. Rich men's sons have a hard road to hoe. It is almost the equivalent of being a beautiful girl. You get it all. You don't have to do a thing for yourself. It's there. The money. The power. The girls. The fast cars and the fast life. Arthur learned that his money did not make him happy, and eventually moved to a ranch in Arizona where he totally changed his lifestyle. He raised cattle, married a lovely girl, and found himself at last. And Syd Chaplin got his act together and made a success on Broadway in *Bells Are Ringing*.

Alas, poor Nicky did not find a way out, and a few years later he was dead . . . from an overdose of drugs.

5

Foxy Lady

'Can you be ready to leave for Tokyo in three days?' my agent's voice, crisp and businesslike on the phone, woke me from a dreamless sleep. My cocoon of baby pillows and sheets was rumpled from last night's lovemaking and my mouth was dry from too much wine and too many cigarettes.

'Shit.' I fumbled for the Visine eyedrops among the bedside table junk. An empty bottle of wine fell off the cluttered table which held scripts, magazines, a clock, Kleenex, a photo of my parents in an antique silver frame, diamond earrings and pearls, tossed carelessly from last night, and an overflowing ashtray.

I pushed the ashtray under the pile of scripts, the smell was vile at that time of the morning and my hangover was in full flower and I tried to collect my thoughts as the Visine did its job on my eyes.

'Three days — that's impossible. I can't be ready in time,' I croaked, pulling the sheet around my naked shoulders and wishing someone would bring me some fresh orange juice, coffee and raisin toast. Oh, for a live-in housekeeper. Alas, my business manager convinced me I couldn't really afford one, although I was earning $2,000 a week, had starred in half a dozen movies, and appeared regularly on the covers of magazines worldwide. I was a commodity now. A young, sexy saleable commodity, and my studio employers took full advantage of this fact and were pushing me into film after film. Movies, unfortunately noted more for their visual beauty and scenic splendour than for their integrity and realism.

My agent was sympathetic but firm. I had to report to the Fox wardrobe department at 11, hairdressing at 1.30 — and see the insurance doctor at 3.00 for whatever shots I might need for Japan and his verification that I was healthy. And then, in the two and a half days that would be left prior to my departure, I had to organise the bits and pieces of my own life as well as I could. It was par for the course. I didn't have much say in the direction my career went. If I ever rebelled I was put on suspension. No work. No money. Not even another studio was allowed to employ me. I was fairly frugal. The apartment on Shoreham Drive — furnished in white/beige and pink Sears-Roebuck Starlet — cost $250 a month. I either ate out or was on a diet so my ice box contained cottage cheese, a few bottles of white wine and little else. The freezer, however, was full of Will Wright's Ice Cream in every different flavour for the odd afternoons when I threw caution to the wind and indulged in an ice cream fit. I had a car befitting my status. A flashy pink Thunderbird, which certainly got attention when I zipped along Sunset well over the speed limit, with the radio blaring Latin American music. The closet contained a large selection of Saks and Magnins sexiest dresses — plus a white mink stole, a black mink coat, a white sheared beaver coat, and a blue fox hat which I had bought in an abandoned moment and never worn. I was sartorially prepared for any eventuality. Of material possessions other than these I had none. And of emotional involvements I also had none, although my date book was filled.

I lay back on the Porthault baby pillows, another indulgence, but I liked to wake up in a field of flowers, and thought about last night. I glanced at the other side of the King-Sized Hollywood bed — a necessity in any young bachelorette's apartment — and could almost see the indentation where his tall, lithe body had lain.

We had talked for hours. And drank wine, and I had smoked endlessly. Although it was the second time we had been to bed together I was nervous. Nervous that we might be seen together. Or that he might be observed by some hawk-eyed neighbour leaving the apartment so suspiciously early in the morning. My reputation as a 'Playgirl' always ready for excitement and adventure would be enhanced no doubt, but the studio would frown on this alliance. I would have to face another lecture on morals and proper behaviour for a young movie personage from Lew Shrieber, an executive who, among his other duties, dispensed advice to the contract players.

I cast my mind back to when it had started. Just a few months ago really, during *Island In The Sun*. I had noticed him immediately, and was stunned by his overwhelming physical appearance. The cast and crew were gathered together for a start of the picture cocktail party. We would all get to know each other, hopefully like each other, and form close attachments which would usually last for as long as the shooting of the movie. Actors are fickle folk. And although closeness develops fast when thrown together on location, it does not always linger longer than the final 'cut'.

I stood chatting to Joan Fontaine whom I knew from *Decameron Nights* and observed him from afar. Tall, dark and handsome was an understatement. About six feet one or two his black hair was close cropped and curly and his skin was the colour of caramel toffee. His body, in tight ivory coloured pants, and a bright red shirt open to the navel revealed that he was slim and muscular and almost hairless. He laughed a lot, I noticed as he, James Mason and Dorothy Dandridge were involved in animated discussion. Full, deep-throated laughter that seemed to come right from his gut as he threw back his head and guffawed lustily. The West Indian waiters, running about with trays of rum punches and platters of fried shrimp, and other delicacies of the island, smiled every time they caught sight of him. To them, he was a local boy who made good and even though he was not from Barbados his songs were indigenous to all parts of the West Indies. He was a folk hero.

He caught my eye, smiled, and wandered over to us.

'Hi', he said, extending his hand with a lazy smile.

Joan Fontaine said a brisk hello and I stood slightly tongue-tied, unusual for me, while she and he discussed their roles in the movie. *Island* had, apart from a main theme of racial miscegenation, three or four different love stories, all concerning the racial issue, a hot and taboo subject in the late fifties. There were four or five interwoven racially mixed stories in the film. I played a girl who discovers that her grandmother was negro, thus giving her 'coloured blood', the euphemism then for being a quarter black. The whole subject — that of black and white people of both sexes becoming involved with one another and falling in love — was considered so shocking and outrageous that there was a tremendous outcry when Darryl Zanuck announced he was making the novel into a movie. Many states instantly announced that they would never allow it to be shown. The controversy was still raging, and Mr Zanuck and Robert Rossen were closeted in their tiny hotel rooms even now trying to placate some of the more stringent censor demands.

None of these issues seemed at all important as I feasted my eyes on his warm brown eyes and aristocratic nose. He was indeed a gorgeous hunk of man — as women from Coast to Coast had been discovering for the past several years. In concert, nightclubs and records his fame was spreading rapidly. His sex appeal made women of all ages go weak at the knees and I, never one to let male beauty go unappreciated, seemed to be no exception to this rule. But, and it was a big but, his reputation was not good. Love 'em and leave 'em seemed to be his credo, and although I liked to be loved, I was cautious of men who were overly conscious of their sexual power. Also, my strict and old fashioned upbringing made me wary of the ramifications that an involvement with a black man could bring. The pages of *Confidential* were filled with innuendos about celebrities involved in relationships with other races. It was not the thing to do. I started to move away but he took my arm and looked into my eyes.

'Where are you going?' he asked, his eyes shining with interest and amusement.

'Oh — I er — said I'd have dinner with some of the camera boys.' I stammered, aware of heat from his hand on my bare arm, and feeling frankly rather aroused. He glanced over to where three or four of the English camera crew, mates of mine from *Sea Wife*, were grouped, observing us and waiting for developments, which from the looks of it seemed inevitable. His grip on my arm did not lessen, and he looked to them and then back to me with even more amusement. My God he was sure of himself.

'An appointment you cannot break?' his voice was husky, sexy and confident.

'That's right,' I said lightly, my eyes locked into his as I removed his persuasive fingers from my rather too receptive flesh. 'We're having dinner and then playing poker.'

'Poker — aahh. Of course. You English ladies always like to play games.'

The innuendo was there. He knew and I knew. Even Joan Fontaine knew as she drifted away in a sea of chiffon.

'Well then, I'll let you go — for now,' he said meaningfully — and bestowed a dazzling and promise-filled smile at my face — blushing under the sun tan.

'Since I don't play games — another time then,' and he smoothly glided off, catlike and elegant leaving the blushing schoolgirl standing trembling and off balance.

I joined my British compatriots, and spent a riotous evening of joking, gossiping and drinking. They went to some lengths to let me know that this fabulous man was considered to be a ladies' man 'Par Excellence', and that one of his ambitions was said to be to make love to as many beautiful women as he could possibly find.

'Come on now Joanie, love,' said Ginger, one of the grips, as he caught me gazing sombrely into my fifth rum punch of the evening. 'Cheer up. For Gawd's sake, don't you start anything with 'im. You're our little mate, girl. We don't want you to get hurt now — do we?'

Ginger was right, As attracted as I was, I would have left myself open to gossip, pain and ridicule if I had become even remotely involved with him. And though my heart beat a little faster when I thought of him, I realised I would have to push all of these thoughts and feelings out.

Although we had no scenes together everyone stayed in the same hotel and our paths crossed often. At breakfast, lunch and dinner — there he was. Smiling, confident — sexy. Throwing me glances and waiting for *me* to make the move. A move I wanted to make but was frightened to do so.

For a week I kept out of his way until the following Sunday when Zanuck arranged a festive Brunch for the cast and crew. A hundred and fifty of us gathered around the tables groaning with Caribbean goodies. I was seated next to him — a Caribbean goody if I ever saw one!

'You've been avoiding me, Joan Collins,' he said nonchalantly spooning up Papaya and melon. 'Have the poker games been that exciting?'

'I'm on a winning streak,' I said lightly, lighting a cigarette with shaking hands.

'Allow me,' he said removing the cigarette from my lips and dumping it in the ashtray. I realised in my nervousness that I had lit the wrong end and the singed filter was burning merrily. Not exactly smooth behaviour for a young sex symbol.

Ginger winked at me from an adjoining table, he and the boys were enjoying the whole scene. God damn them, I thought furiously. Interfering busybodies. I didn't belong to them. They were watching out for me as if I was Little red Riding Hood with the Big Bad Wolf and they were my saviours. I decided to enjoy his engaging personality, and forget about 'the boys'.

He was a spirited conversationalist. Warm and articulate, and so engrossed were we in talking that the heaping plates of chicken gumbo, fried shrimps, lobsters, brown rice and exotic fruits were barely touched. Although the chat was light, the undercurrent of mutual attraction was heavy. Darryl Zanuck sat opposite us, chomping on an immense cigar, wearing little blue and white striped shorts and matching shirt, open to show a protruding, grey-haired belly. He occasionally shot us penetrating looks as if questioning whether or not this conversation was innocent. But I gave him my sweetest, most innocent smile to assure him that all was above board, so he was not aware of my bare leg so close to the well-muscled one next to me.

Zanuck had been instrumental in my coming to Fox. An immensely powerful force in motion pictures, his weak spot was women. Throughout the years he had had a series of affairs with some talented — and not so talented — actresses. His present mistress was absent from this location and he had recently cast his eyes in my direction. In a move which can only be described as brazen and gauche he had grabbed me one afternoon in the corridor of the hotel, pressed me against the wall, cigar still firmly clamped between his fingers and tried to convince me of his endurance, prowess, and endowments as one of the world's best lovers.

'You've had nothing until you've had me,' he muttered, his breath reeking of cigar smoke, as he tried to press grey-moustached lips to mine.

'I've got the biggest and the best. I can go all night and all day.' I tried to wriggle free. Though shorter than me he was powerful in body as well as presence and I was pinned like a beetle to a board. My words could not stop his torrent of lust.

'Why do you waste your time with these boys?' he croaked hoarsely as I skewered my face away from his. 'These Arthur Loews and Nicky Hiltons can't do anything for you. You need a real man.'

Oh God. The oldest line in the business I thought, wondering how to get out of this without having to knee him in the balls. Luckily Dorothy Dandridge suddenly came walking down the corridor and I made my escape — vowing to keep out of Mr Z's way in the future.

One thing I gathered from lunching with my handsome friend — he was smart and he was cool. He was no Zanuck to press his advances on to a woman. Why should he? Women flocked to *him.* I saw them in the hotel lobby, going dithery and weak over his tall, sensual body, always clad in tight pants and shirt open to the waist as he walked by, not at all oblivious to the effect his presence had on them. He also knew that the entire cast and crew were waiting to see what, if any developments were about to happen between him and me. Since I did not wish to be the object of gossip during the movie, and I didn't relish the idea of the *world* knowing about an event which to me should be private, I decided reluctantly that this tropical romantic island was neither the time nor the place for us. I stopped thinking about it. And he, taking my cue, did not pursue it either.

Towards the end of his shooting — he was to be finished before the rest of us as he had contractual commitments, we took a walk along the beach one night. There had been yet another party at the hotel and we had both gone outside for a breath of air. It was hot and the moon was silver and full. I was wearing a bare shouldered, white cotton eyelet dress which showed off my deep tan. I took off my sandals to walk where the ocean lapped at the sand. He was also in white, trousers and shirt, and in the silvery light shimmering on our faces, we seemed the same colour.

I was sad he was leaving. Although we had spent little time together it was only because the circumstances and morals of the time decreed that it was 'wrong' for us to have anything other than the most casual acquaintanceship because of his colour. He was a sensitive and bright man. What the hell difference did it matter if he was black, white or green?

'I guess I won't see you again,' I said quietly after we had walked silently along the surf for a while. He didn't answer, but he stopped and looked up at the moon for a while with a faraway and rather bitter look on his face. I knelt down and picked up some of the pretty little shells that were scattered like uncut gems over the sand. He was still looking out towards the ocean, the moon making his face into a carved bronze statue and the wind blowing the white cotton shirt out from his body like the sails on a ship. There was something so atavistic and powerful about him and his silence seemed so full of meaning for himself that I felt suspended — surrealistic, as though I shouldn't be there. I continued with the shell picking until he suddenly turned — his mood changing — laughing, joking and pulled me up to stand beside him, and said,

'Look,' he pointed to the moon. '200 billion years or more it's been there — what does it matter about us?' He turned to look at me and put his hands on each side of my head and said, 'I'll be in Los Angeles in April. At the Grove. Come then.' It was neither an invitation nor a command. It was a fact. I would be there.

And I was. His opening night at the Coconut Grove was jam-packed. Half the celebrities in Los Angeles were there to see the magnetic personality and performance of this man who was becoming famous throughout America. He was the first man to ever sell over one million LPs. And not for nothing was he called 'King of the Calypso'. He had recently broken all records at a huge sports stadium in New York — and he became one of the first black film idols. He had been mesmerising audiences of every type from true folk aficionados to smitten teenagers, music critics and intellectuals with his honey-voiced and spirited renditions of Calypso folk songs and spiritual jazz performed gutsily, emotionally and honestly.

The Coconut Grove was built in the highly glamorous era of movies, the 1920s. Gable and Lombard had romanced there. Crawford, Harlow, Bogart, all of the great movie stars had wined and dined, brawled and ballroomed in its splendid environs. It had the hot aura of faded glory. If you looked too closely the paint was peeling off the walls and the fringe was falling off the pink lampshades which cast flattering soft lights on the jaded faces who frequented it now. For the age of the nightclub was fast disappearing. But the giant fake palm trees were magnificently showy and tonight the atmosphere had an electric anticipatory mood. Me too.

I had been invited by the studio to attend, and never having seen him perform in front of more than just a few people, casually at some of the gatherings we had in the West Indies, I was eager to see him. And he did not disappoint. As the stage went dark, a spotlight was turned on and to the Calypso rhythm of his theme song he strolled on — casual — confident — singing — dancing, with a slightly arrogant bold and confident style — wholly original.

'If you see me you'll love me' seemed to be his attitude and so certain was he of his magnetism that most of the women there that night were more than overcome. And none more than myself. I sat enthralled, in my lowest cut black satin dress — my hair a masterpiece of curls and velvet bows — the white mink stole gracefully slipping off my shoulders showing abundant cleavage and new diamond earrings from Aspreys on my ears. I looked fetching and knew it. And he knew it too as our eyes connected during his act.

The show over — the applause and encores still echoing, an élite group of invitees trekked through the corridors of the old Ambassador Hotel to the 'Star's' dressing room, which is really the star's hotel room, since the management was too mean to supply both. He was lionised. Bouffant-haired matrons gushed and squealed around him like waves around a lighthouse. Sharply dressed and sharp talking guys hovered on the edge of this, ready to talk deals if they could get to him through the throbbing female hordes.

A valet passed champagne which I sat sipping in the background, too reserved to join the effusive group around him. He looked over at me and smiled as much as to say,

'It's all a bunch of bull-shit but I love it.'

I raised my glass in a silent salute. It was obviously going to be a long party and I didn't feel like sticking around for the grand finale. When my group was ready to leave I went up for the show-biz kiss him on each cheek and the 'Darling you were divine' routine, which I sincerely meant. Too many ladies looked hostile as they saw our exchange. It was all in the eyes, but it was high voltage.

A couple of days later the James Masons gave a party at their attractive home on Pamela Drive, so named for James's vivacious wife Pamela, a charming and talkative lady. It was a convivial group but it was getting almost yawn time for most people, since Hollywood folk still live on the myth that they have to be on the set at 6am and so must be abed by 11. Needless to say, those who do have to be on the set at 6 are rarely on the town at all, and most of the socialising is done by others than working actors and directors.

Then he arrived, and suddenly everyone decided to have another drink and re-light their cigars. He was affable and charming and charismatic as usual, and eventually he came over to where I was sitting and joined me.

'So here we are, Joan Collins,' he said gazing at me with his expressive brown eyes and managing to look sexy whilst devouring a chicken leg. I felt light-hearted and light-headed, and the stars were in the right position. His incredible magnetism and sexuality which I had tried to avoid during the West Indies had won me over. We chatted and laughed, and I eventually gave him my address. I feigned tiredness and an early appointment to my hosts and casually left. Luckily I had come alone.

Back at the apartment it was nervous frenzy time. I rushed about putting on lights — too much light — turning them off — too dark — candles then — I lit them — too contrived. Although I knew why he was coming over I didn't want the place to look like a love nest. Should I slip into something more comfortable', like a character in a thirties movie, or keep on my beige chiffon cocktail dress? God it had a thousand hooks and eyes and a waist cincher underneath. Not very sexy when all the bones have made red indentations in the flesh. I tore it off, threw on a simple blue cotton caftan, brushed down my hair, and downed a large brandy and ten Ritz crackers for my nerves. The doorbell rang and I jumped out of my skin. He stood there — the familiar costume of open shirt, tight pants and wide leather belt moulded to his body, and an engaging smile upon his face.

'Is this where the party is Ma'am?' he inquired — and indeed it was.

Although most people find it hard to believe, I am quite shy. I have overcome the shyness a lot but with a new man in my bed I was always slightly nervous. Although I had had a few lovers, one night stands were not quite my line. One had to start somewhere of course, but usually the first time was far from the best, and I have always found making love became better the longer the relationship lasted. But with him there was the undeniably erotic feeling that I was doing something forbidden and outrageous, and this added enormously to the excitement of the whole thing and my nervousness evaporated. He was very endearing and had, apart from the best body I had ever seen on a man, the most extraordinary skin. Almost as soft as a girl's. It was hard to understand why because I was 'white' and he was 'black' that society felt it was such a shocking thing to make love. Certainly as I looked at our bodies entwined on the sheets there was little difference in the colour of skin. I was nearly the same colour from Barbados and Acapulco — only his skin was smoother than mine!

'Probably in 100 years or so everyone will be the same colour,' I mumbled sleepily. I looked at my bedside clock — four o'clock —definitely bedtime. I wondered if he would stay the night. He seemed as tired as I and he had also done a show. My feelings were ambivalent. I wanted him to stay, and yet the ramifications of his being spotted leaving my house in the morning concerned me. Never mind, can't worry about that, I thought as I drifted off to sleep.

Next morning he was gone. A note on the pillow with a phone number was the only evidence of his visit. I felt good. There is a particular glow that comes to certain women after lovemaking — a certain satisfied and luminous look, which other people seem to notice and react to. Today I seemed to get even more looks than usual as I zipped around Beverly Hills in my pink T-Bird doing errands. I had called him at the hotel and arranged to go the following night to the Grove again. It was even more thrilling to sit amongst his worshipping audience watching him extend his magic, and to know that later that evening we would be together. I found more meaning in some of the lyrics of the songs he sang —

some subtly directed towards me, where I sat understanding now full well why most of the women were spellbound.

When he arrived later that night at my now candle-lit apartment it was more relaxed than before and I realised that I might be getting more involved than could be good for me. My heart always led my mind and with men my relationships either lasted one night or six months. But with the call the next day to get myself together to leave for Japan in three days I realised it was futile to think of this affair as anything more than a ship that passed in the night. There were too many strikes against us to continue. He was married and, although separated, his concert and nightclub tours kept him constantly travelling and who knew when we would meet again.

Two nights before leaving for Japan I went for the last time to the Grove and this time, feeling daring and uninhibited, I stayed with him in his hotel room. It had been a delicious interlude, but it was only an interlude and we both knew it.

I had never in my life seen such a horde of faces as that which greeted Robert Wagner, Edmond O'Brien and myself on our arrival at Tokyo airport. Literally thousands of yelling and screaming excitable Japanese of all ages, whipping themselves into a frenzy at the sight of us. It was quite overwhelming and slightly scary. Even 'R.J.' Wagner, a movie star since his teens, was bowled over by it. The Japanese have always been eager movie fans and a million flashbulbs on a million Nikon cameras seemed to explode in front of us as we forced our way through the *extremely* polite throngs. The Japanese are so polite and well-mannered that they apologise profusely while shoving you violently in the ribs at the same time.

On the way to our hotel in the Ginza district I saw dozens of movie theatres, liberally festooned with giant multi-coloured blow-ups of the stars who were appearing in the movies. John Wayne's face in vivid colours one hundred feet high, with slightly slanted eyes was some sight to behold. But although I enjoyed the ancient charms of Japan I was lonely and miserable.

The script of the film was awful. *Stop-over Tokyo* it was called. I referred to it as *Stop Overacting*. 'R.J.' though friendly and nice, was newly engaged to Natalie Wood and spent most of his off-set time with his parents in his suite or calling Natalie in Los Angeles. His phone bill must have been astronomical since he called at least once a day! The crew, whom I usually hung out with on location, were all men well over fifty, who threw themselves into the male-oriented Japanese society with gusto. Frequenting Geisha houses where they were treated like Lords, fawned over and adored by the Geishas — small-boned, tiny creatures, seemingly from another century in their brightly-coloured gorgeous kimonos and obis, their miniature feet padding softly in white cotton tabis, their faces masked by white powder, carmine lips and intricate eye make-up, and their heads crowned with enormously heavy glossy black wigs. I did not envy the life of a Japanese woman. Most were still virtually chattels to their men, who spent practically every night out with the boys frolicking at the baths, the Geisha Houses and the restaurants, where for women to join in the festivities was taboo. On the few occasions when I did accompany some of the crew to the restaurants and clubs I felt gawky and gauche next to these exquisite little things, and the men made no secret of their preference for the Oriental women.

'A bunch of women haters,' I muttered to my companion, the unit hairdresser, as we sat in the hotel dining room eating our terriyaki and fried rice unenthusiastically, and feeling bored and despondent. One of the camera men, a huge beefy Southern redneck, middle-aged and dressed in a hideous plaid shirt, Stetson hat, and checked trousers with a gross paunch hanging over his belt had dropped by our table with his tiny beautiful Geisha to lay a few comments on us.

'You Western gals should take a few lessons from these Oriental ladies,' he said — his saki-drenched breath causing us to stop eating, lest we gag. 'Now little Tamiko, here — she *really* knows how to treat a man right. Don't you Tamiko?'

Tamiko nodded and smiled subserviently at this lout and I felt revolted that Japanese women thought themselves so inferior to even the most loathsome of the male sex.

Women's liberation was only a glimmer on the horizon. As a so-called 'free' woman, if I chose to sleep with whom I wanted, and when I wanted, I became the butt of coarse jokes, crude remarks and a general attitude amongst less indulgent folk that I was no better than I should be, or a 'tramp'. 'Free Love' it was called — and shocking it was considered. My proclivity for taking as lovers men who were interesting, stimulating, young and good looking did not endear me to a whole section of men in the movie business — producers, directors, heads of studios and general big wigs — because I would never have anything to do with *them* at all. The thought of going to bed with some guy — old, fat, ugly or rich — to get a job, or to do myself some good career-wise was revolting. *That* to me was being a tramp. If I wanted to bed down

98

with ten men a week whom I genuinely fancied and liked, I would do so. It was enjoyable, exciting and non-fattening! But it was only to be done if *I* really wanted to.

However, in Japan there was *no one* I felt even faintly attracted to and I spent my free time with the hairdresser, reading in my hotel room, or with some American friends who lived there.

One evening the phone rang. It was Charles Evans, brother of Bob Evans an actor under contract to Fox. We'd met briefly in Los Angeles and when he invited me to dinner I accepted. A new face was more than welcome in my life. I had killed time having a vast elaborate wardrobe made, choosing from the profusion of glorious fabrics — silks, brocades and chiffon that Japan had in abundance. I had to buy five more suitcases to cart home this loot. There were enough cocktail dresses and evening gowns all copied from the latest *Vogue* and *Harpers* to keep me on the town every night dressed differently for a year.

For my night out with Charles Evans I chose a pink and gold brocade Cheong-sam — a high necked Chinese style dress, tightly fitted with a slit skirt almost to the waist — quite appropriate for anywhere we might go, be it a quiet bistro or a nightclub. However, I was not prepared for what Charles — tall, dark and quite elegant — suggested we do over dinner. We went to what appeared to be an attractive, dimly-lit nightclub — small — very small — and we sat on thick soft cushions on the floor close to a stage, rather tiny for dancing.

The show was an erotic fantasy. There was an amazingly beautiful and nubile young girl who cavorted for a while naked on stage. She had shaved her pubic hair and spent much time massaging that area with an object suspiciously shaped like a penis! After a while two equally nubile young men joined her, and the girl, truly one of the greatest contortionists I have ever seen, knelt and arched her back and bent her head to a 90 degree angle while one of the men fucked her as rapidly as a rabbit and caressed her breasts, and the other had the most expert fellatio performed on him by an eager and practised mouth. All of this was done in utter silence except for some mysterious lute music emanating from an unknown source and the irregular breathing of Mr Evans.

'God. Fantastic!' he whispered, his hand landing light as a butterfly's wing on my over-exposed thigh.

'What do you think?' he breathed nuzzling my left ear, obviously getting wildly aroused.

'I wonder if she's a good cook?' I whispered back, gently

removing the butterfly wing hand.

'Who cares,' he mumbled as another couple joined the threesome on the stage and proceeded to get into every conceivable position. They looked like the Snake Pit and I started to giggle furiously — especially when I caught sight of all the tourists' rapt horny faces in the audience. The more vigorously they writhed and sucked and fucked the more turned off I became. There was nothing erotic or exciting in this flagrant exhibitionism to me. Somewhat of a romantic, I thought the kiss between Montgomery Clift and Elizabeth Taylor in *A Place In The Sun* infinitely more sexy than this.

Charles, his ardour whetted by this display, thought otherwise, and I pleaded every known combination of female ailments at the entrance of my hotel room before I gracefully got rid of him. Maybe there was something wrong with me if I found a group sex scene which many people paid money to watch such a turn *off*. Charles was an attractive man — under the circumstances of being stuck in Japan for over a month, celibate and bored, it was curious that his taking me to a porno show had had the reverse effect on my sexual appetite. Most women would probably have leaped into bed with him and made love imaginatively and passionately for hours, stimulated by all that they had seen. Somehow though I had felt that both sexes were demeaning themselves so much by these acts. They were being used, and to me the degradation was much more apparent than any enjoyment they were probably simulating.

Sex was not a spectator sport, I thought as I got into my lonely bed for the thirty-fifth consecutive night. It was the best indoor sport going and that included poker, scrabble and charades, but I like it straight up — not kinky — not groupy — not bizarre — and definitely heterosexual. He probably thinks I'm a real square, I thought as I drifted off into a sleep filled with nude people writhing in a nest of vipers and boa constrictors. Now I wonder what my analyst would make of that, I thought.

6

A Very Married Man

If I imagined I had been in love with Arthur Loew or Sydney Chaplin those feelings paled in comparison with my infatuation with 'The General'. I had known him, his wife and their rapidly increasing brood of children ever since I had arrived in America. He was a close chum of Sydney, they had gone to Military Academy together, and a friend of Arthur Loew. His wife, who in the 1970s would become one of the biggest television stars, was an actress, pretty, friendly and neurotic, who dedicated her life and herself to 'The General' and the constant breeding and rearing of their children.

Our friends were mutual. As a foursome with Sydney we'd gone to Palm Springs and Tijuana together, and although I knew that they bickered and fought a lot I thought their marriage was okay as most marriages go — not tremendous but not at breaking point either. I was aware of him as an intelligent attractive man with a fabulous sense of humour — but that was all. Married men were a no-no in my book, especially if I was pally with their wives. It was not cricket.

When I mentioned I was going to Chicago and New York on promotions for *Stopover Tokyo*, 'The General' told me he would p. 97? also be in New York at the same time and perhaps we'd get together for dinner one night, schedules permitting. He was coincidentally staying at my hotel, the Plaza, and when he came to pick me up, I was unaware that I was embarking on one of the most traumatic, emotional and unsettling periods of my life.

In retrospect I don't think the highs balanced the lows, but when you are madly, passionately, blindly in love, reason evaporates. On our first date we went to 'Billy Reed's Little Club' for dinner. He was dressed impeccably as always in a dark blue suit from Savile Row's finest tailor, a pale blue Turnbull and Asser silk shirt and a Cardin tie. He had a reputation for being one of the best dressed men in town and sartorially could not be faulted. Aside from his clothes he was devastatingly good looking. Tall (six foot two or three), with light brown hair, going ever so *slightly* thin on top — about the only flaw I noticed as I became increasingly aware of him more as a male than a friend during dinner. He had a wicked wit and a superb mastery of the English language. Indeed he was the perfect advocate of the adage — why use a short word when a six syllable one will do. Words and phrases I seldom heard outside the New Oxford Dictionary tumbled effortlessly from his lips. He was smart as a whip and we seemed to spark each other's funnybone too for he laughed at me as much as I laughed at him.

Ahhh laughter — one of the greatest aphrodisiacs in the world! He ordered a Mouton Rothschild '53 with our Boeuf Wellington and after dinner we drank Calvados, and listened to the tinkling 30s-style music as the pianist played a selection of what suddenly became my favourite tunes. It was too romantic to be true. The wine — the superb dinner — the intimate velvet banquette where we sat next to each other, his hand casually on mine — the Gershwin and Cole Porter songs, some of which he sang softly (he knew the words to the most obscure songs, there was no end to his talents).

We walked hand in hand after dinner through the empty New York streets with the steam rising from the sidewalks, back to the Plaza, and as he accompanied me to my room my heart was pounding. Was it possible to fall in love over *dinner* with someone you had thought of only as a friend for two years? Apparently it was — Vesuvius erupted and I was hopelessly — helplessly — hooked.

For three days I thought of nothing but him. Every possible moment we could share away from my schedule of TV, radio and newspaper interviews, and he from his business meetings, we spent together. We passed a frosty autumnal Sunday walking starry-eyed through Central Park. I was besotted beyond belief and refused to think of the insurmountable problems of wife and three boys — aged six, four, two.

He assured me over and over again that the marriage was, and had been in deep and serious trouble for several years, and that they were only sticking together for the sake of the kids — the cliché line of all time, but so convincing was he that I completely believed him. His influence on me was so strong that he could have demanded I skate naked around Rockefeller Centre and I would have happily done so.

A Very Married Man

On our last evening in New York we went back to 'Billy Reed's Little Club' which I would forever think of as 'our place'. I wore a beige suit and a green felt 'Garbo' hat. I had just read F. Scott Fitzgerald's 'The Girl in the Green Hat' and rather fancied myself as the star-crossed heroine. I sniffled through cocktails — started to cry during dinner — and wept profusely during dessert and coffee. I felt guilty now about our situation but I knew I couldn't and wouldn't give him up. Little did I know I was beginning twenty-one months of the most intense misery of my life.

My best friend was Caprice Caprone Yordan, an exquisitely elegant sophisticated black-haired beauty, married to Philip Yordan, a prolific writer-producer of epics, usually set in Spain or Africa. Cappy and I shared practically every intimate secret of our lives with each other, and since Phil was constantly working she had time to kill. She lived in a huge rambling Spanish hacienda on Benedict Canyon, and spent her days entertaining her myriad groups of friends — dispensing advice and worldly wisdom with a strong dose of astrology thrown in.

'Guess who I've fallen for?' I blurted out. It was the morning after I had arrived in LA and I rushed over to her house to find her languishing elegantly in bed surrounded by satin and lace pillows and a wicker breakfast tray full of delicious croissants, English jams and marmalade and with eleven books on astrology spread over her pink satin coverlet.

'I hope he's rich,' said my friend. 'It's about time you found a rich one.'

'Not only is he not rich — but he's married,' I wailed. 'You know I don't care about the money but the wife bit is a disaster.' I gloomily devoured a croissant covered with honey, while Cappy surveyed me disapprovingly. She was like my big sister and knew the way my mind worked.

'Married and POOR — ha! — wonderful — you've done it again my darling. Enough guessing games — who is he and what's his sign?' She pulled one of the astrology books towards her and looked at me questioningly.

'It's General Electric,' I blurted out using the nickname I had given him. 'I'm MADLY in love with him — and he with me.'

'Oh you fool,' said Cappy. 'Not only is he a Cancer,' she consulted her book with alacrity, 'but he'll hang on *forever* and never let you go — the wife will never let *him* go either. WHAT are you letting yourself in for Joanie?'

103

'It's too late now,' I groaned, grabbing another croissant for succour, 'I can't give him up. It's ghastly. It's as if he's put a spell on me — what am I going to *do* Cappy?'

She looked at me pityingly and did some quick calculations in her head. 'He's perfect for you, of course,' she said as she finished her calculations and I finished her breakfast. 'His moon and his Venus are in the same house as yours, and all other signs are totally compatible. You're a perfect match for each other. But darling, he'll *never* leave that wife and those kids. He's a *Cancer* for goodness sake — THE CRAB — my God, his claws won't ever release *anything*! And his wife thinks so too,' she said, pushing the books away. 'You know she worships the ground he walks on. The best thing for you is to get back to work as quickly as possible and forget him.'

I tried half-heartedly to heed my learned friend's advice, but now that I wanted to work, suddenly I went through a dry spell. Although Fox paid me handsomely each week they did not have any properties suitable for me now, *but* there was a strong rumour on the lot that they were considering making yet another version of *Cleopatra* and that I was being touted as their first choice to play the fabled Queen.

Meanwhile 'The General' and I saw each other four or five times a week; either we lunched at out-of-the-way restaurants — usually near the airport where the sound of jet engines drowned our conversation — or he came to my little apartment for dinner. I never really knew until the last minute when or if I would see him as he had about 47 different projects going at the same time — and was wheeling and dealing on all channels. Although I went out on 'dates' which I kept platonic, I would never commit my evenings until I knew if he was available. It was hell. I was 'back street wife' personified. The worst times were when he said he would be over at 8.00 and didn't show up until 10.00 or 11.00 and sometimes not at all, only a hurried phone call, 'Sorry Babe — can't make it tonight. Have to catch you tomorrow.'

I would go to bed forlorn and miserable trying to understand his problems and trying not to get upset. In the beginning it was easier, but as the weeks passed and his promises of 'trial separations' from his wife came to nothing I began to get immensely depressed.

I tried to become interested in other men, much to his chagrin but no one could hold a candle to his charm, his looks or his personality and I never even tried to find out how they compared in the love-making department. He was certainly a champion in that field, and after the misery of two days of not seeing him, a few hours in his company with his incredible mind bewitching me again, and his humour and his love-making — it was all worth it.

He was also extraordinarily jealous of me — the Cancer crab with his claws out — and when I dated what he considered a possible rival, he would cross-question me afterwards furiously for hours. We had vicious fights, always culminating in blissful making-up sessions.

His best friend at the time was Marlon Brando, the moody and unpredictable charismatic, super-star actor — almost as great an admirer of 'The General' as I was. 'The General' inspired people to worship him. He was so confident, so clever and so aggressively charming that most people, men and women and dogs, found him irresistible.

Marlon adored him, he emulated his vocabulary and mannerisms, his prowess at story-telling, his slightly superior attitude towards others not on his wavelength. Sometimes I found it hard to tell the difference between the two voices on the telephone. Sometimes Marlon would 'beard' for us when we went to restaurants, theatres or screenings together. A photograph was taken of the three of us at the theatre. When it was printed luckily only Marlon and I were in it. I, wearing a pleased as punch expression, beehive hair style and a black point d'esprit evening gown, am sitting in the middle. 'Marlon does the town with the British actress' crowed the New York tabloids. 'Brando and Joan step out together'. 'We're just extremely good friends' said Miss Collins coyly to the *Daily Mirror*. Little did they know how accurate they were. I did, in fact, and had always, found Mr Brando awfully attractive. He had the same sort of charisma, intelligence, curiosity and wit that 'The General' had.

I was somewhat conscious of the fact that I had left school at the age of fifteen and that my vocabulary consisted of about 20,000 words less than these two together. They managed to combine the exuberant enthusiasm of two schoolboys at a baseball game with the sophistication of scholarly jet-set professors. Their humour and whimsicality fed off each other and they would spark each other to new heights of erudite and enlightening prose.

Marlon had an insatiable curiosity about people. What made them tick? What did they think about the world and other people, their feelings, observations, desires? At any gathering Marlon would usually gravitate to the quietest, and what to the unpractised eye appeared the dullest person in the room, and engage them in animated and spirited conversation for hours. He was the master at making the shrinking violet bloom and the wallflower free her blossoms from the wall. His interest was genuine. He really *was* interested in that pimpled be-spectacled young woman whose manner bespoke the library rather than the boudoir. He would draw her out slowly, painstakingly, with questions asked with such intelligence and obvious concern that the girl would flower and blossom before our eyes. He would not — or rarely — converse with the more secure, flamboyant bon vivant seasoned party-going types — he preferred to find his own party fodder. Deeply engrossed, eyeball to eyeball, hunched in the farthest corner of the room, oblivious to the milling about that surrounded them, Marlon and his new-found (albeit temporary) interest, be it male or female, would sit engrossed in each other's company for hours on end.

This amused The General who would make jocular remarks about Marlon's proclivity for turning on the ugliest girl in the room. 'Hey Bud,' he joked, as Brando hove into view after a two hour marathon chat with a mousy little forty-year-old, Pasadena housewife type, now flustered, breathless and glowing from her encounter with the sex star — 'If you play your cards right I think you may get to first base with her!'

Marlon would grunt and grin, unable to resist the blandishments of The General's forceful personality. But.his quest was for truth, to find the person behind the mask, the true feelings behind the facade. When he turned his piercing blue orbs on you, no third degree was necessary. It was confession time. People who had held themselves tightly in check for years would open their floodgates of passion and feeling to Brando and he would receive, and enjoy and share. One of the great qualities in his acting performances is that he brings an amazing realism, truth and authenticity to whatever part he plays. In the late 1950s few, if any, actors brought these attributes to their film roles. With the exception of James Dean and Montgomery Clift, the intensity and depth of feeling was not inherent in actors of the fifties and sixties — indeed they were almost frowned on as the more fashionable attributes of handsomeness, charm and virility were in favour.

Today Dustin Hoffman, Al Pacino and Robert de Niro carry on where Brando pioneered. The age of the 'personality' actor is ending and a breed of thinking and feeling individuals has appeared, to whom the words 'movie star' are odious, and whose egos are sublimated to the personalities of the characters they are portraying.

Marlon's curiosity extended not only to people he met at parties

106

but also to the content of his friends' refrigerators. To say he was fond of food is putting it mildly. Food seemed to be sucked down his throat rapidly, as though by some invisible vacuum. We had discussed the merits and disadvantages of having a 'vomitorium' built into one's house — as in Roman times — a room where after two or three courses of excessive wining and dining, a well-to-do Roman of his day would excuse himself and retire to this quaintly, but appropriately named room and relieve his congested stomach by way of a good old-fashioned puke. He would then return to the dining room to indulge in another four or five courses — tripping to the vomitorium whenever the need arose.

The advantages to those of us (among them me) who like to eat were obvious. Marlon did sometimes practise this odd method of weight watching whilst dieting for a role and trying to get down to fighting weight, but I was never able to do it. My innate squeamishness inhibited me. Ah, the joys of being able to indulge in a four course meal with appropriate wine and liqueurs to follow — and having no tell-tale after effects appearing on the scales next day because of one's perspicacity at the vomitorium.

The General and I caught Marlon red-handed one night at my apartment spooning the last dregs of a quart of Will Wright's Peach Vanilla ice cream into him, whilst two empty quart containers on the side testified to his healthy appetite.

Caught like a guilty seven-year-old with his spoon at half mast, nevertheless his aplomb never faltered and he managed to give the impression of tremendous superiority and savoir faire with a trickle of ice cream at the corner of his mouth.

My fascination with The General moved into high gear. He was *everything* I had ever wanted in a man. Except for the fact that he was married and had little money he was perfect in every way. But his treatment of me was appalling and yet I accepted it. To preserve my sanity and my ego I would occasionally go out on dates with other young men, but such was his rage when he discovered this flagrant breach of conduct that the three or four hours of harassment, fighting, arguing and tears hardly made it worthwhile.

'I am divorcing Mabel,' he announced definitively one afternoon after our own liaison had been going for three or four months. 'We will live together for a while, for the sake of the children — but occupying separate bedrooms, of course,' he added hastily, seeing the spark of anger in my eye.

Round one: it looked like I was ahead. I was thrilled. Subconsciously my suppressed desire to get Daddy away from Mummy was being fulfilled in this relationship. To celebrate his new freedom we flew to Eleuthera, one of the most remote and romantic islands in the Caribbean — where there was nothing but green frothy sea, white sand and a cool blue alcove of a bedroom in which we spent a lot of our time. But he was unsatisfied — edgy, upset and remote.

'Why?' I wailed, sitting on the golden white perfect beach one day — an uninhabited vista of paradise to the north, south, east and west of us. '*Why* do you have to think of Mabel and the kids now for Christ's sake?' I threw myself onto the powdery sand in my white bikini and started to sob. I wondered *how* he could *possibly* — viewing my lithe sun-tanned 22-year-old body, my face recently described as the world's most beautiful, not to mention all the clever things he'd taught me in bed — how could he *possibly* think of wife and kiddies now? What did I *lack* that I seemed to leave him so unfulfilled? Although I was leaning heavily on my 'shrink' I was unable to see that the lacks were not from me alone. His insurmountable guilt at leaving his wife and three children seemed to be fuelled by his obsession with me. Our island paradise became a disaster area. Feuding and fighting and fussing we flew back to the States after only three days in Heaven, and commenced our charade once more.

'Dollink I know a vonderful man who is MAD about you.' Zsa Zsa Gabor bit crisply into a shrimp and surveyed me shrewdly. 'Vat you vant with this — this — son of a bitch married idiot. Dollink, vat he give you?' We sat lunching at Romanoffs, Zsa Zsa dispensing her worldly advice, diamonds glinting in the noonday sun, and I, dark glasses covering the ravages of last night's crying, trying to join in the fun and games of a girls' lunch.

Last night I had operated on a hunch. At 11.00, as the dreary television ended and the even more dreary news had spouted forth, it came to me in a blinding flash that there was no 'spare bedroom' at The General's house! Without thinking I jumped into my car and zoomed over to Westwood. I carefully cruised the alley behind the two-storey white house and observed the action. The house had three bedrooms and six occupants — The General and wife, three sons and a housekeeper. My naivety had gotten the better of me. It was obvious. Three sons in one room, housekeeper in another, Mr and Mrs in the master bedroom. I knew the lay of the land. I'd been there before. As if so prove me right, I saw the two leading actors in my soap opera enter the bedroom and indulge in animated discussion as they proceeded to disrobe. Horrified I gunned my motor and hastily turned into Wilshire Boulevard — had my eyes deceived me or had they indeed been taking off their clothes in the same room with the blinds up yet! I made the turn zombie-like from Wilshire and Westwood Boulevard and cruised the alley more slowly and surely and more observantly. Yes it was he. No mistaking that six foot two tanned and terrific body — clad now only in blue undershorts as he discussed some subject animatedly with her — wearing an orange Juel Park nightgown of gossamer fineness and with shoes off, a good ten inches shorter than he. My eyes filled with tears as my most ghastly suspicions were verified. He had lied to me. Yes — he was cheating on me with his wife!

There was no 'separate bedroom' while they discussed their upcoming divorce. There was a cosy queen-size bed and a thirty-two-year-old man and woman with three children and seven years of marriage behind them ready to go to bed together.

I pressed my foot on the accelerator as hard as I could and zoomed off blindly. At Sunset Boulevard the cop got me.

I had left the apartment so hurriedly I had no identification — not even any money.

'OK lady — where's your ID?' said the gum-chewing middle-aged cop testily, oblivious to my bleary eyed and obvious maiden-in-distress appearance. I thought it best to turn on my British 'Sloane Ranger' accent as fast as possible. 'I'm awfully sorry officer — but I *cahnt* seem to remember putting it in my reticule when I left my flat.' I was summoning up all my talent for my mind was seething. I realised 'reticule' was going a bit far — a Victorian word he probably had never heard of — but 'flat' hit the spot, and I knew Americans were slightly in awe of the plummy, true-blue British diction. He was no exception. Instead of calling in to his headquarters, as he should have done when finding someone driving over the limit — in which event I would have been computer checked and they would have found I had a dozen unpaid traffic tickets which *could* necessitate spending the night in jail, he gallantly offered to escort me on his motorcycle back to my flat whilst I retrieved the licence.

'Oh you American policemen are wonderful,' I gushed admiringly and he, mindful of the tears drying on my cheeks and feeling perhaps that a British damsel in distress coped less well than her Yankee counterpart, gallantly left me to my misery.

And now I listened to Zsa Zsa — grimly — more determined than ever to try and break off this disastrous alliance.

'Dollink he's vonderful,' said Mme Gabor, tossing her blonde and beautifully coiffed curls, her doll-like blue eyes glistening with evangelical fervour at the thought of playing Cupid. I usually avoided blind dates like the plague. Men who were interested in meeting actresses were usually creeps — but I listened to her whilst munching my way through as many courses of lunch, and glasses of wine as possible, to dull the pain.

'His name is Raphael Trujillo — you've heard of him of course?' She looked at me questioningly. I shook my head, mouth full of spinach and bacon salad. Zsa Zsa sighed. Women like Zsa Zsa always seemed to know intimately every head of state, prime minister and tycoon of all the minor countries of the world. Since my involvement with The General and my constant sessions at the analyst, my enthusiasm for current world events had waned, and I had not even read *Time* magazine lately. If I had I would certainly have heard about Sr Trujillo Senior. Zsa Zsa painstakingly started to fill me in, and I listened half-heartedly.

'His father, of course, is the President of the Dominican Republic and' — she bent forward conspiratorially — 'he has sometimes been known as "El Jege", the chief, and "the Caligula" of the Caribbean.' I remembered now reading about him. Although he had successfully lifted his country from a depressed economic state, which it was in when he assumed control and took over the Government in 1930, he had never tolerated any opposition at all to his regime and any suspicion or infraction invited arrests, tortures and political executions. He apparently guarded his country by a curtain of fear, terrorising and exploiting his frightened and hapless people.

Everything of value in his country belonged either to him or his family and it had become a police state in which his glassy-eyed photograph appeared in every public building. Major buildings and streets were re-named for him, and he awarded himself numerous titles of importance although he came from a poor peasant family and was one of eleven children. All in all a very unsavoury character indeed. A sort of Idi Amin of his day. A holiday in the Dominican Republic would be at bottom of my list of favourite places to visit.

But dismissing the father's injustices with an airy wave, Zsa Zsa proceeded to fill me in on sonny boy. He was a polo-playing friend of Zsa Zsa's great friend, Porfiro Rubiroso. He had recently finished an army stint at Fort Leavenworth in Kansas and now, therefore, had the title of General Raphael Trujillo. (All these Generals could become confusing I thought.) '. . . And . . .' Zsa

110

Zsa finished triumphantly, 'he's twenty-nine-years old —
unmarried, *very* handsome, very rich and dying to meet you. Vat
do you say dollink?' I considered carefully whilst devouring
chicken pancakes. Well why not? Even if his father was the
Great Dictator it didn't necessarily mean the son had to be a
baddie too. I had been on dozens of dates. It didn't constitute an
engagement.

'Will you come along too?' I asked Zsa Zsa, who was now
surveying me like a mother hen looking at her first new laid egg.

'Oh dollink — I can't — I can't get to Palm Beach right now —
I'm doing a show.'

'Palm *Beach!*' I gasped, 'you didn't say anything about *Palm
Beach.* I mean this is Beverly Hills — I'm not going 4000 miles for
a *blind date.*'

'But dollink,' she wheedled, 'his boat is there now — he has to
be in Palm Beach for the next ten days on business — he can't get
here — surely dollink,' she lowered her voice conspiratorially and
bent her blonde coy head closer to mine — I could smell Arpège
and observe she wore navy blue mascara on her false lashes —
'Surely you can leave this awful General of yours for a couple of
days — it *might* be worth your while.' She smiled mysteriously
and leaned back to sip some more Chablis, her mission, if not
accomplished, at least message delivered.

'No dice, Zsa Zsa.' I lit a cigarette and shook my head violently.
'I'm not about to shlepp 4000 miles for a date with a guy I don't
even *know* — however cute and rich he may be.'

'But dollink, you told me you were going to be in New York
next week for the opening of your movie. Palm Beach is next *door*
practically. He'll send his plane for you naturally.' She continued
her argument through the raspberries and ice cream but I was
unenthused about the idea. Besides I had to get back to the
apartment. The General was coming over at 3.30 and even though
he was always late — nevertheless I was always ready — and
today I had things to discuss.

We said hasty goodbyes and I dashed back to Shoreham Drive.
It was a beautiful, sunny Californian afternoon but I felt chilly.
He arrived at 4.00. Handsome and tanned as ever, wearing an
immaculate Prince of Wales plaid suit, which on any other man
would have looked tacky and on him looked like the cover of
Gentleman's Quarterly. His socks matched his tie I noticed, and
the new shoes obviously cost more than 50 dollars.

I tried to remember a present or trinket — or even a flower he
had ever bought me and realised he had never brought me

anything but himself. I wondered if that was supposed to suffice.

Our usual afternoon ritual was to kiss, hug, chat and get into bed, but I was only in the mood for the third item on the agenda. And I needed a drink. To broach this subject was not going to be easy. He also accepted the vodka and tonic I handed him and then sat opposite me in the armchair, jacket off, leaning back, arms behind head — surveying me with benign satisfaction and a faint smile. I was his property, his little princess in an ivory tower in the hills of Hollywood. Behind him the afternoon sun glinted on his shiny shoes, his gold cufflinks and — it gave me a moment of bitchiness to note — his slightly receding hair line. 'Serves him right,' I thought to myself bitterly. 'I hope it all falls out *soon*.' I downed the vodka in one great gulp and came right out with it.

'You told me that you and Mabel sleep in separate rooms, but I don't believe you.' I stared at him, hoping against hope he would come up with a good story and that it had all been just a figment of my imagination.

He stared back. He drowned his vodka. Pain came to his face. He lit a cigarette. My God he *never* smoked — what the hell was going on? OK, admit it now. Admit you slept with the wife; come out with all the old clichés; she was there you weren't; I thought about you all the time; I only did it once; she tried but I couldn't do it; say *something* but don't sit there at half past four in the afternoon looking like Paris has fallen and smoking cigarettes and drinking vodka. Admit it — tell me — I'll cry a bit — and then we'll make up and go to bed. These thoughts raced through my head as he continued to stare and smoke.

'She's pregnant,' he said finally, 'but we only did it once, believe me Joanie and she's goddam pregnant again.' I stared at him numbly. Pregnant — it wasn't possible — or was it? She already had three kids, with about two years between each one.

'How . . I mean why . . . when . . ?' I couldn't speak. There was a lump in my throat the size of a fist, that only vodka would make go away. I silently filled our empty glasses with straight Smirnoff while he filled me in on the details.

One afternoon seven or eight weeks previously when he had been in my apartment she had suddenly started knocking on the front door and screaming frenziedly, 'He's here — I know he's here — make him come out — oh God — how can you do this to me . . .' and other histrionic phrases. We sat fearfully up in bed clutching each other and he motioning me to shut up as I attempted to go to the door and assure her he wasn't with me. After five or ten minutes the neighbours complained about the

shenanigans and she was hustled, still weeping and wailing, away.
I was in a mild state of shock for I was not aware she knew about
me, but rumours fly like moths in Hollywood and obviously word
had reached her that his Cadillac was parked on Shoreham Drive
several times a week. At that time — according to him — they
were in fact occupying separate bedrooms. He slept in the study
on a couch and they were going through some sort of separation
whilst he was trying to sort out his very mixed up emotions. But
that evening when he returned she threw the book at him — tears,
hysteria, threats of suicide. To protect me, and prove to her that
he was *not* involved with me, he slept with her — just the once —
and the result was this pregnancy.

'So now you'll be a father of four,' I said, my voice sounding as
if it came from the grave. I picked up the vodka bottle and tilted it
to my lips. I drank it all down — about a quarter of a bottle and
then hurled it across the room at him with all the force I could
muster. It crashed into the window behind his head and glass flew
everywhere. He jumped up amazed. I took an ashtray and threw it
at another pane in the middle of the bay window, and then a glass,
and then a pillow — anything I could lay my hands on, whilst
sobbing and screaming at him incoherently, 'That's *my* baby she's
having — it should be mine — how dare you make another baby
with her. It's mine — it's mine — it's mine!' As I threw myself
about the room, all reason gone, he tried to calm me. He knew I
detested physical violence, had never hit anyone or anything in
my life and that this awful outbreak was the signal that I was at
breaking point.

I wouldn't let him touch me. My lungs were raw from yelling at
him and screaming. All the pent up months of patience, hoping, of
putting up with his lateness, his lies and his deceptions were
unleashed. If I had had a gun I might even have killed him. A true
'crime passionel'. I never knew I had such a build-up of feelings of
rage inside me. The dam indeed burst and the floodgates opened
wide. A tiny cynical part of me watched the proceedings with
great interest. As an actress I would be able to call on this
experience for future roles. 'Well done,' said the little voice
admiringly, 'what a great performance dear' — but the grief, rage
and passion that overcame me at four o'clock on a sunny
afternoon in North Hollywood has never been matched in my life
— thank the Lord.

Hours later he left. To his credit he saw me through the tempest
and to the shore of oblivion — sleep. As he tiptoed out of the
apartment at nine o'clock he left a groggy, helpless wreck lying in

bed exhausted, overwrought, filled still with rage and a desire for revenge.

The next afternoon I called Zsa Zsa. 'I'm leaving for New York tonight,' I said crisply. 'Tell your friend Mr Trujillo to call me at the Plaza.'

She had not been too wrong about Trujillo. He was quite good looking in a glossy, black haired, olive skinned, Latin way. His manners were impeccable and his admiration for me was apparent. We dined on his palatial 350-foot yacht, the *Angelita*, surrounded by the trappings of wealth that only the very richest of rich men can afford. The vast table was set with a hand-embroidered white organdie cloth; the dishes were gold, as was the cutlery; the glasses at each place setting were the most beautiful pale amber Venetian glass; flowers were everywhere — orchids, lilies and lush tropical plants. There was caviar in profusion, wines of extraordinary vintage, and exquisite food. It was a balmy beautiful night in Palm Beach. The moon was full and reflecting on the water which lapped gently at the boat.

Apart from the crew of about eighty, not counting the band, there were a few people there — Palm Beach socialites, his equerry and some aides from the Dominican Republic. The talk was light, typical jet-set chat about parties and places and people. Some of them I knew, some of them I didn't. I didn't really care. It was good once again to be in the company of a man who obviously found me thrilling, paid me lavish compliments and appeared to wait on me hand and foot. Your word is my command, seemed to be his attitude. What a change from trying so hard to please and not succeeding.

We had coffee and liqueurs on the upper deck where, on the distant shore silhouetted against the navy blue sky, the palm trees waved lazily in the breeze and the Calypso songs brought me back memories of locations in the Caribbean. We danced. His desire was obvious and I felt light-headed, light-hearted and more than a little drunk. I had not slept the previous night — thoughts of The General's impending fatherhood tormented me. I wanted to go back to the hotel at Palm Beach and sleep for a week. I was tired and told him so, but he insisted that I stay the night in the luxurious state room that had been prepared for me.

So what the hell. I was young, footloose and fancy free. My love-affair and commitment with The General still occupied all my thoughts, but it seemed doomed. Why not stay the night with this attractive strange gentleman who treated me like a piece of rare crystal. I had never before gone to bed with anyone unless totally carried away by passion, lust, love. This time my motivation was mental and physical exhaustion, mixed with gratitude for a consolation missing from my life for months. I had always been faithful to The General, and he had not to me, so this finally would be how our affair would end. On a beautiful boat, on a perfect Florida night, with the son of the President of the Dominican Republic.

Autumn in New York and it was a frenzy: interviews, photo sessions, press luncheons and guest shots on TV. *Stopover Tokyo* opened to mediocre to poor reviews. Most of the movies I was making at Fox seemed to get mediocre reviews, and I would get comments like: 'Joan Collins seems to be an actress with more talent than she is able to show in the purely decorative roles she has been playing.'

It was party time too. Late August and the New Yorkers returned to their favourite haunts of 21, Pavillon, El Morocco and Billy Reed's Little Club from their summers in St Tropez, the Hamptons and the Greek Islands. I started dating a young Greek, Peter Theadoracopolis. Short, dark and handsome, Peter or 'Taki' as his friends called him, was the son of a powerful Greek shipping tycoon. He was very much the jet-set playboy — never seeming to linger long enough in one playground or the other to form lasting attachments. This suited me down to the ground — lasting attachments were for the birds so far as I was concerned right now.

One night I would see him and we would drink champagne at El Morocco and dance until sun-up, and the next I would see Nicky Hilton, who was also in town and at his father's hotel the Plaza, and once again pursuing me.

Around my neck I now sported a dazzling diamond necklace from Van Cleef and Arpels, a gift from Trujillo which had arrived the day after I returned to New York from Palm Beach. It was an exceptionally beautiful choker in the shape of seven or eight flowers and consisting of about 25 carats, and although I had tried to contact Trujillo to return it, his aides informed me he had returned to Santo Domingo and would be most offended if his 'token of esteem' was returned. It would be insulting, they informed me frostily.

When I phoned Cappy Yordan in Beverly Hills she was horrified at the thought that I should return it, and so was Zsa Zsa. 'Dollink, from him, he is so rich it is like sending a basket of flowers,' she scoffed. So what the hell again. I kept it. If you've got it, flaunt it was one of Cappy's jokey phrases and so I did. It was the first piece of valuable jewellery I had ever received. Arthur Loew, with all the family millions, had only given me little gold pins and rings with a few quarter carat diamonds strewn around and Nicky was not noted for his largesse with women since being bitten by Elizabeth Taylor. It's a pity, I thought, that the one piece of jewellery of any value was given to me by a man from a relationship that had no value to me. True, he was nice, charming, handsome, but I had no desire to see him again.

My week's whirl of hedonism and work ended when I was called back to Los Angeles to start another picture. Nicky and Taki had almost come to blows one night at the Plaza, and it was time to get out of town and get down to work.

The General was out of my system now I thought.

One red rose and a note 'Forgive Me. G.' was delivered the day after I got home. I didn't need to know who it was from. I tried to pretend that I didn't care as I sped to the studio to fit costumes for *Rally Round the Flag Boys* but I couldn't deny that I was exceptionally cheery and full of joie de vivre today; was it just because of the note?

The message service called me as I sat in consultation with Charles Le Maire, who was designing the clothes for *Rally*.

'Mr Cunningham's called you three times today,' said Teddy, who knew how many times I would casually ask on a check in: 'Has Mr Cunningham called?' and how disappointed I was if the answer was negative. Mr Cunningham was The General's telephone alias.

My heart did a definite lurch. The mind is controllable but not the heart — mine certainly isn't.

'If he calls again tell him where I am,' I said and went back to discussing the dresses with Charles, my heart not in it now. Ten minutes later he called again. 'Before you say anything,' he said hastily, 'I just want to say three things — I love you, I miss you and who the fuck is Taki Theador whatever-the-fuck-his-name is?' I giggled. I couldn't help it.

'We're just good friends,' I laughed — fingering the antique diamond anchor brooch that Peter had given me as a parting gift. Suddenly the men I met became Santa Claus. The General didn't have to beg too hard for me to agree to see him, since he whetted my appetite by telling me he had portentous news of great benefit to both of us. But I insisted we meet at La Scala. Since I considered our affair over, what was there to hide?

116

'Mabel lost the baby,' he said flatly. 'It happened a couple of days after you went to New York. We had a lot of fights — heavy ones.' He paused to sip his vodka — I hung on his words.

'We've decided to definitely get a divorce. I've consulted a lawyer and . . .' He took another sip. I leaned forward not really believing what I was hearing.

'. . . And I've moved into an apartment on Wilshire — the Beverly Comstock — 'The boulevard of broken dreams" ', he referred to the fact that there were dozens of hotels along Wilshire in the Westwood area where newly separated or divorced men went to sort out their lives whilst their lawyers fought it out with their wives for custody of their property, houses, Cadillacs, paintings, and children. The wives usuall got it all anyway — unlike my farcical divorce settlement with Maxwell Reed, and that Wilshire Boulevard section which also housed a lot of stewardesses, models, and actresses had become a swinging singles paradise.

'So where do I fit into all this?' I asked, fingering Taki's diamond pin and wishing I hadn't worn it.

'With me you fit in, of course. I mean I love you — do you still love me?' My look should have told him that. 'And when it's all over maybe we can . . .' he took another drink — this seemed hard for him to get out — but I had to hear it. He smiled at me boyishly. 'D'you fancy being stepmother to three boys?' Did I!!

It was all too much to take. He had finally decided to commit himself. I felt like the happiest girl in the world. We ordered a bottle of Dom Perignon to celebrate — and while we drank it he informed me that his lawyers had advised him that he must not be seen publicly with a woman alone — especially me — since Mabel was considering naming me as co-respondent. In the unenlightened days of 1958 scandal could still be ruinous to an actor or actress's reputation and career and I knew I had as much to lose as he. So we agreed on complete discretion until the divorce was final.

We started going to obscure restaurants at the beach and in the Valley. Sometimes we would double date with Marlon Brando and his pretty and dynamic Puerto Rican girlfriend Rita Moreno — an actress usually typecast in 'spitfire' roles but in life a faithful worshipper at Marlon's shrine. She adored him but he, in turn, treated her in a rather cavalier manner — never letting her know where she stood in their stormy affair which lasted on and off for eight years, and culminated in her taking a near fatal overdose of pills. I sympathised with her. Marlon too was having marital problems with his estranged Indian wife Anna Kashfi. I don't think Marlon ever went out with a blonde, he loved the exotic girls. Now Marlon and The General were preparing to make a film together and I hoped that The General might find a feeling of nepotism overtake him and would cast me in the role of Marlon's wife.

Alas it was not to be. An unknown actress — unknown before the film and also after — got the part, but I at least was finally playing a role I really liked and had fun with; man-baiting, outrageous Angela in *Rally Round the Flag Boys*. Fox had originally wanted Jayne Mansfield to play the sexy young vamp, living in a small town, married to a boring business man, who goes all out to seduce Paul Newman away from Joanne Woodward. But Joanne and Paul insisted to director Leo McCarey that Mansfield was far too tarty and obvious, that the character should have a touch of class and an impish sense of humour and persuaded him to cast me. They were good friends and I appreciated their loyalty. Few actors go out of their way to try and get a part for a friend, but the Newmans have always been generous and supportive in their relationships with people they care about. The picture was a happy experience — although again like most of my movies neither a critical nor a financial success — but Leo McCarey was a famous and beloved director having made such films as *Going My Way* with Bing Crosby, for which he won an Oscar.

My love life was lyrical, working with the Newmans was a treat and I finally was allowed to express my comedic talents again which had been lying dormant since *Skin of Our Teeth*. Critically this turned out to be my most favourable film. I received rapturous and sometimes surprised reviews that a sexy and attractive woman should be able to play comedy too. I was able to be inventive in ways I had not been allowed to be before. The laughing scene, where Paul and I get drunk together while I try to teach him how to cha-cha had some hysterically funny moments. We had to laugh all day — take after take — from dawn till dusk. Mascara ran endlessly down my cheeks and we became so hysterical that just the sight of each other would set us off. 'Angela — I'd know that face anywhere,' groaned Paul between gasps of laughter as he came face to face with my rear end. I was doubled over on the floor, bottom up, gasping for air, and when he said the line I deflated like a balloon and fell flat on my face. Another cut, and Paul was swinging literally from the chandelier back and forth whilst I hung onto a pillar for support, weak from laughing. We became so carried away that we couldn't stop even

The anguished look comes from trying to hold in my stomach. The ruby was there to satisfy the censor.

MAGNUM

Sydney and me — off set and on.

TOP LEFT: Twentieth Century Fox's 'foxy lady'. The publicity machine goes to work on me.
TOP RIGHT: Watch the birdie! BOTTOM LEFT: Being pinned to within an inch of my life.
BOTTOM RIGHT: Hi Hollywood! Some funny things happened on the way there . . .

TWENTIETH CENTURY FOX

The American publicity machine tried to give me a much more glamorous image than the Rank publicity machine. Here are some examples.

TOP LEFT: Evelyn Nesbit in 1907 and . . . TOP RIGHT: . . . how Hollywood saw her in 1955.
BOTTOM LEFT: 'The Girl in the Red Velvet Swing' made the cover of *Life* Magazine. BOTTOM
RIGHT: The real Evelyn Nesbit, 1955 vintage.

TWENTIETH CENTURY FOX

TOP LEFT: From a fan photo . . . TOP RIGHT: . . . to the real thing! BOTTOM: We couldn't kiss in the film — but Fox allowed me this symbolic palm tree as a substitute . . . *Sea Wife*, 1956.

TWENTIETH CENTURY FOX

TWENTIETH CENTURY FOX

TOP LEFT: Having a farewell drink with Arthur Loew and Errol Flynn before leaving for Jamaica. TOP RIGHT: Playing the dating game at Mocombo's Night Club in Hollywood. With Nicky Hilton from the hotel of the same name (fat faces were 'in' that year!). CENTRE: On location in Barbados for *Island in the Sun*, 1956 with Harry Belafonte, Patricia Owens and Michael Rennie. BOTTOM: Peter Townsend, escaping from his problems, visits Robert Wagner and me in Tokyo while shooting *Stopover Tokyo* which we fondly referred to as 'stop overacting'!

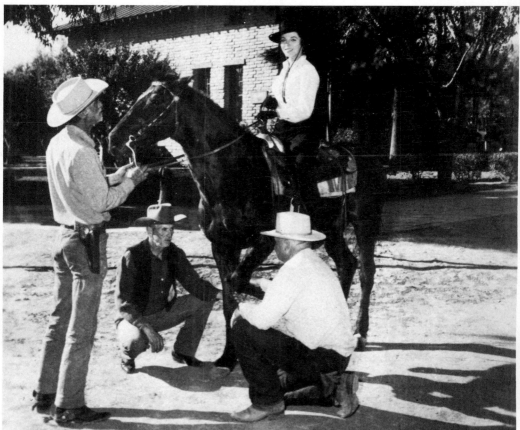

TOP: I may look as if I'm enjoying myself but my rear end was raw and a few moments later I was served with a subpoena! *The Opposite Sex*, 1956. BOTTOM: Trying to remain cool for a close-up — while three assistants hold Pancho down — on the set of *The Bravados*, Mexico, 1958.

when we sat on canvas chairs between takes and tried to be coherent. It was catching. The crew were laughing like crazy too. Everyone was having a wonderful time. Pity it didn't work so well on the cinemascope screen.

In the five and a half years I was contracted to Fox, and in fact for several years before and after my tenure there their record at the box office was appalling. And artistically it was even worse. The studio which had turned out such hits as *Gentleman's Agreement, Grapes of Wrath, Razor's Edge* and *Letter to Three Wives*, now turned out things like Jayne Mansfield in *The Girl Can't Help It* and Sheree North in *How to be very, very Popular.* Depressing. Especially for the stock holders. Zanuck was less and less involved in the everyday production. Buddy Adler was head of the studio now, and everything he did turned to dross. But the studio were deciding to make an expensive blockbuster. *Cleopatra*, story of the femme fatale to end them all, and in first position for the role of the fascinating serpent of the Nile was the contender from Great Britain — the pouting panther herself — J. Collins. But the studio, and Walter Wanger the producer could not accept me as I was, no sirree. Grooming had to take place. I had to learn to walk and talk and move like a Queen. Specialists in the art of walking and deportment (what have I been doing so wrong all these years pray?) were called in to turn this sow's ear into a silk purse. My body must be slimmed down. At 9 stone I was too curvy for Cleo so they told me (Liz wasn't exactly sylph-like when she played it eventually).

I dieted; I exercised; I sat for hours in the make-up and hairdressing rooms whilst Whitney Snyder, my make-up man, applied unusual and elaborate designs on my face. 'I know she had slanted eyes but this is *ridiculous.*' I gazed into a pair of astonished green eyes outlined from nose to temple in black and purple eyeliner, silver sequins outlined the liner, and a glistening blue-black wig cascaded to my shoulders. No less astounding was my costume for the test I was about to make.

A pleated toga of pale violet chiffon stopped at thigh level. Silver sandals laced to the knee — causing me to worry about early varicose veins. A teeny weeny silver bikini bra from which hung baubles, bangles and bric-a-brac of various hues of purple and silver. A giant collar of amethyst and silver inhibited my vocal chords and made moving my head an effort. Immense silver earrings jangled to and fro and constantly tangled themselves in the wig.

119

The costume was finished off with arm bracelets from wrist to elbow of sturdy sterling silver, nine or ten large rings all representing snakes in one way or another, and a billowing cloak of purple velvet and silver lamé. This was attached to the giant collar and was so long that if I misjudged my step I tripped and almost strangled myself. In this sensuous, enticing gear I hobbled to Stage 16 to try and act some of the most appalling dialogue ever written opposite an actor who, though obviously chosen for his looks and virility, had as much acting talent as Minnie Mouse — maybe less.

But Walter Wanger and Co persevered. If the first test wasn't too good, maybe it was because the costuming was wrong. Try again and again — and we did. Three tests in three outrageous outfits I made for the coveted role of the Queen, and I ached to play her. Shaw's Cleopatra had been my test piece for the RADA entrance exam and I knew it was a role perfectly suited to me. Of course they were considering others too, and eventually the casting couch reared its all too ugly head. Spyros Skouras, an elderly Greek gentleman, was the Chairman of the board of directors at Fox. He had much to say about the casting of Cleo and he said it. To me and aften. Phone calls, suggestions and skittish forays around his desk. He should know better I thought. He's old enough to be my grandpa.

But with typical Greek tenacity he continued his entreaties and persuasions. An eye for an eye, a tooth for a tooth — a fuck for a part. No thank you very much Mr Grandfatherly Greek — I have my hands full at home. I tried to be as graceful about it as I could in the circumstances. Greeks don't take kindly to rejection, but he still persisted in calling me often to tell me what a terrible career mistake I was making by my unreceptiveness towards him.

This did not help my relationship with The General who now spent several nights a week at my apartment and heard the 'phone calls. He became enraged at the ancient Greek's audacity. Stupidly I had told him about the young Greek, Taki, and endured several hours of tongue lashing. I had hidden the little diamond anchor he'd given me and when Taki came out for a quick visit I hastily sent him back to Jet Set land. But The General's jealousy was boundless. Too broad a smile at the delivery boy and his dander was up and off we went again — 'Why did you . . .' 'How could you . . .' 'Why can't you . . .' All he needed was to put a record on the stereo, I knew his dialogue inside out. He was making me nervous. I started to get occasional attacks of hives, especially after I'd eaten lobster or shrimp. After several tests my doctor discovered I was allergic to shell fish and must stop eating it completely. Quite a blow, I adored it, but my reactions had been getting worse each time I ate it and Doctor Sellars had warned me that these allergies could become dangerous.

I gave a little dinner party at the end of the shooting of *Rally Round the Flag Boys*. Although I went to many parties I was not accustomed to giving them, and most of the friends who crowded into my tiny apartment were, I thought, used to a more lavish setting for their revels. My insecurity reared its ugly head, and I fluttered around trying to be the perfect hostess to people like Milton Berle, Paul Newman, Joanne Woodward, Sammy Davis, Stanley and Marion Donen and about twenty others, and on the way imbibing quite a lot of whisky.

La Scala were doing the catering and I had chosen the menu with care. But not quite enough thought had gone into my choice. After a heaping platter of Chicken Sinatra con Risotto I started to feel my cheeks flaming and large welts appeared on my neck and shoulders. 'Oh my God you look like a suet pudding!' shouted one of my English girlfriends. I rushed to the bathroom mirror and saw a flushed and swollen face and startled green eyes set in a sea of broken red capillaries and puffed up eyelids. Dr Sellars had told me to call him at any hour if this allergy came upon me. The hour had come. I leaped to the 'phone in the bedroom. Sammy was on it talking earnestly with his hand over his ear to shut out the babble of voices around him. 'Kim, baby, you know I care — I don't give a shit what the papers say baby . . . .' I interrupted him in mid-Kim. 'Sam — I've *got* to use the phone — please.' He didn't hear my frenzied plea and continued his soliloquy . . . .' 'Of course not baby — how can that bastard Harry push you around like that . . . .'

'Sammy *please!!*' He looked up and gasped, 'Christ, what happened to your face kid?' I grabbed the phone from him, yelled a breathless 'sorry Kim!' and dialled Al Sellars. A group of concerned onlookers had gathered to observe my transformation from dazzling hostess to Dracula. I felt hives swelling like ripe tomatoes all over my face as I breathlessly explained to Sellars my predicament. 'Get over here immediately,' he said authoritatively.

'I'll drive you' said an anxious Stanley Donen. 'Quickly!' I yelped, my desire to escape from my own party and the anxious stares of the guests uppermost in my mind. I grabbed a scarf and we rushed down the stairs, my breathing already starting to feel strange and forced.

As he drove fast and erratically through semi-deserted Sunset Boulevard, my face felt as if it was being blown up by a bicycle pump. I shot a feverish glance into the rear view mirror. 'Oh my *God!!* Stanley, don't look at me!!' I threw the scarf over what was the most grotesque and revolting sight I had ever seen. My face was the size of a football. It was getting bigger by the second, purplish red, and my eyes were disappearing into the rapidly swelling surrounding tissue. My lips were bananas, so thick I couldn't talk, and worst of all, I realised that I could not get enough air into my throat to breathe properly. It too was swelling rapidly.

'Jesus H. Christ!' Stanley's look of frozen horror and his sudden acceleration to 100 miles an hour and through all the red lights was proof enough of my plight. I couldn't speak — I could hardly breathe — I lay back with the scarf over my face so no-one could glimpse this horror, and realised I was probably dying.

'I'm dying . . . .' I gasped.

'You'll make it kid — you'll make it.' Stanley's desperate voice was reassuring but his face, a study in paralysed fear, was not. At the same time as I was facing death the little voice in the back of my head was telling me to keep the scarf over my head so no-one would have to see how hideous I had become. 'Live fast, die young and have a good-looking corpse.' It was a Bogart line from *Knock on any Door*. I had done the first, was about to do the second, but the last was by now beyond me.

I hope they cremate me, before anyone can see what I look like I thought hazily and then fainted, right into the loving arms of the most beautiful sight I'd ever seen — a nurse. As they wheeled me through the corridor — yes, the wheelchair had been waiting, too — Sellars pumped some sort of injection into my arm and I heard through a haze his Dr Kildare voice saying . . . . .' Probably have to give her tracheotomy.' That's all I need. A tube through my throat. That should photograph nicely — if I live to ever appear on the silver screen again.

The prognosis seemed unlikely, my face was like a revolting barrage balloon floating above me, alien from my body which felt like ten thousand mosquitoes had just had lunch on it. As I was propelled through the hygienic corridors of the Roxbury Medical Centre a few odd passers-by observed this curious creature obviously in final death throes and her entourage. A solicitous nurse pumping adrenalin into her arm, calm yet concerned doctor taking her pulse, a harassed and frantic-looking tousle-haired film director, and the creature herself, oblivious to her imminent death, concerned only with keeping her ghastly visage far from the madding crowd.

Magically my body responded instantly to the adrenalin injection the nurse had administered in the lobby. By the time we reached the doctor's office, I could at least breathe a little easier and the dirigible that used to be my face was deflating slightly.

Death did not claim this young victim just yet. My astrologer had told me that I would always 'be saved at the eleventh hour' whether from financial ruin, certain death or bad emotional involvements. I was just happy to get my face back. Stanley couldn't get over the fact that at death's door my main concern had been that I should not let anyone see my ugliness. Such is the vanity and insecurity of a young actress under contract to a studio whose entire emphasis throughout her working day is placed on the illusion of retaining perfection of face and body at all times. I couldn't let myself look awful in front of somebody else, even if I was at death's door.

The General came back from his nineteenth trip to the Orient — he spent more time there than Chiang Kai-Shek. We rather daringly decided to attend a large industry party together.

In the private room upstairs at Romanoffs all was glitter, glamour and glib talk. *Toute* Hollywood was there. Everyone, from Buddy Adler to Darryl Zanuck had put on their best bib and tuckers and, the hell with those early calls, decided to have a ball.

I wore the Trujillo necklace. It looked divine with the white strapless silk dress and diamond earrings, which I had bought myself from my *Island in the Sun* expense money while in London. Clever kid, living at home and not having to pay those hotel bills. Much smarter to blow the money at Cartier than the Connaught.

The General and I made an attractive couple, and also several people present knew of our relationship. It was thrilling to be out with him, to feel as though I belonged to him, and he to me. Soon — he had assured me only yesterday — we would be married, a thought too exciting to contemplate without chills running up and down my spine. It was a delicious evening. To be out with the man I loved, publicly for once, to be able to dance with him, touch him, look into his eyes, talk to him, and not have to pretend to be enjoying the company of someone else.

'Is that the necklace Trujillo gave you?' I couldn't believe my ears. One of my girlfriends, the only one other than Zsa Zsa and

Cappy who knew of it, had plopped herself down next to us as we were having a tête à tête on a banquette. She was somewhat the worse for wine.

'N-n-no — it's wardrobe,' I stammered, noticing out of the corner of my eye The General's nostrils flare suspiciously.

'It looks just like the one you described to me,' she tattled on, squinting close to get a good look.

'Mmm — yes, well they really are doing good things with costume jewellery these days aren't they.' Her husband mercifully appeared to whisk her onto the dance floor, and I turned, flushing hotly, face to face with The General's angry brown eyes.

'Trujillo?' His questioning and menacing tone sent shivers down my spine of a different kind to those I was experiencing only a few minutes ago.

'Trujillo who? — may I ask?' His tone became even more menacing and his hand which had been gently on my knee now turned into a vice. There was no possible denial — my flaming cheeks and blazing diamonds were proof enough. I was undone, unfaithful to my unfaithful lover — bad, bad girl. I falteringly, stammeringly, haltingly told him all. He extracted every detail from me, his face a thunderous mask of rage which he was trying extremely hard and unsuccessfully to control. My tactless friend had realised her faux pas and was grimacing 'I'm sorrys' at me across the room. By now the nearest onlookers were riveted to our obvious 'discussion'.

'You fucking little slut,' he whispered savagely into my ear. 'You're worse than a street corner tart.' His fingers gripped my knee even harder and I winced in agony, tears of pain and humiliation squeezing themselves from under my carefully painted eyelids, and making little grey rivers down pretty pink cheeks. With an uncontrollable 'Whore!' bursting from his lips, he ripped the necklace from around my throat, and flung it savagely across the room, to the astonishment of the observant ladies to whom diamonds have always been a girl's best friend. And he was off and away, leaving me to grovel for the broken baubles on hands and knees in front of half Hollywood.

My girl friend and a few of the others joined in the general hunt for those tiny carats — so precious, so valuable and so useless — but which certain women could not do without. Well I was not joining their ranks. The insurance alone on this thing was too high and The General's attitude and my humiliation did not seem enough of a price to pay for the privilege of parading this bit of chemical junk around the 'A' party circuit. I knew a lot of the older wives of men in the business did not approve of me. They felt I was a 'threat' to them because of my 'loose' morals. Strangely enough, with the paradoxical double standard, it was considered 'OK' for a girl to sleep around with casting directors, producers, agents to get on and up the ladder. But going to bed with men because it was fun and enjoyable branded one as cheap and frivolous. So, no doubt, some of those ladies contemplating this sad little scene at chic Romanoff's restaurant, were smugly thinking that I was getting what I deserved. Having an affair with a married man indeed. Some of their morality was positively Victorian.

We stayed until 3.00 piecing together the bits of necklace on a table like some glittering jigsaw puzzle. It had shattered into about 150 pieces — but none of the diamonds themselves were broken and although it was in pieces it was not irreparable. The waiters joined in the treasure hunt with gusto and eventually we retrieved it all. 'Into the vault with this as soon as it's fixed,' I said grimly, 'it's more trouble than it's worth,'

We made up of course. We always did. It seemed half of our relationship was making up. We both apologised. He for making a nasty spectacle of me and me for being a faithless sex fiend when his wife was pregnant. And for a few weeks all was harmony until suddenly the papers got the goods on Trujillo.

'Gifts for the Girls' screamed headlines. 'Diamonds for Kim Novak and Joan Collins' yelled the tabloids. ' "Say it again and I'll sue" says Zsa Zsa.' The yellow presses were running at full speed to print startling and colourful stories of sex, sin and costly baubles in Hollywood.

It started when Congress, whilst voting on foreign aid to the Dominican Republic, was asked by a Congressman if the Republic really *needed* help when it had been discovered that the young Trujillo on top of having a wife and six children, appeared to have lined his pockets with over six million dollars, which could only possibly have come from American Aid, and had proceeded to lavish gifts on various well known film actresses. The catalogue was impressive. To Zsa Zsa Gabor: 1 Empress Chinchilla Coat — value $8,500; 1 Mercedes Benz — value $5,500. To Kim Novak (whom he now professed to love and hoped to marry in spite of the six kiddies at home in Dictator-land):1 diamond and pearl ring — value $3,500; 1 pair of diamond earrings — value $1,500; 1 Mercedes Benz (he obviously liked that car) at $8,500. And — in spite of some weak 'No comments' and half-hearted denials to the press — Collins finally joined the gold diggers and admitted all: 1

diamond necklace — value $10,000. Well, well,well!

Zsa Zsa sprang to Trujillo's defence, and to her own, when the Congressman accused her of being 'the most expensive courtesan since Madame Pompadour'. Zsa Zsa with her typical resilient wit countered: 'I was born in the wrong century — I would have made a bum out of Mme Pompadour.' One up to Hungary.

Miss Novak also jumped to his defence. Photos of their hand holding had been appearing in the tabloids. 'He is a wonderful gentleman and an honour to his great father who is doing a world of good for his country. He is a real Goodwill Ambassador.' So much for Poland.

The British contingent, after grudgingly admitting the existence of the trinket, categorically refused to discuss the man and his affairs at all. I desperately wanted my name out of the headlines and revealing nothing was the surest way of achieving that.

But the publicity rekindled my General's anger and jealousy. There were more scenes, even more tears, more making up. I started getting minor allergic reactions again. 'It's nervous' tension,' said my doctor. 'Get out of town for a while until this blows over.'

I went to New York to do a television show. Walking down Madison Avenue one fine afternoon I stumbled upon an adorable shop. 'Jolie Gabor Jeweller' it was called.

The boutique was filled to overflowing with authentic looking jewellery, which was in fact paste, glass and rhinestones, but so cleverly designed that they looked like the most expensive diamond, emerald, pearl, and ruby jewellery. The shop had a liberal amount of pictures of the three Gabor girls and Mama, looking delicious and wearing Jolie's jewellery creations which she designed herself. Madame Gabor Senior was there that afternoon in person. A vision in pale beige crepe and pearls, smelling wonderful, and looking like a younger, more glamorous Barbara Cartland. My inferiority complex jumped bolt upright. In my grey pleated skirt, loafers and polo-neck I looked like a gauche college girl next to a wise woman of the world.

She obviously didn't think someone dressed as I was would do anything more than browse, so when I pointed to a 'diamond' necklace in one of the showcases, she showed it to me with a marked lack of enthusiasm.

'For your mother dear?' she enquired in her Zsa-Zsa like Hungarian husky voice.

'No, for me!' I said excitedly examining the necklace. It was incredible. It was practically identical to the one Trujillo had given me. An idea had formulated in my mind.

'How much?'

'One hundred and twenty-five dollars,' said Madame Gabor, quite surprised to see this student-type fish out that much money for something that would be out of place at Vassar. With no make-up and simple clothes I could pass for seventeen or eighteen.

'I'm a friend of your daughter's,' I explained as I scribbled the cheque and showed her my ID.

'Ahh of course!' she smiled — no longer surprised. With Zsa Zsa anything was possible, and who knew what possibilities lay behind that baggy sweater and skirt and innocent face.

'I wish you much success with it darlink,' she husked, giving me the package. 'It vill look vunderful on you, I think. With the right clothes of course,' she added hastily.

'Thank you Madame,' I trilled happily tripping into the Madison Avenue sunshine. The General had a surprise in store for him.

We had a romantic candlelit dinner for two at a cosy bistro on the beach at Malibu. It was a perfect California night — a little chilly but the moon was a miniature crescent, the sea dark and calm, and the pebbled beach crushed softly underneath our feet as we walked hand in hand along the shore. I had drunk a bottle of Liebfraumilch single-handedly and was feeling rather giddy and nervous. We were celebrating our first anniversary of on and off togetherness. Ups and downs seemed to be my destiny and I was adjusting and adapting to them like a trouper. He wasn't an easy man. Fascinating yes, witty and goodlooking certainly, but his tempers, his jealousy and his ambivalent attitude towards his divorce proceedings did not make me feel at all secure. I *still* never knew where I really stood with him. I was about to play a trump card.

'Darling,' I cooed. 'I know how upset you have been about the necklace.' I put my fingers to his mouth to stop his retort. 'No, don't say anything darling. I realise it was an idiotic thing to do, to accept a gift from someone I had . . . er . . . hardly known.' Again he started to speak but I stopped him. 'So, because I love you so much I'm going to do something that I hope will stop us bringing this subject up *ever* again.' I fished in my handbag and brought out the necklace. The diamonds glittered in the moonlight and I dangled them in front of his eyes. 'Look, darling, look, your love means more to me than all the diamond necklaces in the world,' and with that I hurled Jolie Gabor's 125 dollar masterpiece into the waves where it sank instantly — hopefully to be swallowed by a passing shark.

He looked at me in stunned amazement. 'Jesus, babe, you just threw ten thousand dollars to the fish.'

'I know,' I said softly and serenely. 'Oscar-time,' said my inner voice. 'Because I love you so much I don't want anything like this to ever come between us again.' He seemed truly moved by this noble gesture and gathered me into a passionate embrace. I felt it was a devious and underhand ploy — one I was not proud of — but I hoped that this would close the Trujillo chapter for ever.

It did. But when, a week later, I found him locked in yet another passionate embrace in a car on Beverly Drive, with the wife of one of TV's handsomest Italian singers, I knew that I was dicing with disaster.

I walked into his office the next day, unannounced and confronted him. He denied it. He was a brilliant liar (I'd heard him with his wife) and he almost convinced me. But not quite. I called the singer's wife in Palm Springs: 'You're playing it too close to home my dear,' I said icily. 'Lay off The General or I'll tell your husband, I swear I will.' She spluttered and cried and finally admitted it was true and I dropped the phone, disgusted. God, was I becoming a hard brittle bitch? Or were circumstances just ganging up on me to turn me into one.

The phone range. My agent.

'Can you ride a horse?' he enquired.

'Of course not' I replied testily 'they scare the hell out of me.'

'You'll have to learn then,' he said, 'you've been cast opposite Peck in a Western to shoot in two weeks time in Mexico. Get your ass down to the Fox Ranch in Santa Monica tomorrow morning at nine o'clock. You leave for Mexico in ten days so you'd better learn fast.'

'But I'm *terrified* of horses,' I bleated piteously. 'What happens if I can't learn to ride?'

'You'll go on suspension again' he said crisply. 'Get it together kid.' And he hung up.

I lay back on the bed and gazed at the cottage cheese ceiling, a fixture in most West Hollywood apartments. A Western! Me! A British bombshell in the saddle — what a joke. But at least it would get me out of town, and away from him. He had a hold on me like Svengali had on Trilby. I knew it, I hated it and loved it; was I becoming a total masochist? My analyst assured me I was still looking to conquer Daddy and that The General represented him but I felt that there was more in it than only that. His all-round attractiveness was so strong that I felt it couldn't just be a father fascination. When things were going well with us I felt so completely *right* with him, infinitely more than I had ever done with anyone else before. It was total 'oneness'. The kind I had only read about.

I believe that loving someone, whether it be a lover, parent or friend is accepting them for the way they really are and not trying to change or shape them into a behaviour image of what *you* want them to be. Loving is being happy that the other person is doing something that is making them happy, even if it means that you are not always together. Therefore I let him have his own way a lot more than most women would. He was still full of doubts and guilt about his divorce — fine, I'd try and help him, and support him, and not make him feel more guilt ridden by bringing *our* relationship problems into an already difficult situation. He felt a need to see other women occasionally because he'd been trapped in his marriage for so long and had gone straight from that into an affair with me with never a chance to look around to see where the action was — well that was a hard pill to swallow, but I understood. I bloody well tried like hell to understand, because I loved him so much that that's all that mattered. My own pride and self respect were becoming eroded. My blossoming self confidence was on the wane. Being an understanding mistress to a mixed up and often thoughtless lover was taking its toll. But I was resilient, persistent and tough and I hung on in. Looking back, he obviously didn't love me enough. Maybe he was only infatuated with me as some men were because of my looks.

On the occasions that we bumped into each other throughout the following years, he was always enormously complimentary, flattering and ruefully reflective about the fact that 'if only' I had been more patient and understanding we would have been together. I wonder. There is a limit to anyone's endurance.

Brooding endlessly about my romantic problems, bottom hurting violently from two weeks of riding practice, I flew to the primitive little village of Moralia in the wilds of Mexico for *The Bravados*. On location again. My God did I ever seem to spend more than two or three months in one place without whisking off to foreign parts. Ben Gary's words came back again as I looked around the dank and insect-ridden little adobe hut that was to be my home for the next seven weeks.

The Bravados had a good script, a fairly good director,

blustering, blunt Henry King, and an excellent cast: Gregory Peck, Henry Silva, Stephen Boyd, Albert Salmi and Lee Van Cleef. I was not cast to advantage as an arrogant, tough, hard-riding American ranch-owner. I was meant to look as if I'd been born in the saddle and as though I and the horse were married to each other. Instead I felt I looked out of place and awkward.

I had dutifully spent every morning in comfortable jeans and T-shirt riding with Henry, Albert and Stephen stiffly round and around the Fox ranch on a docile nag called Dulcie, who had a temperament like an old shoe, and whose age seemed to put her in the running as a candidate for the glue factory. Now, dressed in stiff black jodhpurs, narrow boots constricting my feet so that all circulation immediately left my toes, a ruffled white shirt, black gauntlets and a black Stetson slanted sharply over my eye (over a heavy wig of course), I was shown the horse I would ride in the picture. Imagine a diesel engine attached to a dragon and you will get a picture of Pancho. A black stallion, in his prime and raring to go. Glossy, glistening, beautiful and *dangerous!!* I could feel his animal energy palpitating beneath me as four husky handlers forced me protestingly into the saddle.

Pancho of course knew I was nervous. Scared shitless was more like it. I leaned over and patted his nose reassuringly to let him know I cared. I offered him two large lumps of sugar. He practically took off my hand. I wrenched it back startled. He was snorting and tossing his great black mane. His hooves were doing a tap dance on the grass. This baby wanted to *go*. He was about to show this crew of strange people lolling about and moving arc lamps and cameras who was the boss. I already knew. I leaned over and whispered to the handlers, and my riding teacher to stay nearby at all times. Pancho pricked up his ears, half turned his head and neighed jeeringly. He had heard me. I swear that horse knew how scared I was. 'Nothing to worry about honey,' my tough, tobacco-chewing teacher, fifty years in the saddle, patted the horse's rump and gave me a reassuring wink. 'It's safe as houses if you'll just *relax* — I told you a thousand times. *Relax* honey, Pancho can feel your tension.'

'Stay there, all of you until Henry calls action.' I hissed to the four laconic, weathered old ranch hands, all highly amused by this nervous English Miss sitting petrified but proudly in the saddle of Mexico's wickedest horse.

As the shooting progressed Pancho and I became even less close. As soon as he sensed me in the vicinity he reared up. His eyes rolled around in his head, and he bared his yellow teeth in a sadistic smile to welcome me to his back. I had begged for a double for the long shots, and finally Henry King, a stickler for realism and a man who couldn't fathom how anyone couldn't *adore* horses, let alone be frightened of them, had grudgingly agreed. However I think his motives were more for artistic than altruistic reasons. I had put on about ten pounds in two weeks through eating. A mixture of terror and boredom had driven me into the arms of the great God FOOD!! Every night the hotel served delicious Pecan Pie, my favourite dish. Every night I would persuade the jovial Mexican cook, who loved my appreciation of his food, to give me the leftover pies. I took them to my lonely prefabricated Holiday Inn, Mexican-style hotel room, with the 15 watt sole light bulb, put on the record player, and gorged. To the sentimental ballads of Sinatra, Tony Bennett and Johnny Mathis I devoured slice after slice of pie until satiated, like some early Roman glutton. I fell into an exhausted nightmare sleep, filled with grinningly ghoulish red-eyed fearsome horses, ready to eat me with their bale of hay. The next morning I'd stuff what remained of the pie in my bag with the script, and finish it off as a little mid morning snack. After ten days of this gluttony the wordrobe woman unsuccessfully tried to zip me into the pants which, tight before, now fitted like a sausage skin. This necessitated her constantly having to reinforce the splitting seams. She asked me if I was pregnant! I knew I wasn't but looking at my once curved waist, which had gone from 22" to 27" in less than a fortnight, I could see where she, and the rest of the crew could possibly imagine I was three months gone. Round chubby cheeks hid my once photogenic cheekbones, and my bosoms could rival Monroe's.

My midnight feasts were not unnoticed by everyone, and the director decided to use my riding double as often as possible which would relax me more and keep me away from food. They even got a double for Pancho. As though to prove me right about horses being extremely dangerous, and out of pique at having been thwarted of his fun every morning by terrifying me when I mounted him, Pancho kicked up his heels in retaliation one day at my riding teacher. He broke the poor man's ankle in three places and from then on everyone had a healthy respect for this noble and cunning beast.

I gave up Pecan Pie in favour of a more stimulating evening pastime, and with a sudden new-found equestrian skill in the saddle of my friendlier new horse, Adonis, started to do most of the riding myself. Greg and I had a scene where we have been riding together for three days searching for a kidnapped girl. The hairdresser insisted on setting my wig each night, pin curl perfect, and then glumly watched me as I pushed dirt and twigs through it and messed it up as much as I could. I rubbed mud and dirt in my face and scrubbed off as much globby make-up as I could. 'That girl's going to ruin her career,' said the hairdresser bitterly to the make-up artiste, watching her attractive hair style being destroyed, as I tore bits and strands out to try and look as though I'd been authentically riding for three days. I still looked like a Hollywood actress sitting fully made up on a prop horse, with my tight slacks and well fitting blouse and wig. Realism was an unattractive word for actresses in 1959. They were supposed to be Goddesses. Untouchable. Plastic. Looking as pristine as a band box. I'm sure that the public's idea of beautiful movie actresses not being able to act, is partly the result of over-zealousness on the part of the costumier, hairdresser and make-up man. We looked like wax store window mannequins. I managed in *The Bravados* to look fairly unpresentable, but by today's standards I was still impossibly well-groomed.

I had not exchanged many words with Gregory Peck until we came to the scene where he and I ride side by side, hard and fast and expertly for days. He did not mix with the cast, spending his time with Veronique, his attractive, chic French wife. The cast and I were in awe of him, he was a big star and seemed rather austere, aloof and disinterested in the rest of us.

He was a wonderful looking man, tall and rangy with a classically handsome profile, saved from actual beauty by a strongly carved nose. His aloofness, I found out when we rode for so long, was a form of shyness. He was basically not at ease around new people. I found he had a droll sense of humour and, knowing my fear of riding, was considerate. But on the last day he teased me unmercifully by riding so fast that my behind was sore for a week. 'Come on Collins!' he yelled in a loud whisper that the sound couldn't pick up as we cantered faster and faster next to a deep canyon that I knew with a sickening lurch meant plunging to certain death if Adonis put a hoof wrong. They say you English women can ride,' he said mock-scornfully, digging his spurs in and making his mount fly even faster. 'Let's see you show 'em *all* Collins — show 'em you're a real horsewoman eh?' He galloped even faster, the wind almost took off my stetson and I jammed it down like Peck's until it covered my eyes. It was enormously exhilarating. I felt in command of that 300 pounds of moving sinew and muscle beneath me, I wasn't afraid at all, in fact it was a wonderful, free and joyous feeling I had of space, power and purity.

The camera car was hard put to keep up with us. They hadn't expected Peck to gallop so fast, and even less expected that I would be right alongside him, urging my horse to greater and greater speed. Even when Henry yelled 'Cut,' we continued galloping faster and faster into the distance. I was laughing now and so was Peck, as we heard the assistant director plaintively calling us back to our positions. We reined in the horses. I amazed myself with my new-found expertise and galloped back.

'Thank you Greg,' I yelled over my shoulder, now I was outracing him!

'For what?' he called back.

'For curing me of my fear of horses — you really got me over it.'

'Don't mention it Ma'm' he yelled gallantly.

I still am not a mad fan of horses but thanks to Gregory Peck I can at least get on one now without becoming a basket case.

7

Warren Who?

I sat in 'La Scala Good Evening' with Barbara and Mort Viner, drinking red wine and feeling despondent. My relationship with 'The General' had been dragging on for over a year and in spite of six or seven separations he had eventually always returned to his wife. Although he was still separated now, and vowed that when he returned from the Orient he would definitely divorce her, I felt cynical about it.

I had been in trouble with Fox several times in the past year for turning down scripts that I thought were wrong for me — and had gone on suspension. I had spent the early part of 1959 extensively preparing for *Cleopatra* but in spite of several tests I did not hold out too much hope for it now. So I was drowning my sorrows in wine and cannelloni when I became aware of a young man, staring at me from the opposite table.

As I returned his stare which was becoming a bit too bold, he raised his glass and silently toasted me. I blushed and looked away. Flirting with attractive strangers in restaurants can get one into trouble in Hollywood or anywhere else for that matter and I had other things on my mind. But I couldn't resist another look when Barbara said, 'That boy who's looking at you is Shirley MacLaine's brother, Warren something or other.' I looked over and studied him covertly. He was about 21 or 22. He had blondish, slightly curly hair, worn rather longer than was fashionable, a square-cut, Clark Kent type of jaw with a Kirk Douglas dimple in the chin — rather small greenish eyes, but a cute turned-up nose and a very sensual mouth. From where I sat it also looked as though he suffered from the same problem I had as a teenager — SPOTS! He wore a blue Brooks Brothers' shirt and a tweed jacket. All in all, he looked rather appealing and vulnerable and my interest was slightly aroused.

'Who's the girl he's with?' I asked Mort, who was an agent with

MCA and usually knew everyone. 'That's Hank Fonda's daughter, Jane,' he said. 'She's out here to make some basketball picture with Tony Perkins. It's her first movie.' 'Are they an item?' I asked casually, sipping my drink. Mort looked at me amused. 'Aha — so Joanie's got eyes for him, has she?' 'Oh for Christ's sake, Mort, can't I even ask about somebody, without the world thinking I've got eyes for them!'

I only had to look at a man and people would start surmising I was having a flirt. Because of my secret affair for the past year, I had dated a lot, and the gossip columns were full of my supposed 'Latest Loves'. What they didn't know was that my dating was a cover up.

'She's quite pretty,' I said taking a look at Jane. 'A bit fat in the face though, I wonder how she'll photograph?' 'They're working on her face,' said Barbara. 'She goes to that woman in the Valley, Louise Something — you know, she can do wonders with problem areas.' I looked at Jane Fonda. She was pretty — in a fresh, scrubbed, wholesome way and she bore a strong resemblance to her father, Henry. She had long, fair thick hair which I envied. She was hanging on to Warren's every word, and they made the perfect all-American couple. I turned back to my cannelloni and we continued talking about other things. Out of the corner of my eye I saw Warren looking me over occasionally, but I didn't return his glances.

I thought nothing more of young Mr Beatty. I was busy rehearsing every day at Fox with Candy Barr. I was playing a stripper in *Seven Thieves* and Candy, who was about the best stripper in America, was my teacher! For two or three hours every day, she taught me how to bump and grind, and take off my gloves and stockings in the most provocative and sexiest manner. We had enormous fun. Candy was a down-to-earth girl with an incredible body and an angelic face. Although she had recently been sentenced to a long jail term for possession of a tiny amount of marijuana, from her attitude you would never know this was hanging over her. She was funny and gay and we had a ball together rehearsing.

Needless to say, Stage 6 at Fox where we rehearsed became the most popular spot on the Fox lot. It was amazing how many agents, writers, producers and crew members used Stage 6 as a short cut to Stage 5, or Stage 4, or the commissary, and then would linger while Candy put me through my paces. Actually we rather enjoyed it — it was good to get an audience reaction, and the guys were most appreciative. But she was a hard taskmaster, so when John Foreman called and asked me to a party at Debbie Power's house, I tried to beg off, exhausted from all the bumping and grinding. Stripping may look easy, but to do it well is really a work of art, and very demanding.

John was insistent we go and so I reluctantly agreed. I didn't feel like getting dressed up. I was getting bored with having to look like a glamour queen every time I went out. The studio frowned on my Bohemian hippy look. I was trying half-heartedly to be chic — but not succeeding very well, because I had recently made Louella Parsons' '10 Worst dressed Women' list. 'I think I'll live up to it tonight,' I thought — and took from my wardrobe a pair of grey flannel boy's Bermuda shorts, some long grey socks, sneakers and a green Brooks Brothers' shirt. I scraped my hair into a pony tail and didn't put on make-up. I liked the look. A cross between Jackie Cooper and Betty Co-ed.

Debbie Power was the young widow of Tyrone Power. Rumours abounded that she was about to marry my ex-boyfriend, Arthur Loew. Her house, in the flats of Beverly Hills, was filled with people when we arrived. The usual mob doing the usual things — drinking, gossiping, talking box-office grosses, whiling away another forgettable evening. I wandered around chatting to a few people and wishing I hadn't come. My outfit caused a few amused remarks. I was pleased. I liked being outrageous sometimes, although at other times I needed to be conventional. The Gemini in me coming out again.

'That piano player is really good,' I said to John, 'I wonder who it is.' John, who was tall, craned his neck above the crowd and said, 'I think it's Shirley MacLaine's brother, Warren, something or other.' Aha, so there he is again, I thought. Even if he couldn't make it as an actor, he was a superb pianist and could definitely make a living in a cocktail lounge of his choice. He was doing imitations of various pianistic styles, Errol Garner, George Shearing, Oscar Peterson. It was clever stuff and I drew closer and watched and listened. He noticed I was there and smiled, but appeared totally absorbed in his music. When John and I left after a couple of hours he was still happily immersed at the piano.

The next day was Sunday and a gorgeous sunny day. I rushed to the beach for some sun and then came back for a cocktail party for songwriter Jimmy McHugh. Gardener McKay was my date. When I checked my answering service, there were six messages to call Warren Beatty at the Chateau Marmont. Surprise! surprise! We had not even exchanged a word and yet he had managed to get my number. As I sat wondering what to do, the

phone rang, and a soft voice said, 'Hi, did you get my messages?'
He didn't say who he was, and I admired his self confidence in
being so sure that I would know him.

'Yes I did,' I said crisply. 'You must be rich. It costs 25 cents a
call from the Chateau.' He chuckled softly and then said, 'Do you
want to have dinner tonight?' I thought swiftly. The party was
from 5.30 - 7.30 and although Gardener probably thought I would
have dinner with him after, nevertheless, I had not actually made
a date to do so. Gardener, a black-haired six foot four actor at
Fox, was according to *Life* magazine the handsomest man in
America — we had been dating in a semi-platonic way for a few
months. Fox was thrilled to have two of its sexy stars out together
and we went to various industry functions with their approval.

'OK — I have to go somewhere first though — I'll meet you in
Beverly Hills.' I didn't want him coming to the house and
bumping into Gardener.

'Eight o'clock at the corner of Rodeo and Santa Monica,' he
said. 'I can hardly wait.' Strangely enough neither could I. This
was odd. Somebody I hadn't met — hadn't spoken to — and I was
getting excited at going out to dinner with him.

I hadn't had this feeling about anyone other than The General in
ages. I rushed home after the party — pleading exhaustion and an
early call to Gardener — ripped off the black faille cocktail dress
and the flowered organdie hat and jumped into a pair of jeans and
a shirt. I brushed out my hair and took off some of my make-up.
He was obviously slightly younger than I so I didn't want to look
too made-up.

He was waiting at Rodeo and Santa Monica in a rented Chevy. I
locked my rented yellow Ford and joined him.

'Hi,' we said simultaneously and looked at each other. 'Do you
like Mexican?' he said, after we had each taken a good look.
'Mexican what?' I asked, coming down to earth. He was better
looking than I had imagined. True he did have a few spots —
probably left over from his adolescence which couldn't have been
too far behind him, but his eyes, although small, were clear
greenish-blue, and I noticed that his hands were beautiful.

'Food of course,' he said as we moved into the Santa Monica
traffic.

'I thought we'd go to the Casa Escobar — they make terrific
Margaritas.'

'Sounds good to me,' I said gaily.

Over dinner and countless Margaritas we couldn't stop talking
— or looking at each other. He was in Hollywood to hopefully

start his movie career. He had done stock and a lot of TV and made a few tests — all the usual things young actors do, and was hoping to get the lead in William Inge's new play *A Loss of Roses*. He was an Aries and, curiously, was born on March 30th — the same date as Sydney Chaplin. I had always gravitated to Aries men. Although only recently interested in astrology, I had realised that my sign of Gemini had certain signs with whom I was more compatible and these were Aries, Libra and Aquarius.

We talked and laughed until the restaurant closed. It was past midnight. He dropped me back at my car and then said he would follow me home to see that I got there safely.

My apartment on Shoreham Drive was in Hollywood, off the Sunset Strip. It was about half a mile from the Chateau Marmont where he was staying. As I drove through the deserted Beverly Hills streets, I wondered if I should ask him up for a night cap. I realised what this could mean. I was not an innocent virgin and asking him for a drink was tantamount to going to bed together. I was already in love with a married man, wasn't I? If I asked Warren up, I was taking one giant step, not just being disloyal to The General. I had, after all, had a couple of flings when he was doing his usual on-again off-again with his wife, but they had meant very little and slightly salved my damaged ego. But this time I felt would not be just a one-night stand with somebody I couldn't bear to look at the next morning.

But I really liked Warren. I liked his mind. I liked his humour and his conversation — and, I liked his physical packaging.

My brain was buzzing with 'ifs' and 'buts' and pros and cons. I couldn't make a decision. As I drove into the underground garage he decided for me. 'I'm coming up,' he announced, pulling his car in behind mine, 'For coffee,' — and the die was cast.

We became inseparable. Apart from the incredibly strong physical attraction, we seemed to have everything in common. We would stay up all night talking, laughing, exploring each other's minds and bodies, and I would stagger to the studio to work on *Seven Thieves* and he would call me 18 times a day. We couldn't bear to be apart. Every second we could be together we were. He visited the set and hung around for hours. We drove to the beach and sat gazing at the ocean and each other; we went to piano bars and listened to music and he would sometimes play. He played magnificently — after acting it was his main passion — other than me of course. We played poker with my friends, who were all surprised by this new and sudden romance. 'Don't you think he's a touch young for you?' said Cappy, one afternoon after Warren and I had been entwined on a beach chair sunbathing and necking all day. 'He looks about seventeen — and how can you stand those *spots!*'

'Oh, Cappy, for Christ's sake, he's not that young. He's twenty-one and I'm only a couple of years older. Don't you think he's the best thing that's ever happened to me?' Sexually, it's true, he was, and we had all the time in the world to experiment. With The General, who I was trying hard to forget, there was never enough time.

'But darling,' she said, 'he's penniless, he's not successful, he's an unknown actor, and he's probably using you to get ahead.' Dear Cappy! — she usually called the shots right — and although I ignored her remarks this time — her advice, especially about The General, had always been on the nose.

'Bullshit,' I said rudely. 'For once in my life, someone is making me happy. Someone is caring about how *I* feel, someone is taking an interest in my mind and in my work and helping me over my insecurities. It doesn't matter that he's poor and not successful. He's a terrific actor and he's going to make it. You can bet on it.' Cappy looked dubious, but she knew when not to fight City Hall.

'Have you told The General yet?' she asked. We were in her lavish dressing room doing our hair for the evening.

'Oh, God, Cappy. I don't know how to tell him!' I wailed. 'He's in Hong Kong with Marlon and every time he's phoned, I've been out.'

'You must send him a cable,' she said firmly. 'You've been seeing no-one else but this Warren for three weeks now. You know he'll find out as soon as he gets here — send it now Joanie!'

I sat down and reluctantly composed a 'Dear John' cable. Although Warren and I were in the midst of a flaming love affair, it was still very hard for me to break off with my married lover after over a year and a half of being together. He had treated me callously, I know — but I also empathised with his marriage problems and the three kids. I understood his problems *too* well — that was the problem!

'Can't see you any more,' I wrote, 'in love with someone else — very sorry — love JC'. 'How's that?' I said, showing it to Cappy.

'Awful,' she said, 'But better than nothing — send it.'

He returned from the Orient two days later and immediately called. He was charming and persuasive and he made me shiver again. He couldn't believe I had fallen for someone else. Not after all we had meant to each other. He would definitely and absolutely get the divorce and then we would be together for ever.

I had heard this so many times, but he was my weakness and he knew how to manipulate me. He persuaded me to meet him for a drink the following afternoon at the Cock and Bull, an English-style pub on the Strip.

'At least you owe it to me to say goodbye properly,' he said, 'and not just one fucking "Dear John" telegram.'

When I told Warren, he became extremely jealous. 'How long will it take?' he asked petulantly.

'Oh, just 45 minutes or an hour,' I said, airily. 'Just to end it all like friends — we owe it to each other.'

'You'll probably realise it's him you love and not me,' he said moodily, doodling on a piece of paper and fiddling with the phone. He *loved* the telephone. He made 20-30 calls a day and often to the same people three or four times.

'I won't,' I said, putting my arms around him. 'I know I won't. You don't have a thing to worry about.'

I left him doodling on his pad, the phone — like some extra part of his body—hanging from his ear, and went to meet The General. He was tanned from his trip, and beautifully turned out as usual in a beige suit, pale green shirt, obviously from Hong Kong, and a dark green tie. He looked extremely handsome. My heart danced around a bit. I was about to kiss off over a year of my life. I was about to get rid of Daddy!! I was about to say goodbye to 15 months of misery, unhappiness, jealousy and hysteria, but also to closeness, intellectual stimulation, and at times more fun than I'd ever had before.

He ordered me a Pimms and got down to business. He already knew all about Warren. He's a kid,' he laughed. 'How can you, a sophisticated woman of twenty-three be interested in a *kid?*' I started to protest that he was nearly twenty-two, but he went on. 'Listen, Joanie, I know how tough it's been for you this past year — I know I've been a shit and I understand this little fling of yours had to come. I understand it — and I forgive it and I'll forget it ever happened if you just end it now and come back to me . . .' He went on in this vein, ordering more Pimms and talking in his clever and fascinating way. I began to waver. Maybe he was right. He was a man — Warren was a boy. He knew about life and, although Warren was clever and bright and razor sharp, he was still inexperienced and naive and gauche. My good intentions started to falter. I was so weak! So stupid. After all the lies and promises The General had made to me, I was starting to believe them all over again.

I looked at my watch. It was eight o'clock. We had been

drinking for three hours. 'I've got to go.' I got up hurriedly and he threw 10 dollars on the table and followed me to the parking lot. He grabbed my shoulders as I stood trying to open my car door and talked firmly. 'I'm going to give you a week to decide,' he said, conceding heavily. 'You're a smart girl, you're *not* going to throw your life away on an out-of-work child actor.' He bent down and kissed me. A fervent kiss. It felt good. Too good.

'Goodbye,' I mumbled, as I stumbled into the driver's seat, trembling violently. Oh God — could I love two men?

'I'll call you tomorrow — I know it's not easy Baby, but don't forget what we had and what we *can* have when I get the divorce.'

I pulled away into the Sunset Strip traffic, my mind a turmoil. Warren was not in the apartment when I came in. He arrived five minutes later. Furious. 'I saw you,' he said, ripping off his glasses and jacket, throwing them on the sofa. 'I saw you necking in the parking lot!' He tried to look menacing and walked towards me. He tripped over a stool — without his glasses he was practically blind!

'We weren't,' I said helplessly, more than a little drunk and suppressing a chuckle at Warren's trip. 'He just kissed me goodbye, that's all.'

'Oh sure,' he sneered. He had been driving around and around the Cock and Bull for two hours, steaming with jealousy and rage. We fought all night. Screaming and yelling, crying, recriminations, and declamations of a passion neither of us were positive about. We ran the gamut of emotions as only actor and actress can. My indecisiveness drove him mad, but it drove *me* mad, too. I wanted to do the right thing for me. Did I really love Warren. Enough??

The next day I had an early call on *Seven Thieves* to shoot a scene in the Monte Carlo Casino with Rod Steiger. I was a wreck. I had hardly slept and my eyes were swollen from crying. The make-up man, used to the overly developed emotions of young actresses did his magic tricks and I was poured into a tight black satin evening dress, my hair swept into a chignon and diamonds in my ears. I looked nearly new, but I couldn't play the scene. I kept blowing my lines. Something I *never* did. Henry Hathaway became furious with me. The angrier he became, the more I blew my lines until finally I broke down completely and left the set in tears. Rod came to console me. He was a kind and considerate actor — hard to reach on a personal level but wonderful to work with.

Warren came for lunch in the commissary and we again hashed

over our problems. I told him I was going to see my shrink at 5.30 and that I was sure I could sort things out in my confused mind.

On the familiar brown couch I tried to be analytical about my problem. I owed nothing to anybody. I should not go to The General just because of my 'investment' of time but only if he could make me truly happy which most of the time he had not managed to do. If Warren made me happy I should be with him. An hour backwards, forwards, inside out — get rid of my father — for that's what the married man represented. But to chuck out that year and a half when attainment was so close? — or was it? — he had lied so much — maybe this was another one. I decided. I left Dr Greenleigh's office and walked elated down Bedford Drive to my car. A tap on the shoulder. It was The General. Full of confidence and vigour from the hour of uninterrupted soul searching, I told him, 'I love you. A lot. I probably always will. You're the brightest, cleverest man I know, but you haven't made me happy. I want and *need* happiness now. I want to be with Warren — he loves me, and we're good for each other now. And there is nothing that is going to stop me.' He tried to plead and remonstrate but I wouldn't listen. 'I hope we can always be friends,' I said, cornily but meaning it, and walked away. Strangely enough we did remain friends. He was, until I met Ron, the love of my life — the man with whom I always felt exactly right. But he never did leave his wife. Ben was right again!

That night Warren and I celebrated our eternal love and commitment with his sister Shirley MacLaine at La Scala. We had been together nearly a month and everything was coming up roses.

Warren left the following week for New York to start rehearsals for Inge's *A Loss of Roses*, with Carol Haney and Betty Field. It was a tremendous break for him, and one for which he had been waiting for several months. Inge's plays were always critical and commercial successes and the part — that of a tormented young man with a slight Oedipus complex who falls in love with a much older woman — was meaty enough to guarantee he would be noticed and hopefully discovered for films. For, unlike me, Warren's first love and preference was for movies rather than theatre.

Inge's plays included *Bus Stop, Come Back Little Sheba, Picnic,* and *Dark at the Top of the Stairs,* all major dramatic works which had earned him the accolade as one of America's most important playwrights. Warren was nervous and excited about this

assignment and he plunged into rehearsals with enthusiasm
and optimism. I stayed in Hollywood to finish *Seven Thieves* and
then planned to join him. We talked on the phone constantly. I
watched him in a TV show called 'The Affairs of Dobie Gillis' —
he was good. He had talent and looks and I felt he was bound to
succeed.

In November, *Seven Thieves* finished finally and I caught the
midnight plane to Washington where *Loss of Roses* had just
opened to less than rave reviews. I was tired, as apart from
shooting, the strip sequences for *Seven Thieves* were very
arduous. I had also been cramming in photographic tests for the
next film I was supposed to start — D. H. Lawrence's *Sons and
Lovers*.

We stayed at the Willard Hotel in Washington and became
closer. I met his parents who lived in nearby Arlington. They were
kind, humorous people whom I liked instantly and I could see
from where Warren and Shirley inherited their intelligence and good
manners.

He was busy rehearsing all day and performing at night, so I
had time to myself, something I relished. I took long walks and
read, went to the Smithsonian Institute and thought about our
relationship, and what I wanted from it. I didn't know — I was
happy just taking each day as it came. Warren and I were in a
good space, and we were good for each other.

When the final script of *Sons and Lovers* arrived we decided I shouldn't do it. Not only did he think the story not
appealing, but he did not want me to go to England and leave *him!*
Had the film been a comedy I would probably have done it. I had
been nagging Fox to let me do more comedy roles, but apart from
Rally Round the Flag Boys, the funny parts went to other
actresses. So I rebelled, realising this would mean a suspension of
salary. It was not the first time I had been suspended. The
previous year I had refused two roles. One in *The Last Wagon* and
the other in *Madison Avenue*. Both turned out to be mediocre
films, but for the duration of the shooting of these films I not only
did not get paid, but could not accept another job. Since I was by
now earning $2,000 a week, 40 weeks a year, this financial
sacrifice was not easy, but I was becoming very discontented with
not having any say at all in my career. Now Warren — the bossy
Aries side of him coming out — was making career decisions for
me.

I was a 'utility infielder'. If they couldn't get Susan Hayward or
Gene Tierney, they'd use me. I was usually cast at the last minute

in decorative and unrewarding roles. My agent would call and tell me to get my ass over to wardrobe right away. Once there, old Lana Turner or Maureen O'Hara costumes were refitted and refurbished to fit me and off I would go, to Tokyo, Mexico or wherever the wind blew me, my second-hand finery following. I was not being allowed to stretch myself as an actress and Warren understood this more than anyone.

Jerry Wald, the producer of *Sons and Lovers*, had promised various script changes that would have made the part in *Sons and Lovers* more palatable, but when I read the final script these changes had not been incorporated. Warren encouraged me to walk out of the film. Of course his motives were not exactly selfless. He needed me with him — he was getting publicity over our liaison and it was a tricky time of his life. With me in England he would feel forlorn and lonely. 'Don't go Butterfly,' he begged. 'Don't leave your Bee.' We moved back to New York into the Blackstone Hotel together and *Loss of Roses* opened.

It was not Inge's greatest work. The critics were unkind but Warren's personal reviews were good and he was excellent as the sensitive boy. Interest was stirring for him in Hollywood. The play only ran for three weeks but after it closed we stayed on in New York partying and seeing plays, going to the Harwyn club, a chic Manhattan boite where they let us eat for free because of the publicity they got from us going there, arguing and making up — neither of us earning a bean, broke, but loving life and each other a lot.

We moved back to California at the beginning of the year. We took a small studio apartment at the Chateau Marmont, a rather rundown and seedy but fashionable hotel-apartment where out of work New York actors lodged, and started looking for work. Financially I was in good shape again. My suspension from *Sons and Lovers* had ended and I was back on salary and preparing to test for a little epic called *Big River, Big Man*.

Warren coached me and helped me to prepare for this test. He was an excellent director and teacher, very patient, with an intense and intellectual approach to exploring the depths and details of a characterisation.

The endlessly sunny winter and spring California days passed quickly. We spent a lot of time at the Aware Inn, eating healthburgers and drinking carrot juice, for he was a health freak, and was trying to persuade me to stop both drinking and smoking. After we ate we would walk to Turners' drug store and flick through a pyramid of movie magazines looking for pictures of us together. We were a new twosome and the movie magazines loved us.

Warren was heavily involved in trying to get the lead in Elia Kazan's *Splendour in the Grass*, again written by his friend, William Inge. This necessitated his making 350 phone calls a day — 250 to his agent, 25 to Bill Inge, who was doing all he could to get Kazan to test Warren, 25 to me wherever I was (although when I was working, or doing an interview, he was never far away), and the rest to his by now numerous friends and business acquaintances. He was never happier than when he was on the phone, and he didn't need a phone book to remember the important numbers he constantly called. Ten years later, meeting him at a party he said, 'CR———— do you remember what that was?' I didn't but he told me it was the number of the apartment on Shoreham Drive where I lived when we met.

Telephoning, however, was secondary to his main passion which was making love. He was insatiable. Three, four, five times a day, every day was not unusual for him, and he was also able to accept phone calls at the same time. I had heard that men were at their sexual peak between the ages of seventeen and twenty-three and if Warren was anything to go by, this was definitely true — and he had 18 months left! I had never known anything like it, and although it was exciting for the first few months, after a while, I found myself feeling somewhat like a sex object. 'An oyster in a slot machine,' I said wearily to Cappy.

One Sunday morning, feeling exhausted and depleted after several bouts, I left him sleeping soundly, another thing he did well, and staggered upstairs to visit an actress girlfriend. She had been happily married for several years to a handsome superstar and idol of millions. 'I don't think I can take it any more,' I moaned, falling into the couch and lighting a much needed cigarette — frowned upon by Warren. 'He never *stops* — he's like an animal — it's unnatural. It must be all those vitamins he takes all the time.'

She smiled warmly and passed me a cup of coffee. 'Just like my husband,' she said proudly.

'After all the *years* you've been together!' I said incredulously.

'Oh, yes. In fact it gets better.'

'Better — Oh God. Please.' I leaned back and took a drag on the cigarette. 'In a few years, I'll be worn away.'

'Take my advice, Joan,' said my friend warmly, 'Don't push

him away. Just go along with it and enjoy it. If you don't he may find it necessary to go with other women.'

'Perish the thought,' I said jealously. But the warning lingered in the back of my mind and I let him continue his favourite occupation whenever it suited him. Of course, the inevitable happened, just like a bad novel.

'I think I'm pregnant,' I said coming into the kitchen one day where he was preparing one of his health concoctions in the blender. He stopped slicing bananas and pouring wheat-germ, took off his glasses and stared at me. Without his glasses he was quite myopic and I wondered why he didn't want to see me. 'Pregnant?' he said in a puzzled voice. 'How did that happen?'

'Perhaps the butler did it,' I said sarcastically, 'Or maybe it's an immaculate conception.'

'This is terrible,' he said, putting back on his glasses and looking at me as if for the first time. 'Terrible!' He threw down seven or eight vitamin E tablets.

'I know,' I said in a small voice. 'I'm sorry.' Not only did I feel awful about it, but I remembered what happened to my girlfriend Jackie at RADA. She had gone to a butcher in Ladbroke Grove, was cut up and almost died. She would be unable to have any children, ever. I did not want that to happen to me. Although I did not feel ready for motherhood, nevertheless, I felt that one day my maternal instincts would rise, and when that day came I wanted to have the option to be able to fulfil them.

We sat on the faded red sofa in the living room, I, with a stiff vodka, and he with his health drink and discussed what to do. Abortion was a dirty word in the early 1960s. In fact, so was sex, and even living together as Warren and I were was considered very risqué. But abortions, of a kind, were available. I had recently gone to Tijuana, the tacky border town of Mexico, accompanying a girlfriend and her married lover, and listened horrified with him to her cries and screams of agony as a Mexican 'doctor' performed the operation *without* an anaesthetic.

I shuddered at the memory and downed my vodka. We could get married of course. But I was not in favour of 'shotgun' weddings, and on the few times we had discussed marriage we had both decided that we were too young and immature to make it work. Besides which, he was practically penniless and exceedingly ambitious and to get tied down in marriage at the age of twenty-two was totally impractical. So marriage was out. And having a baby was *definitely* out. So there was only one solution.

He called a friend in New York. New York was slightly more

lenient with their abortion practices, and we had heard that it could be done in clinical circumstances without risk to health. I would not consider a Ladbroke Grove or a Tijuana type deal. The 'friend' arranged it. Warren had to go to New York to start preparing for *Splendour in the Grass* and I followed a few days later.

Early in the morning of 'A' Day, I woke up trembling with the old nightmare. It was as terrifying as ever. I was going alone up a very dark and winding staircase. To get an abortion. I was terrified about getting cut up. The stairs creaked and the wind howled outside. In the distance I heard dogs barking and an owl hooted and then silence — only my footsteps which went faster and faster up the crumbling stone stairs. Rats and mice scurried ahead of me — their tiny furry bodies brushing my bare legs. Suddenly I heard breathing. It was behind me. It was getting closer. I ran faster and faster up the endless stairs hearing the breathing getting closer all the time. And then I came to the top of the stairs to a door that said 'Doctor'. I rapped furiously. The footsteps were gaining behind me. Slowly the door opened. A grinning old man stood there, his white apron covered in blood, a bloody knife in his hand. He came towards me to take me by the hand. Behind I heard the moans of a woman. I stepped back. A hand grabbed my arm and swung me backwards. 'I've got you at last little girl' screamed Maxwell Reed dementedly, his face a mask of encrusted caked makeup, his eyes those of a madman. 'Now you'll really get cut up, and carved-up and no-one will ever look at you again!!' He raised the bloody knife in his hand to bring it slashing to my face. I screamed.

'What is it, what's the matter?' said Warren, groggy with sleep, as I sat up sobbing, the vivid dream still gripping me.

'I can't go through with it,' I sobbed. 'I can't, I can't. Please don't make me go there, Warren, I'm scared — I'll have the baby — we'll get it adopted — but I can't go there.' He comforted me as I sobbed hysterically. It was true. It is an ironic fact of life that the metabolistic and hormonal changes that women go through when pregnant bring them closer each day to a protective feeling towards this life inside them. I had been feeling, perish the thought, maternal for a couple of weeks now, almost accepting what was happening to me, and now that it was going to be taken from me, I wanted to keep it.

'Butterfly, we *can't*, we can't do it,' he said helplessly, trying to comfort me. 'Having a baby now will wreck *both* of our careers — you know it will.'

He was right and I knew it. Ingrid Bergman, a far bigger star than I, had almost wrecked hers by having an out-of-wedlock child by Rossellini. It was a very serious and far reaching step. There had been rumours of various actresses throughout the years who had disappeared for several months, and a few months after their re-appearance had 'adopted' a tiny baby, but it was all very hush-hush and with the eyes of the gossip columnists on us, constantly nagging in print for us to 'tie the knot', it would have been an impossibility. So, I dried my tears, putting his ambition and my career first, and mooched about the hotel room until dusk when it was time to drive to New Jersey.

I wore thick black stockings, a sweater and a full plaid skirt. 'Don't wear slacks,' I had been told by a sterile, sibilant voice over the telephone when I received my instructions. My eyes, which were swollen and red from crying, were covered by the biggest black sunglasses I could find at Bloomingdales, and a headscarf covered my untidy hair. I did not wish to be recognised by anyone going in for this dreadful course of action.

I chain-smoked as Warren drove a rented stationwagon through the endless freeways and turnpikes to New Jersey. We exchanged little conversation. He glanced at me with concern several times. I desperately wished I could keep the baby, although practically I knew it was impossible. But the fact that he would not even *consider* that possibility hurt me terribly. He was a man. He took none of the responsibility for me becoming pregnant. That was supposed to be the woman's department. But however careful one is, accidents happen, and she is the one to face the emotional upheaval that pregnancy causes — and then the unbearable ambivalent feelings it generates.

I tried to convince myself that we were doing the right thing as we crossed the New Jersey turnpike and Warren started consulting a piece of paper on which were written the directions. I was not yet twenty-five, and I had a thriving career, which if not exactly to my liking as far as the roles I was playing were concerned, was lucrative and rewarding in many ways. A baby would change all that. I would have to stop working. Fox would suspend me. I might lose my figure. I might be a lousy mother. He and I were not suited to each other in the long run. Was our love just a physical thing? I didn't seem to be able to be with *any* man for a long period of time. We were both selfish, careless, argumentative, combative and just plain immature. It was stupid to think otherwise. Thus I convinced myself — whilst my mind shrieked 'No — No — No!!'

I dried my eyes and blew my nose as the car drew to a halt in front of an ominous-looking, maroon high-rise apartment building on the wrong side of the tracks of Newark.

'We're — um — here,' said my gallant lover, nervously wiping his glasses on the sleeve of his tweed jacket. I noticed his face was covered with perspiration. He was probably more scared than I was. We looked at each other and I swallowed hard. 'If anything goes wrong . . .' I started to say, but he interrupted me, almost screaming, 'Nothing's going to go wrong — NOTHING. He's the best in New York. Don't even *think* about *that* Butterfly.'

He was close to tears himself. My maternal instinct went into comforting him, and hand-in-hand we walked to the green, paint-peeling elevator.

I awoke to hear someone pounding on the door.

'Are you still there?' yelled a coarse voice. I looked at my watch. It was one o'clock in the afternoon. I pulled the covers back over my head and tried to sleep again. The voice kept on yelling.

'Open up in there. I'se gotta clean the room.'

'Oh, go to Hell,' I yelled back. 'I don't want it cleaned. Leave me alone.'

The voice sniffed. 'If that's what you all want, you just go ahead and sleep all day, sees if ah care.' It shuffled down the corridor and left me in peace.

I tried to go back to sleep. Warren had gone to rehearsal and I didn't want to think about what had happened last night. It was too vivid and too painful. We've got to get out of this flea-bag hotel and find an apartment, I thought as I drifted back to sleep again.

The next day I felt much better and full of pep again. I pushed the horrifying abortion out of my head. Done. Over. Forgotten. That was yesterday — no point in brooding about it — and — oh good — I didn't feel maternal any more. — Not even to Warren. I called a house agent and went apartment hunting in New York. It was a beautiful, clear, crisp May day. A rare day in New York. New born — I felt new-born myself, as though a great weight had been lifted and I could get back to living again.

As I rummaged through the drawers to find sweater and stockings, I noticed my jewellery case under the sweaters. I opened it up and looked at the diamond necklace. It was scrunched up with some junk jewellery, some Greek worry beads — could've used those a couple of nights ago — and my gold chains. I put on the gold chains, and slid the leather box back under the pile of sweaters. That necklace. What trouble it had caused me. Much more trouble than it was worth. I toyed with the idea of putting it in the safe, then forgot as the phone rang and the switchboard announced that the real estate agent was downstairs.

Two nights later, dressing in a pretty black dress to go to El Morocco, I looked for the necklace. Gone. Stolen. Probably by the maid, angry because she couldn't make up the room. 'I think jewellery is a drag,' I announced to Warren, as I heaped Mikimoto pearls from Tokyo around my neck and waited for the police to arrive. 'I really don't care if I never have any expensive jewellery again.' He smiled at me and squinted in the mirror to try and fasten his tie. He was neatly dressed and looked cute in a tie.

'Zsa Zsa, you're *not*, Butterfly, but don't tell me you could give up Buccelatti?'

'No more than I could give up you,' I said, helping the poor near-sighted thing to do up his tie as the police arrived.

We moved into a tiny apartment on Fifth Avenue. It was furnished in blue and white chintz and English antiques and had bad plumbing. Warren started filming *Splendour in the Grass* with Natalie Wood, and I went to Berlitz every day and took Italian lessons preparatory to leaving the following month for Italy to film *Esther and the King*. I was unhappy about leaving and so was he, but I was not going to let him get in the way of my career again. Also, I needed the money. *Sons and Lovers* turned out to be quite a good picture, infinitely better than most of the stuff I had done at Fox and I deeply regretted having turned it down.

I had now been on suspension so many times that Fox must have thought I was crazed. In five years, five suspensions. Is this a record, I wondered as I sat on the set of Filmway's studios and watched Elia Kazan direct Warren and Natalie in a scene.

He was such a sympathetic, sensitive brilliant director. Lauded and rightly so for a multitude of great movies: *Streetcar Named Desire*, *Viva Zapata*, *On The Waterfront*, *East of Eden*, and many more. He was the discoverer of Marlon Brando and James Dean. Would Warren be next, I wondered as I saw 'Gadge' Kazan, his arms around his two young stars, patiently talking, explaining, extracting from them every nuance of thought, meaning and expression for the scene. Warren was very lucky to have Kazan as his first director. Maybe he really will become a big star.

I thought back to what my astrologer Ben Gary had said recently, when he had done my chart in conjunction with

Warren's. Ben was a psychic astrologer and his predictions had always been uncannily accurate. 'You know Warren's birthday is March 30th, the same as Sydney Chaplin's,' said Ben triumphantly. 'He's got all the usual Aries traits,' continued Ben. 'The ram of course.' I nodded agreement on that. 'The Ram is the first sign in the zodiac — it represents Birth. "I want" is the Aries credo and they usually get what they want.'

'Hmmm, Maxwell Reed was an Aries too,' I remembered. 'They can't be all good.'

Ben fixed me with his beady eyes and I shut up. 'He is stubborn and aggressive, but he is unyielding in his ambition and because of his tremendous drive and energy will have an early and immense success.' I listened carefully as Ben continued. 'However, after a short period of success, he will go into a dry period for a couple of years, make several career mistakes, but finally will become a major star again — probably in the late 60s. He's very sexual you know,' he looked at me questioningly. I looked demure. 'Most Aries are, of course. Ruled by their cock. How delightful for you my dear.'

'Sometimes,' I said cryptically. 'What else — go on Ben — what about us?' He consulted the hieroglyphics on his chart, peering through his near-sighted eyes, and taking a long draught of beer. 'You have an affinity for Aries men, you know my dear — you'll probably marry at least one more of them. But it won't be him!'

'It won't?' I said disappointedly. 'Why not?'

'He will not marry for a long time,' said my soothsayer. 'Probably not until he's 45 or older. I do see many, many women though.'

'Terrific,' I said gloomily. 'Are they around him now?'

'No, dear, now he only needs you — later he will need . . .' He pored again over the chart and paused, making little notations with red pencil on the indecipherable squiggles on the paper. 'He will need a constant inflation of his ego — one woman will not suffice.'

'So where does that leave me?' I asked, trying to look over his shoulder at the squiggles. 'Watching, while he does it with all the other birds?'

'Ah, no, my dear — you have only just begun to live your life.'

This is encouraging I thought. I seem to have lived so much already.

'There will be many more men in your future.'

'One at a time I hope,' said I. 'I'm not much for menages à trois.'

Ben fixed me with a steely stare. 'You will marry next within two years to a . . . .' He squinted again, 'a writer, no a producer or director —also an actor — a very multi-faceted man — he does many things.'

I giggled and looked over at Cappy sitting over on the couch. Although I believed in astrology, I couldn't really take it completely seriously, but it was fascinating to hear one's future, even if one took it with a pinch of salt. 'This marriage will last six or seven years,' continued Ben. 'From it will come two or three children — two of them probably twins, or very close in age.' Oh God, there goes my figure, I thought. 'Shortly thereafter you'll marry again' . . . he stared at the paper thoughtfully. 'It's hard to see that far — I think he is a business man — maybe an executive in some company.'

'Rich?' I said hopefully. 'My dear, you never go for rich men,' said Ben. 'Your heart rules your head — you will always make enough money to take care of yourself — you will continue working for a long, long time — your career will have many ups and downs but you were born under a lucky star. You are a survivor.'

I thought about Ben's prophecies years later. He had always said that he would die when he was thirty-two. On his thirty-second birthday he shut himself in his house with a close friend to take care of his needs. He was ultra-careful. He did not touch anything electrical, or mechanical, not even a telephone or a fridge. He insulated himself from anything that could cause him physical harm. A year later he was dead. From malnutrition. His diet of beer, pretzels and potato chips had finally caught up with him.

As of this writing all his prophecies to me have come true.

'I feel like having some chopped liver,' said Warren, looking up from studying his script. It was three o'clock on Saturday afternoon — we had only recently finished lunch. 'Well that's rather different from what you usually feel like having,' I said bawdily.

'It's in the ice box,' he said going back to his script, 'I got it yesterday at Reubens.' I opened the fridge and got the white plastic carton. 'Did you find it?' he yelled from the living room. 'Yes,' I shouted. 'What do you think of it?' I opened it up. 'Umm — it smells delicious,' I said. 'Chicken fat too, I see.'

'Does it fit?' he called.

'Fit??? Fit where, on a bagel?'

The man was going round the twist — working too hard no

doubt. 'Well try it on,' he said anxiously appearing in the doorway of the kitchen. 'Oh,' he looked sheepishly at my surprised face. 'Oh, you haven't found it yet.' I followed his eyes to the carton of chopped liver and gasped. There, smack in the middle of the brown paste was a gorgeous gold ring. With diamonds too. *And* pearls. 'Oh, darling — it's beautiful,' I cried, extracting it from the liver and licking it quickly so I could see its full glory. 'Absolutely beautiful — what's it for?'

'It's your engagement ring dummy,' he said, grinning like a schoolboy who's just found the jam. 'I figured — since you're going away soon and we'll be separated we should um, well, um, you know . . .' he shuffled embarrassedly. Took the glasses off. Put them on again. Grabbed a couple of vitamin C tablets and crunched them. 'Get — well, engaged. What do you think?' he looked anxious.

'I think it's a great idea — just terrific,' I squealed happily. 'Are you sure you really want to — I mean you're not just doing this to make me feel secure are you?'

'No, Butterfly, I'm not — you know I don't do anything unless I want to . . . and . . . um . . . well . . . um . . . I guess I want to. We . . . er, could get married at the end of the year.' He took his glasses off again and we looked at each other and burst out laughing.

Only Warren could think of putting an engagement ring in a carton of chopped liver. It was whimsical, off-beat and imaginative, and somehow it was absolutely right. The fact that he may have done it out of a strong feeling of guilt about the abortion also crossed my mind. I put it on the third finger of my left hand and left it there for a long, long time. I wore it all the way through *Esther and the King* — luckily it fitted in with the period costumes.

That night we celebrated our new engagement by going to hear Bobby Short at The Carlyle, and dining at Danny's Hideaway. I flashed my left hand casually wherever we went and within a week the columnists were pleased to announce that we had officially become engaged at last.

I was dismal about going to Rome. Although it was my favourite city in the world, I was desolate at leaving Warren, and so was he. He was very jealous at the thought of me being around other men. *Especially* Italian men. I tried to convince him not to worry, that I would be true-blue fidelity personified — but Aries are exceedingly possessive, terribly jealous and monstrously stubborn and he would not be convinced.

At Fuimicino airport I was greeted by Raoul Walsh, the roistering one-eyed director, bearing pink roses, my Italian agent, two Italian actors from the film, two producers from the film, a bunch of staring tourists and twenty paparazzi.

I was surprised at the amount of paparazzi. The word is Italian slang for photographers who make their living from photographing celebrities outside restaurants, at airports, shopping along the Via Veneto and, oh major coup, coming out of a lovers' apartment after a 'romantic interlude'. Some are better than others, and have ethics and respect for people's privacy, and others are scavengers feeding on tit-bits of celebrities' love-lives. One of their favourite tricks is to incite an actor to such extreme rage that he will attempt to either smash the photographer, or the camera. These photos, the more irate the actor the better, are usually worth several hundred lira and will garner a two page spread in *Tempo*, *Gente*, or *Oggi*.

I was quite popular in Italy, and the amount of photographers proved that they still liked me although I hadn't set foot there since *Land of The Pharaohs*.

Instead of staying in a hotel, where I might get lonely and prone then to accept dinner invitations, Warren had insisted that I stay with Marion Donen in her apartment, and immediately I arrived he started bombarding me with telegrams, protesting love, fidelity and commitment for ever. When we talked on the phone, he sounded so forlorn and depressed that I decided that I would surprise him and fly to New York the following week-end. Twelve days after leaving New York I was back again. I had not yet started shooting the movie and he was over the moon to see me. Not many fiancées usually fly eight thousand miles just for three days, so he had every right to be *deeply* thrilled. We spent the week-end, what was left of it, in bed and partying at various clubs and restaurants in Manhattan. Monday and Tuesday I watched him filming again and Tuesday night I was back on Alitalia to the Eternal city. Exhausted but happy.

We had decided to marry in January and he wanted me to get my dress designed in London. I called my dressmaker's, told them to start making up some designs and started filming *Esther*.

It was not a good film. It was full of pseudo-biblical, banal, Hollywood dialogue and, with the exception of Richard Egan, Denis O'Dea and myself, an all Italian cast who spoke their dialogue in Italian to which we replied in English! There were also a Spanish and a French actor who spoke their lines in Spanish and French respectively. It was a veritable league of nations.

It really was crap. Warren had advised me not to do it, and to behave so badly when I arrived in Rome that they would fire me, but bad as it was, my professionalism got the better of my romanticism and I faced up to it.

Warren's first letter contained some jocular rules and regulations on 'How to make a Biblical film.' They included:

1. It is always best to try to show as much emotion in all scenes as can be possible. It is generally best if the actor does his best to cry in each scene, taking special pains not to be out of control or realistic to the extent that members of the crew or other actors will be made to be embarrassed or feel uncomfortable. All gestures and facial expressions should be planned and worked out in front of a large mirror. These should not be deviated from. Remember that the audience is not involved until the actor cries. But be very careful not to let the mascara run.

2. In doing biblical pictures it is best to try to imagine how Jesus Christ would have said the necessary lines and done the prescribed movements and then to emulate his work.

3. Never change the words in a movie script. These words have been written by great creative forces.

4. Do not challenge the director, or especially the producer. These are dedicated men.

5. Do not tire yourself out with thinking about the script between takes or at night away from the set. This destroys spontaneity.

I had been trying for months to re-negotiate my contract with Fox to have some freedom to do outside offers. But for some reason they wouldn't let me go, although they were dropping other contract players like hot potatoes.

Every night I was in bed reading, or had early dinner with Marion or my agent. I was bored and miserable, hating the movie and missing Bee desperately. I constantly wore, besides the flashy engagement ring, a tiny gold butterfly that he gave me from my favourite jeweller, Buccelatti.

I visited London one week-end and started choosing wedding dress fabrics, and the phone calls and the letters got more intense and desperate every day . . . 'Can't wait to see you in dress', were the gist of most of them, and . . . 'Missing you more than I can bear.'

Eventually I could stand it no more and after a pleading consultation with the production manager, he let me fly to New York again for the week-end. Three and one half weeks later, an exhausted wreck deplaned at Idlewild airport on Saturday night and left again on Monday night. In those 48 hours we did nothing but fight. He was convinced I was having an affair with someone — nothing I did or said could persuade him otherwise. We snarled and hissed, screamed and ranted and raved at each other. The fact that I had flown eight thousand miles twice in five weeks should have been proof enough to him that I still loved him, but apparently it went for naught. His insecurities got the better of him, and I became the butt of them. Could it be — I wondered on the plane back to Rome — that *he* was the one who had been unfaithful? His was a heavy habit to break.

Sullen and angry, I returned to the awful film. I mouthed pious and pontificating language while I seethed with rage inside. How dare he treat me as if I were his piece of private property with 'For Warren's personal use only' stamped in large letters all over the packaging. I had spent $3,000 on air fares alone, never mind the phone bills which must be massive. Why should I suffer for his insecurities?

If I was being blamed and criticised and yelled at for something I hadn't done, maybe I *should* do it. He probably was. 'Ruled by the cock' Ben had said. — Hmmm.

I started returning the flirtatious glances and remarks from a young Italian actor on the movie.

I always had a penchant for Italian men. I like their appreciation, often verbalised, of women, I like their attitude towards life and I like the way they dress. This year everyone, including the young actor, wore black shirts open to the waist, a plethora of gold amulets and charms around the neck, to ward off evil, to make them more virile, or just to glisten invitingly on a tanned hairy chest, and white cotton or linen pants. Quite a devastating look when teamed with black curly hair, sparkling white teeth in a brown and unbelievably handsome face and amazing slanted green eyes. Thinking of pimply, be-spectacled, white-faced Warren, seriously emoting his way through his first movie role and getting angry at *me* all the time, the young Italian was a welcome change.

We launched into what the Italians call a 'flirt'. My mother and brother Bill were by now staying with me, so I was chaperoned at all times which suited me fine. This was to be a 'flirt' and nothing more, since my deep-down monogamous instincts and loyalty to Warren won out over the Italian's passion. But oh, what sitting hand-holding in a corner of the studio and being told one was 'Bellissima!' and 'Marvellosa!' 'Simpatica!' 'Piu Bella del Mondo!' could do for one's fragile, slightly fractured ego. Not to mention

156

the boost in the arm it gave my Italian vocabulary.

Although I wouldn't go out with him officially, since I was *'fidanzata'* to Warren, I spent half an hour a night on the phone listening to his protestations of 'amore'. Somehow in Italian. the words had far more meaning, but I could not take them seriously. Italian men love to use flowery phrases to their women — just as Englishmen court a woman between going to soccer matches and boozing it up with their mates at the pub. It's all part of the international mating call of men, and one has to read between the lines (or lack of them) to understand what the man is really *saying*. But when all was said and done I was in love with Bee. And this 'flirt' was my usual, immature way of getting some sort of revenge for the pain he caused me.

His suspicions solidified when he tried to call for an hour one evening, with the line constantly busy. He would only be assuaged by another visit from me, which I dutifully and foolishly did. Accomplishing nothing more than to alienate the producer and director of *Esther*, get splashed all over the New York and English tabloids, including the front page of the *Daily News* as a runaway, renegade actress and generally achieve nothing more than a temporary truce in our battles. He never visited me in Rome — but I didn't think of that — then. He sent me a telegram on the first anniversary of our meeting. 'My life began one year ago.' The letters and phone calls and cables continued, but the quality of the relationship started deteriorating.

The phone in the rented house of Sunset Plaza Drive rang, waking me out of a deep sleep. I picked it up, noticing it was barely nine o'clock. Our friends knew better than to call before ten.

'Joan, it's me,' said the anxious voice of my agent. 'Can you be packed and ready to leave for London by the end of the day?'

'Oh God,' I sat up and searched fruitlessly for my eye-drops. 'I've only been home a couple of weeks, whatever is all the rush for?'

'It's Liz. They think she's dying. They want you to replace her in *Cleopatra*,' he said tersely.

Dying!! Liz Taylor — God I *don't* believe it — this is some sort of ghastly joke — my eyes snapped open without the drops. I nudged Warren — curled up like a foetus — awake.

'It's not a joke sweetheart,' he went on. 'I wish it was. She's so ill they don't think she's going to pull through. All the sets are finished. The cast and crew are already on payroll. It's already costing them thousands of dollars a day while she's in the clinic and if she dies they've got to start shooting with a new Cleopatra within three days. Fox are way over budget already. They can't afford to screw around any more.'

I listened horrified. I couldn't believe the crassness of the Fox moguls. All that mattered was money — and power, of course — but this was a matter of dollars and cents. What did they care if Elizabeth Taylor, young and beautiful, was dying of pneumonia — all that mattered was that the show must go on. Get someone, anyone, to take her place. Alter her costumes, put her wigs and make-up on — lights, camera, action — instant *Cleopatra* — just like Nescafé. It was awful. It was Hollywood. Except that it was happening in London and Elizabeth was fighting for her life in the London Clinic — exactly opposite Harley House where I had spent so much of my life.

I looked at Warren who had woken up and was trying to listen to what was going on. 'I can't — I couldn't do it — I know Elizabeth . . . I would feel too *ghoulish* stepping into her shoes like this.' It was true — my whole body had turned to goosebumps during this conversation. However desperately I had wanted the part in *Cleopatra* last year, the thought of finally playing it because the favoured choice had died was appalling.

'Sweetheart — don't get so emotional,' said my agent, trying to calm me down. 'Let's hope she doesn't die — on the other hand, *think* of your *career!* This is Fox's biggest movie of the year — it's going to cost over $6 million. It'll make you a Big Star. Besides which, if you don't do it, you'll go on suspension again,' he said flatly.

'I'll call you in a couple of hours after the next medical report.' He hung up and I stared at the receiver numbly.

'What do you think?' said Warren getting up and jumping into his jeans.

'It's shitty,' I said lying back with my arms folded behind my neck and staring at the ceiling, 'Really shitty.'

'Show Biz — Baby,' said Bee, pulling a crumpled blue Brooks Brothers' shirt out of the eternally half-unpacked suitcase lying on the floor. 'Show must go on y'know. Give the people what they want.' He looked at me seriously, his unspectacled eyes squinting slightly. 'But I think it's shitty too!'

'God, I hope she doesn't die,' I said.

'She won't,' he said confidently, going out to the kitchen to squeeze fresh orange juice and take his Brewer's Yeast and more of the 15 other mysterious vitamins he fortified himself with.

'She's got nine lives, that woman. So don't worry about it,

Butterfly. All you have to worry about is making us breakfast.' He disappeared into the kitchen.

I refused to pack as much as a powder puff until I heard anything officially. On the other hand, my agent had told me not to leave the house and to be available. I prowled around unhappily, chain-smoking, biting my nails and fervently wishing for Liz's recovery. We talked on the phone to friends who had the 'inside' track on her condition. All the radio and TV news reports seemed to differ. Some said she had pneumonia, others, a chest infection. Some said three doctors were in attendance, some said there were nine doctors — including the Queen's personal physician.

I imagined myself in Elizabeth's place. Hovering between life and death in a sterile hospital room — tubes in my throat and in my arms — what must she be thinking? Did she live her life enough? Or did she feel cheated of many more decades? Did she know she was possibly dying? Or was she in a somnambulistic state?

The last time I had seen her she was married to the English actor Michael Wilding, and Arthur Loew and I had dinner with them at LaRue in Hollywood. She was indeed extraordinarily beautiful: deep blue eyes, hundreds of black eyelashes and a perfect heart-shaped face. She was down to earth and warm, and we chattered and gossiped about the usual things girls talk about animatedly all evening, with Michael and Arthur trying to get a word in edgewise. And now she was dying — it seemed unbelievable.

At six o'clock my agent phoned once more, gave me permission to go out to dinner but to leave a message on the service as to where I could be reached at all times. Warren and I munched on nut, celery and carrot salad at The Aware Inn and gloomily discussed the situation. The next morning my agent called bright and early.

'Good morning Sweetheart,' he said cheerily. 'You're off the hook. Liz is going to make it.'

I heaved a deep sigh of relief. 'Thank God,' I breathed. 'I guess she does have nine lives after all.'

Warren went to London to make *The Roman Spring of Mrs Stone* opposite Vivien Leigh. I went too, but for a two-fold purpose. My mother had been operated on for a malignancy and I wanted to be close to her. Jackie got married — amidst great pomp and ceremony. I had tried to dissuade her from this marriage as she was very young, and my own mistake was still fresh in my

159

memory, and I thought her fiancé was a jerk. But she did it anyway.

Warren and I were not getting along well. The idea of marriage no longer seemed appealing. The beige chiffon wedding dress lay carefully packed in tissue paper in my closet in Hollywood, and I moved once more into Harley House in the bedroom recently vacated by Jackie.

We were spending less time together. He did his two or three weeks reserve duty at George Air Force Base in Victorville before he left for London. Whilst there he bombarded me with telegrams and phone calls expressing his misery, loneliness and infatuation and his undying love. So why did he fight and harass me all the time when we were together? I know Aries are fiery, but this was ridiculous.

Many of the cables stressed how much he was longing to see me in the wedding dress, and so naturally, being unable to resist him when he was enchantingly persuasive, I jumped on a plane and went to spend the week-end near him at the Apple Valley Inn, a sweet, run-down, old world hotel in Victorville close to George Air Force Base.

Being in the service definitely did not agree with Bee. He was upset, nervous, depressed and argumentative — furious that he had to take precious time from his career and dedicate it to his country. After the initial elation of our first glorious meeting we, yet again, deteriorated into petty fights and arguments, culminating with me getting on a plane and away from Victorville as fast as possible.

We seemed to argue about anything and everything. Since Maxwell Reed, and maybe even *because* of him, I have never been the type of woman who is in any way subservient to a man. I believed in total equality in all things and would not tolerate the idea that women were inferior to men. Consequently I was over-assertive sometimes when it wasn't necessary. Warren, being insecure and aggressive and determined to always get his way no matter what, and I made a volatile combination, since I would not give in to his often very childish demands and he wanted his own way all of the time. I had finally been released from my Fox contract after six years of slavery, and was eager to accept some of the tempting offers I was receiving, but as soon as he read the scripts he would contemptuously throw them aside.

'It's crap, Sweetheart, junk — you can't do it.'

'But darling, it's $75,000,' I demurred — and the row would start. True, he was a perfectionist, but he had been spoiled by his first film being of high artistic calibre, and now he wouldn't settle for anything less . . . consequently, neither should I. But unfortunately, ninety percent of the films made are *not* of a high artistic calibre. I had made eighteen movies, and of these eighteen only two or three had any artistic merit at all. But, acting is a business as well as an art, and sitting around waiting for the phone to ring and for my agent to come up with the plum role of the decade was not likely in the foreseeable future. I wanted to work — to pay the rent (Warren wasn't contributing much there) and to practise my craft until the day when, and if, a fulfilling role would come along. And meanwhile Warren threw the scripts I was offered into the waste paper basket.

I went to see a producer about a part I really wanted. He sat behind his giant mahogany desk, his five-feet five-inches elevated by an extremely long-legged chair, and surveyed me through a haze of cigar smoke.

'You've been around a while now dear,' he said. 'How old are you?'

'I'm twenty-five,' I said.

'Twenty-five . . . hmmmm — y'know, that's not young in this business any more, dear.'

I was speechless. Not young in the business any more! What cheek! This elderly asshole — fifty if he's a day, telling ME that twenty-five is not young any more. That epitomised the bullshit that pervaded so much of the Hollywood hierarchy at that time.

Discovered at sixteen — Hollywood star at nineteen — washed up at twenty-five, I thought despondently. No wonder Daddy wanted me to become a secretary. I surveyed my face in my compact as the elevator glided me smoothly away from this repulsive man. Didn't look like I was over the hill quite yet own hair; own teeth; no wrinkles. What a stupid jerk I thought, angrily shutting the compact and striding out on to Sunset Boulevard. He's trying to make me feel insecure, and he's angry because he tried to seduce me once in New York and I rejected him. Men.

'Men. They only want one thing,' said a tiny voice in the back of my mind. 'They use you. They abuse you. They're all a bunch of bastards.'

I sat in Warren's canvas chair on a dark and dank stage at Elstree Studios outside London and watched Warren, dressed and made-up like a young Italian gigolo, make love to Vivien Leigh. Vivien was a beautiful woman in her late forties. As the ageing Mrs

Stone, an American lady looking for love and companionship in Rome, she was cast perfectly. The great beauty of her early films was no longer much in evidence. Her life, never very happy, was compounded by ill health and drinking, and she looked tired and older than her years. 'Beauty is a gift. You should not destroy it,' someone said to me once at a party, as I downed my fifth vodka and tonic. And looking at Vivien, and how her lifestyle had taken its toll on her looks, I hastily ground out my cigarette and vowed to take better care of myself. She did not take kindly to me, Miss Leigh, but she was certainly taken by Warren. He, never one to miss an opportunity, was his most beguiling and adorable self around her.

'Why do you spend so much money on clothes?' she asked me peremptorily at lunch in the studio restaurant one day. 'It's an absolute waste of good money. Why, I've never seen you in the same outfit twice.' She looked at me accusingly. 'And what is that you are wearing today? It looks like a man's suit.'

'It is,' said I, digging into my steak and kidney pie. 'Made for me though.' Men's suits for women were unusual in the early 1960s. London had a couple of years yet before it became the trend setting capital of the world, and ladies wore skirts in England.

'You should spend your money on jewellery, my dear,' said Vivien, elegantly lifting a glass of wine with her be-ringed and braceleted hand.

'Jewellery is such a good investment. Why with good jewellery — some pearls and rings, or an attractive brooch — you could wear a little black dress every day and look marvellous.'

A little black dress every day! How ludicrous, I thought, looking at Warren busily devouring fish and chips, and apparently oblivious to this catty exchange. He looked devastatingly handsome today. There was little trace of the adolescent boy I had first observed sixteen months ago.

His hair had been darkened for the part of the Italian gigolo and he was deeply tanned, which, although it came out of a bottle, looked as if it came straight from Portofino. He wore a beautifully cut beige silk suit from Brioni, a cream crepe de chine shirt from Battaglia, and a brown and beige St Laurent tie. No wonder half the females in the restaurant were tripping over themselves to get a glimpse of him. The Warren Beatty sex symbol image was finally emerging for the world to see and the women to adore, and he was loving every minute of it.

'What do you think, Warren, darling?' asked Vivien, lightly

resting her aristocratic hand on his arm and fluttering her beautiful pale blue eyes.

'Um, she looks cute,' said Warren, giving me a sly wink. 'No use trying to get Joanie to change her way of dressing. She does what she wants. You look like — umm — a little man,' he said fondly. I raised my eyes heavenward at this back-handed compliment, and observed Vivien's eyelashes batting in his direction. I was not above having a touch of the green-eyed monsters myself, so I gave him a swift kick under the table and he quickly resumed his lunch. Vivien gave me a sharp look. She was a perceptive lady and she knew, that I knew, that she fancied Warren. Whether this May-December flirtation was ever consummated I do not know, but Warren was now getting plenty of opportunities to be unfaithful if he chose to do so. Women were going ga-ga at the sight of this vision and he was pleased and flattered by their attentions.

I was worried about my mother. After the operation to remove the cancer, she seemed in good health and spirits, but the surgery had been debilitating and upsetting to her. With Jackie married and out of the house, I now, again, became the live-in daughter, which made her extremely happy.

She worried about me. Would I ever settle down like Jackie and find a man to make me happy? She adored Warren — most women did: he charmed them all — but she was aware of our fights and bickering, and realised he was not really the kind of man who could make a woman happy for ever. I knew marriage with Warren was not the answer, but I was still in love with him and since I found it hard to make any major decisions in my life I continued to let the relationship drift along.

Warren had rented Peter Glenville's house in a charming Square near Harrods for the duration of filming. He was up at dawn every morning, so I preferred to luxuriate in my old familiar bed in the mornings and have Mummy bring me tea and toast and marmalade and sit and chat.

We took a trip to Paris one week-end to visit Joanne Woodward and Paul Newman, who were making a movie. We took long walks along the Seine; browsed through the bookstalls and the endless art galleries; and whiled away happy hours in the cafes. I toyed with the idea of buying some paintings. After six years in Hollywood, making a healthy salary, I had almost no possessions except clothes, hundreds of books, a stereo and thousands of records. Not a chair, a tea pot or a lampshade had I ever purchased. I had been encouraged by my business manager to always rent furnished apartments and to lease my car whilst my money was 'invested' for me — so I had nothing, which meant I was free to go where the wind blew me. And just then the wind was still blowing in Warren's direction. But I knew little about art, and looking at some of Vasarely's abstract lithographs, I found the idea of spending lots of money on these funny squares and triangles rather formidable.

The Newmans took us one evening to a gay nightclub in Montmartre, The Carousel. It specialised in beautiful young men and boys dressed in women's clothing who sang, danced and mimed on the tiny stage. The club was packed, mostly with tourists, but also a sprinkling of 'Tout Paris', and, of course, a large selection of homosexuals. All eyes focused on our table as Newman, of the fabled blue eyes, and Beatty, not so famous but definitely with an aura about him, sat and sipped Poire, a particularly potent liquor made from pears.

The 'girls' who performed were gorgeous. Divine creatures, each with her hair style, make-up and clothes patterned after a particular movie star. There was Marilyn Monroe — Ava Gardner — Audrey Hepburn — each one a vision, and each one more breathtaking than the last. Joanne and I began to feel rather ordinary next to all this glamour. The 'girls' performed especially for our table. 'Diamonds Are A Girl's Best Friend', sang huskily a vision in red lamé and feathers as 'she' slithered her boa invitingly over Warren's shoulder blades. 'Je t'aime, Je t'aime', intoned a masculine but soft voice, looking into the eyes of Paul, 'her' make-up so fastidiously applied that it must have taken three hours.

Paul and Warren grinned sheepishly at all this attention, while Joanne and I got a good attack of the giggles. All the songs were for the two men, with suggestive glances and gestures directed towards them.

'I should take lessons in sex appeal from this bunch,' I thought. Eventually came the finale. A dozen pairs of false bosoms and false eyelashes shook and batted triumphantly from the stage as they performed their final number, with bobbing ostrich feathers, beehive hairdos, and slit skirts, cleverly covering their strategic areas.

The 'proprietress' came up to us after the show. 'The ladies would like to 'ave you visit zem backstage — oui?' she breathed, an ancient crone in a three-foot high red wig and black sequins who, on closer inspection proved to have a heavy five o'clock shadow under her pancake.

164

'Oh, c'mon, let's,' I giggled, the Poire liquor having loosened my inhibitions.

'Um — er — do'ya think we should?' said Warren, nervously glancing at the crone, whose vast false bust was resting on the shoulder of his best blue suit, whilst she gazed smoulderingly into his eyes.

'Yes — Yes — I want to see them up close. Come *ON* — don't be a square.'

The two men reluctantly trailed behind us while Joanne and I followed 'Madame' backstage to the dressing room. We walked in. Squeals and shrieks of joy from the assembled gentlemen — or ladies. It was hard to tell. Some had on full make-up, but had taken off their hairpieces to reveal short-cropped hair. Some were in 'undies' so elaborate, with lace and frills and garter belts, that *Playboy* would have paid them a fortune. One or two had removed their lower garments, revealing that they definitely were not of the female gender.

The smell of perfume and powder was intense, as was another more subtle scent that would become more familiar as the decade progressed. They passed the joint to me but I refused. I was trying to drink it all in: the drying stockings; the photos of Jean Paul Belmondo and Marlon Brando taped to the mirrors; the high-pitched, girlish chattering (in French, of course); and these were men, and more beautiful than most of the women I knew.

The excitement was feverish, but it was not Paul and Warren who they oohed and aahed over. It was Joanne and me!

'Your 'air — eet ees so beautiful,' crooned the Monroe look-alike to Joanne. 'Ow you get that colaire — ees natural non?'

'Mais oui — naturalemente c'est natural,' indignantly said 'Jayne Mansfield', running her fingers through Joanne's bob, as she tried to suppress a smile.

'Ooh — regardez — regardez les *eyelashes*', said a ringer for Sophia Loren pointing excitedly at my eyelashes. I backed off, while three or four of them descended on me, avidly admiring and discussing my lashes.

'On ze *bottom* — oh c'est très, très originale,' said 'Sophia', her eyes staring into mine. ''ow you do eet?'

I explained how I sometimes stuck fake eyelashes on my bottom lids — a recent fashion trend in London, and they listened as spellbound as if I were telling them the secret of nuclear energy.

Our dresses were examined and fingered, and our jewellery, and our hair. The two men stood forgotten in the corner of the cramped dressing room watching amusedly whilst Joanne and I played twenty questions about our looks. Eventually we escaped, laughing hysterically, into the Place Pigalle, and strolled over to a nearby bar to continue our revels. The evening was unforgettable for giving me the worst hangover I have ever experienced in my life. On waking my head felt like a balloon, and a sledgehammer was inside that balloon pounding it so hard I thought it would explode.

'It's the Poire!' gasped Warren who, although not a drinker, had done his share that night. 'It's 90 per cent proof.'

'Oh God,' I gasped — catching a glimpse of my dissipated white face in the mirror. 'If the "girls" could only see me now!'

'Somehow I think that tonight in Montmartre there will be two new stars,' said Warren giving up and falling back into bed. 'Joanne Woodward and Joan Collins starring at The Carousel — authentic down to the last bottom eyelash.'

'We *won't* be there to see it,' I mumbled, closing my eyes and hoping for sleep or death. 'Never again!'

After Warren finished filming in Rome we returned to Los Angeles and the house on Sunset Plaza Drive — and the smog and the rows. We argued so much and over such mundane and petty things that the last few months of our relationship are a hazy blur. My mother came to visit with Bill, who was now fifteen and tended to hero-worship Warren.

'Why did you let them come?' Warren hissed at me loud enough for Mummy, who was sunbathing in the garden, to overhear. 'We never have any privacy now — ever,' he rummaged through his usual messy suitcase which was lying on the floor with his shirts and jeans falling out of it, and glared at me accusingly.

I glared back. 'She's my *mother*,' I said flatly. 'And I pay most of the rent on this house, and I have every right to have her visit, so stop being such a shit.'

I left the room, my eyes filling up with tears. I didn't let him know how much he hurt me by his antagonism towards Mummy. I tried to never let him know he hurt me now. I was full of guilts and recriminations about her recent illness and I wanted to try and be the perfect daughter to her and try and make her happy as I hadn't done since I was a child. My sister was pregnant now, and Mummy was thrilled, and hinting strongly that it was time I took a turn in that direction.

It was obvious I had to be the one to end it with Warren. He seemed content to let it drift sloppily along. What happened to the glorious romantic fun we used to have? Why did all of my relationships with men turn sour? Was it my fault? Was I too strong? Or was I too weak? Or was it — and this I knew deep down to be the truth — that I still only really *wanted* the neurotic ones, the men unable truly to love — truly to support and truly to give. Only by gaining the love of one of these impossible men could I prove to myself that I was a worthy person. But I wasn't learning from my mistakes.

Finally I accepted an offer from Panama and Frank to go to London to play opposite Bob Hope and Bing Crosby in *The Road to Hong Kong*.

'It's crap,' said Warren throwing the script to the floor. 'Crap! Why do you need to do it?'

I looked at him. 'Two reasons,' I said simply. 'For the money — and to get away from you.'

We looked at each other and I started to cry. It was the end, and we knew it. We held each other tightly. Nearly two years of loving and fighting had passed. He had become a man and almost a star, and I had marked time. It was time to move on.

8

Newley Discovered

The Sixties were youth. They were freedom. They were 'doing your own thing'; 'letting it all hang out', and throwing convention to the winds. Nowhere epitomised the Swinging Sixties more than London. It was the place to be, and that's where I was. Although the decade was young, there was excitement in the air, a feeling of vibrancy and great expectations in people's attitudes. Optimism and enthusiasm were the key words of the day. Everyone seemed young, swinging and smart.

The 'Mersey Beat' was starting to drift down from Liverpool where four mop-headed youths in their early twenties were getting started and a new kind of music was beginning to be heard. They called themselves 'The Beatles'. Discotheques were opening all over the place. The youth culture was upon us and Mary Quant had just burst upon the scene with the mini-skirt. Girls were showing more and more of their legs.

I sat in the White Elephant, one of the most fashionable of London's new restaurants and observed the scene at lunch. Half of Hollywood seemed to be there making deals — setting up pictures, or just hustling. Many American movie people had decided to leave smog-ridden, heavily-taxed Los Angeles and move to tranquil, civilised non-foggy (thanks to an Act of Parliament in the mid 1950s) London, and the restaurant was abuzz with conversation and activity. The delicate crystal sconces glittered; the Italian waiters moved swiftly from table to table. Cubby Brocolli, an American producer, stopped by my table to say hello and we chatted for a few minutes. He told me he was producing a film based on Ian Fleming's James Bond spy stories and they were off to the Caribbean soon. I wished him luck and watched him as he said hello to two young men seated at a nearby table.

'That's Tony Newley,' said my girlfriend. 'You know, the fellow who's just had a big success with that new show *Stop the World I want to get Off.'* Ah, yes. Of course, I remembered reading the reviews when it had opened a few weeks previously. The critics had been harsh but also intrigued by this practically one-man show, in which Newley, in white clown-type make-up and baggy pants, played an amalgam of Everyman. He also directed it, and wrote the book, music and lyrics with Leslie Bricusse, who my friend informed my was the man lunching with him.

Newley looked familiar, and I stared, trying to remember where I had seen that face before. Then it came to me. The Artful Dodger in David Lean's *Oliver Twist*. He was about fourteen then, the same cheeky Cockney face, darting intelligent eyes and strong Romanesque nose. He was older now, in his late twenties I would have thought, very satanic and intense looking, with thick, dark brown hair and beautiful expressive hands that he used constantly in the conversation. He glanced at me as I looked at him and a flicker of recognition crossed his face. I looked away feigning disinterest. I was heavily off men right now. Besides, glances in restaurants had caused me trouble before. That's how it had started with Warren.

I thought no more about him until Robert Wagner, who was also making a movie in London, called and said he had tickets for *Stop the World* that night and invited me to go with him. 'R.J.' and I had been friends since the disastrous *Stopover Tokyo*, and since his separation from Natalie Wood we had gone out together several times in London.

The newspapers and gossip magazines jumped on this hot 'new twosome' immediately and a bunch of articles were immediately printed to the effect that we were 'consoling' each other whilst Natalie and Warren were now dating openly. These reports were fairly irksome. Enough that Warren and I had ended our relationship with honesty and objectivity, and with the understanding that we would try to remain friends, but to have the eager eyes of the yellow press announcing avidly that Natalie and Warren had been carrying on a passionate affair whilst she was still married to 'R.J.' and Warren was engaged to me was not only aggravating but untrue.

However, Warren, ever quick to make hay whilst the sun shone, had not found it disadvantageous to his burgeoning career to be seen dating Natalie, a major star, and since he was fond of seeing himself in photographs with pretty actresses, it served him well. As one wit remarked recently — 'I knew Warren before he only bedded household names.' While their relationship developed, R.J.'s and mine did not. Although he was attractive, I was still neurotic enough to only be truly interested in complex, difficult men — and R.J. was gentle and sweet and too nice for me to become involved with. We were — hello cliché! — 'just good friends'. The tabloid-reading public, however, found it hard to believe that an attractive man and woman can be merely friends, and consequently there was idle gossip and speculation about our friendship.

I was completely enthralled by *Stop The World I Want To Get Off*. It was one of the most brilliant, creative, and excitingly original shows I had ever seen, made all the more so by the magical presence of Tony Newley. His was a tour de force bravura performance, and although many of the critics had belittled and dispraised it, his shining genuine talent was the maypole from which the ribbons and form of the musical flowed.

The premise of the show was simple. It was the story of 'Littlechap', a sort of 'Everyman' of the world, alternately bumptious and belligerent, vulnerable and sensitive, ageing from brash youth to elder statesman, and in between running a veritable gamut of emotional highs and lows punctuated by show-stopping songs culminating in the classic 'What Kind of Fool Am I'.

At the end of the show I was drained but exhilarated. I hadn't witnessed anything in the theatre that had moved me so much for ages, not only the show, which I had been informed was autobiographical in flavour, but by Newley himself.

'Let's go backstage and say hello,' I eagerly asked R.J., as the cast took their final bows to tumultuous applause. He, as impressed with the show as I was, agreed and we made our way through the labyrinthine, musty back corridors of the Queen's Theatre to Newley's dressing room. A gruff, heavy-set middle-aged man greeted us suspiciously, asked our names and told us rather uncharmingly to wait as the 'young master' was removing his make up.

R.J. and I raised our eyebrows at each other at this rather grand nickname, used previously I recall only by Noel Coward himself. We waited. And waited. And waited. After twenty minutes of staring at the seedy, cracked and water-logged walls of this far from elegant ante-room, and without being offered so much as a glass of water, my Gemini impatience got the better of me and I jumped up and suggested we leave.

'We're going,' I called coldly to a shabby green velvet curtain, which separated the waiting room from the star's dressing area.

'Oh — hang on a minute love. Just putting on me drawers,' called a beguiling Cockney accent, and the curtains were drawn back with a flourish and there stood Littlechap in the flesh. Little indeed, he was. Not much more than five foot nine or so. Thin as a rail, white as a sheet, blue of eye and black of hair — and rather sexy. He was towelling traces of white pancake from behind his ears, and his intelligent, deep-set eyes were still encircled by the heavy black eyeliner he wore in the show.

'How d'ja do — How d'ja do, sorry to keep you waiting. This muck takes forever to scrub off.' We shook hands and I gushed fan-like about how much we *loved* the show, and him. He seemed genuinely pleased to hear this and listened with deep interest to all our comments.

The heavy-set man hovered disapprovingly in the background — fiddling about with stuff on the dressing table and making it obvious we were not too welcome.

'Well we better take off and get something to eat,' said R.J., intercepting a basilisk stare from the vigilante at the dressing table.

'Why don't we have a bite together,' said Tony. 'Unless you two have other plans?'

'No, no, come on — come with us,' said I, my interest in young 'Master' Newley slightly piqued.

'Shall we go to the Trat?' said Tony, putting an old green tweed jacket on top of his baggy grey flannels and black polo neck. 'I usually have a table there.'

'Sounds good,' said R.J., and after Tony bade his surly retainer a brusque, 'Ta Ta Ter,' we crossed Shaftesbury Avenue to the brand new Italian bistro, the Trattoria Terrazza. We were greeted effusively by Mario and Franco, and led down the tiny winding staircase to a marble-floored, white stucco painted room, hung with Chianti bottles and humming with conversation. In fact, the acoustics at the 'Trat' were such that conversation had to be conducted three pitches above normal level. This, added to the proximity of the tiny tables to each other, the excitable Italian waiters — who occasionally burst into either song or rage (a trolley laden with desserts was constantly getting in the way of one of the waiters and he would angrily ram it against the patrons' tables) — and the appetising smells of Saltimbocca, Lasagne and other Italian yummies gave the evening a stimulating light-headed feeling, a bit like being in a giant goldfish bowl.

'What will you have, Pretty Lady?' said Mr Newley, frowning at the wine list as if it were a term paper on biology. Pretty

Lady!!! — an effusive compliment for an Englishman, I thought.

'Verdicchio, please,' I said, that being my favourite wine — and the three of us plunged into animated conversation.

We had friends in common, and the talk flowed easily, punctuated by Tony's sudden bursts of staccato laughter. He had a keen Cockney humour, which I appreciated. I was able to slip easily into the vernacular of London slang or Beverly Hills small talk, having spent all my adult life between these two opposite poles. Two hours and several bottles of Verdicchio later we bade each other fond farewells outside the restaurant and wended our respective ways home. It had been a lovely evening. Tony was bright, amusing and attractive, intelligent and likeable.

Joyce Blair came to lunch at Shepperton a couple of days later and I was surprised to hear: 'Whatever did you do to Tony? He fancies you like mad.'

I sprawled on the couch in my portable dressing room and peeled an apple.

'What did he say then?'

'Oh, you know. The usual. How fantastic you look and what a great body. All that sort of thing.'

'Oh, did he say anything about my mind?'

Joyce giggled. 'I think Old Tone's a bit of a male chauvinist. He didn't mention your mind. He thought you were funny though.'

'Oh, goody, goody,' I said sarcastically, taking·a bite from the apple. 'That must mean then he *does* think I've got a mind.'

'I'll tell you something about Tone,' said Joyce leaning forward confidentially. 'He's a super person — really super — I mean we were at Aida Foster's together so we've known each other since we were kids and I've always adored him, but do you know,' she lowered her voice and leaned forward even more. 'Do you know — that he's *NEVER* been in love!?'

I stopped in mid-munch. 'Never?' I said incredulously. 'What is he — some sort of faggot?'

'No, No. Come off it darling. He loves the ladies. No, he's just never been able to fall in love with anyone. Can you imagine, darling, twenty-nine and never been in love. Awful isn't it?'

'*Very* interesting,' I said studying my apple core. 'Is that where the song comes from at the end? You know, the fool song?'

'Yes, Yes,' she said excitedly. 'Those lyrics are *exactly* the story of his life. What kind of fool am I, who never fell in love, it seems that I'm the only one that I have been thinking of.'

'Oh God, save me from *that*,' I said, throwing the apple core in the waste basket, and feeling a little bit like a bull who has just had the red flag waved in his direction. A man who has never been in love. How sad — how challenging. I looked at Joyce and she looked back mischievously.

'Oh no, sweetheart. I'm *NOT* interested in making him change his ways,' I said hastily. 'I've had enough of selfish, uncaring, unloving, unable-to-commit themselves guys to last me a *lifetime.*'

'Well, a little lunch wouldn't hurt,' she said lightly. 'He called me yesterday and drove me *mad* for your number. I finally agreed that I might be able to persuade you to have lunch with him — and me too, of course,' she added quickly, seeing my dubious look.

'Oh, come on darling. What ever can happen at *lunch*?'

'You'd be surprised,' I said darkly, finding myself against my will, suddenly being highly intrigued by this ambiguous Newley character. '*Everything* happens at lunch.' I stood up to get ready for the scene. We looked at each other and I smiled.

'Never been in love, eh? Well, we'll see about that.'

I found myself thinking about Anthony Newley during the next twenty-four hours. I was, for nearly the first time in my life, absolutely free of all entanglements of an emotional nature. I had no roots; no home; no house or apartment; no husband or lover to answer to; no children to look after; no contractual obligations. I could do what I liked, when I liked. It was bliss. If I wanted to fly to Paris or Rome for the week-end all I had to do was pack a bag and jump on a plane, which I often did. This feeling of total freedom and disencumbrance was so heady and refreshing after my disciplined childhood, early disastrous marriage, studio contracts with Rank and Fox who controlled every career move, and then heavy involvements sequentially with Sydney, Arthur, 'The General' and Warren, that I almost didn't know how to handle it.

I was like a bird that had just learned to flap its wings and fly. The world was mine and I intended to keep it that way — at least for a while.

Occasionally I would get a flicker of envy as I would see some cherubic infant being fondled and caressed by its loving mother. Feeling 'broody' came upon me now and then, but I pushed these strange maternal feelings away without stopping to analyse and dissect them. I knew I had felt a sense of loss since the abortion despite myself. Whenever I saw a baby I would automatically compare it as to what age mine would have been had I had it. But, as with all my deep and subliminal feelings I would not allow myself to dwell on them. Life was gay. Life was fun. Life was for doing, and seeing and going places. There was no time for ruminative self pity or unhappiness. I wanted to live life to the hilt, but in doing so I lost touch with a certain basic reality. Never stopping to analyse my constant mistakes, I blindly went in where angels feared to tread . . . and Tony Newley was no exception to this.

Any woman with any horse sense does not fall in love with a man who openly proclaims to the world in song and verse that he is unable to love. She might like him. She may admire his talent and personality — but if she is smart and clever she will not get involved thus leaving herself open to the pain that being involved with that man can bring.

Poles apart — we were worlds apart. He was a Libra. Quiet, placid, home-based, deeply involved in his work and himself. His capacity for loving life was not great, indeed he was uncomfortable and felt out of place anywhere except with close, old friends and in surroundings that he knew well. He was nothing at all like my father, and yet the feelings he generated in me, as in all the men to whom I became deeply attached, were exactly those of that little Joan of so long ago — trying to make Daddy love her. I was everything that he shouldn't have wanted in a woman: Gemini — mercurial — moody — exuberant — inexhaustible — extraverted — highly energised and quick tempered — thinking only of today, dismissing yesterday and letting tomorrow take care of itself.

But, despite our different lifestyles and personalities, we became involved. It did not, of course, happen simultaneously. First I became infatuated, and then used my wiles to persuade him to feel the same way. It was a struggle. Not too long to make the battle seem lost, but swift enough to give me the sweet smell of success. Three weeks after our first meeting we became lovers. And not long after that he *professed* to love me.

So now that I had won his hard earned 'love', what did I intend to do? Was I going to cook liver and onions every lunchtime for him at Leslie and Evie Bricusse's flat in Stanmore? Was I going to sit night after night applauding wildly in the stalls as he performed, revelling in the adulation of his enthusiastic audiences?

As a lover he was not the greatest I had experienced. I had the distinct feeling that his mind was elsewhere during our 'romantic interludes'. I had not succumbed for several weeks. I instinctively felt he was a man to whom a woman who gave in too quickly was an 'easy lay'. Consequently we had circled and played the game but I had kept him more or less at arm's length.

One day when I had the flu he visited me in my parents' flat before his show. Weak, protesting, and feverish, I feebly tried to fend off the advances I had been anticipating. With a runny nose, red eyes and a sore throat, sex was the farthest thing from my mind, and the bed was full of cookie crumbs, damp Kleenex, and dog-eared magazines.

'No Tony. My parents might come in, for Christ's sake,' I moaned, whilst he, intent on his task, took no notice. I realised instantly how Sydney had felt in his father's house in Switzerland. Of course. It was positively *sacrilegious* to make love in the same house as your parents. God, the shame of discovery. The agony of your father or mother realising that their baby was a grown person, and doing and feeling things with their body that were . . . well . . . not quite nice. Anyone with any regard for their parents would feel the same way. I was certainly no child, but that every evening in September I felt fourteen years old and guilty as hell.

'I think I've just played my trump card,' I said weakly, lying back exhausted against the red padded satin headboard, eyes and nose watering, and feeling slightly used. He twinkled triumphantly. Why shouldn't he. He had just got to first base whilst I had never left the dugout. I wondered if he had 'lost respect for me' — another of Mummy's favourite expressions.

'Got to go to the factory, Sweet Lady,' he said. He was looking extremely pleased with himself. I found out why a couple of days later. He had spent the afternoon with the torrid American actress Linda Christian — noted for being very sexy on the screen and off — and who was not letting grass grow under her feet during her London stay.

Two home runs in one day. Not bad for a Cockney kid from South London.

My mother was dying. I knew she was dying — so did Daddy — so did Jackie. Only sixteen-year-old Bill was protected from the truth, although with the wisdom of childhood he no doubt suspected. The illness came upon her so swiftly that it took us all by surprise.

After a brief period of hospitalisation she came back to Harley House to spend her final days with the family. I had to be there. I could not face the fact that she was dying. I refused to believe it. Even now I cannot really believe she is gone. Her photographs are with me all the time: her always smiling happy face, with the fair curly hair, sparkling blue eyes and high cheekbones, which I inherited from her, as well as her joie de vivre and tremendous zest for life.

Unfortunately my mother was the product of a strict Victorian authoritarian upbringing. She was nervous about her intellectual capabilities, and consequently had a tendency to sometimes play the dumb blonde role. She was a slave to my father's whims, even to giving up all of her own friends when they first married and adopting his friends as hers. He was extremely critical of her and seemed to delight in never letting her be her own person and enjoy herself. He, being an absolute male chauvinist before we even knew the meaning of the word, ruled the roost totally. His word was law, and woe betide any of us who disobeyed it.

'I pay the bills around here,' he would roar if any one even dared to remonstrate and argue with him. 'If you're so clever, you make the money to support us all. Then I'll listen to you.'

He would shout and yell at her for the slightest reasons. He gave a new meaning to the word irascible. Unfortunately, from him I inherited *my* temper and tendency to fly off the handle at petty irritations, and I have been trying to control it for years. But it didn't matter how much he yelled at her — she *adored* him! I could never understand how she could be so warm and loving and cuddly to someone who often treated her so badly. Her mentality was such that she believed in the superiority of the male, but at the same time acknowledged them as 'The Enemy'.

She was filled with a host of misconceptions and superstitions that were drummed into me at an early age, and painstakingly exorcised on the analyst's couch years later. A lot of these old adages I deliberately set out to disprove as soon as I became aware of the male sex. *But*, there is a lingering residue of her teachings bouncing around in the back of the brain somewhere that agrees with a lot of her philosophies: 'Men are no good.' 'They only want *one thing* from a woman.' 'He'll have *no respect* for you if you let him *have his way* with you.' 'Nice girls don't let men *touch them* unless they are married,' . . . and so on . . . and so on . . .

She was not alone in her viewpoints. Millions of women in the 1930s, 1940s and 1950s felt the same way, and brought up their little girls to feel the same guilts and unclean feelings about their sexuality. But today my generation of women have hopefully been able to learn from the sexual revolution of the sixties, and from their own ashamed and furtive early years how *not* to indoctrinate *their* children.

Be that as it may, I loved my mother and it was unbearable to know that she was leaving me. Her forte, of course, was motherhood. The kind of mothering that keeps you home from school if you wake up with so much as a sneeze; that checks every day to see that you've been to the toilet; that sees that you get three good nourishing meals a day, plus at least ten hours sleep; that makes sure all the doors and windows are locked and that there is a light on in the hallway when you go to sleep, in case you get frightened during the night. And who, after nagging you to pick up your dirty clothes, will sigh heavily and pick them up and do it for you. We were taken care of very well. Even during the years of rationing during the war we always had meat and eggs and sugar, thanks to a little judicial dealing on the 'Black Market'.

Mummy had her reward from Jackie: a beautiful little baby girl, Tracy, a few months old and the apple of her eye. 'If only Joan would get married and settle down,' she would say wistfully to Jackie, as they played each afternoon with Tracy in the photograph-laden living room of Harley House. The room was now an absolute shrine to the Collins sisters. Hundreds, literally hundreds of pictures of us hung on the walls, clustered on the mantelpiece, sideboard and TV. One even hung in the toilet! Me in a lurex sweater, wearing shorts and a hood, looking saucily over my shoulder at whoever was sitting there. Yes, she certainly was proud of her children and I felt guilt pangs that I had not been able to be closer to her in the past few years.

I refused to leave England and go back to the States while Mummy was so sick. We had taken her to many different doctors and specialists but the prognosis had always been pessimistic. We were told she had only a few months to live and I was determined to be with her as much as I could.

The Road To Hong Kong had finished. It had been fun. I liked Bob Hope immensely. He was the consummate comic: confident, aggressive, always completely in command and never at a loss for a joke or a quip. He was consistently charming, warm and down to earth. He was also a Gemini, which I always cottoned to. Bing Crosby, on the other hand, was a different breed: off-hand, grumpy and vague. He appeared to me as an old man acting very young, or a young man who looked old. His face was like a piece of crumpled tissue paper and I never felt his eyes when he looked at me. They looked *through* me. He did not endear himself to the crew and had the cute habit of spitting on the set, or wherever he happened to be. We spent some time shooting on a stage, which had sawdust on the floor and he would clear his throat and aim a great wad of pipe spittle on the piles of sawdust scattered around, to the chagrin of the tiny Cockney in charge of sweeping the set.

'Blimey if I 'as to clean up any more of that old geezer's spittle, I'm goin' to ram it dahn 'is bleedin' throat, I swear I will,' he muttered furiously, as he collected the debris in his spade and deposited it in a bucket. Mr C puffed away on his pipe, oblivious to all the activity going on around him. We were standing in the middle of the set getting the final light checks for our love scene, and Bing had spat at least three times that morning.

'How'd you like to have to kiss him?' I whispered to the little Cockney as he angrily brushed at the sawdust around my feet. 'Ooohh, you poor little darlin'. I'd rather go down on Hitler,' said he, and sniffing disgustedly he walked away.

I arranged my face into the correct loving expression to gaze into Crosby's bland blue eyes and smell his rancid breath, and wondered again how people could think an actress's life was just a bowl of cherries.

Tony — Tony Newley . . . I was obsessed with the bloody man; obsessed by his outrageous talent, by his brilliant performances. He astounded me with his virtuosity and I, and many other people, including himself, thought he was a genius. But geniuses are complicated. And being infatuated with one wasn't a bowl of cherries, either, for he had an obsession too. Although professing love for me, *he* was infatuated with a nubile, sixteen-year-old blonde, one half of a pair of twins, who played his daughters in *Stop the World.* This little mini-affair had been gathering momentum ever since rehearsals had first commenced in April and although Daisy, as I shall call her, was usually heavily chaperoned by either her mother or her twin sister, the difficulties of consummation only increased Newley's ardour.

I wasn't aware of Daisy for many months. Blissfully involved in the first passionate throes of an exciting affair with an exciting man, working hard on *Hong Kong*, and devoting what time I had left to spending it with my ailing mother, I had blinkers on as far as another girl in his life was concerned. It wasn't really until six years later when he wrote, produced, directed and starred in an erotic autobiographical film called *Can Hieronymus Merkin Ever Forget Mercy Humpe and Find True Happiness?* that the full extent of his involvement with the girl was crystallised to me.

And, in fact, was a strong contributing factor in the break-up of our marriage.

But these were the early days, and months, of what to me have always been the best time of a relationship — the icing on the cake. First you taste the icing — and then you get to eat the cake. Not as delicious, and often difficult to finish. And I liked to have my cake and eat it too. All of my relationships with men had by now followed this destructive pattern. Months, or a year or so of happiness and joy, followed by gradual disillusionment, and a mutual wearing away of the fabric of love until it was no longer bearable, and then it ended. I was well aware of this familiar pattern. I knew I expected too much from men. I expected them to be perfect. I couldn't seem to cope with human frailties and idiosyncrasies. God knows I was not perfect myself so it was presumptuous of me to demand such faultlessness from others. But knowing this was the way my love affairs had gone, I was giving Newley the benefit of the doubt, and making myself well aware of all his failing and foibles before I committed myself.

We discussed the fact that he had an eye for the ladies. Especially those between the ages of fourteen and seventeen. This was not so unusual. Hadn't Maxwell Reed's interest in me started because of my tender years? But I felt myself mature and adult enough to be able to accept it. I convinced myself that I could wean him away from these tendencies once we were married, for I had decided he would make a fine father for the children I felt I was now ready to have. All I had to do was convince *him*.

I threw myself into the role of 'camp follower' with a vengeance. I turned down all movie offers, to the despair of my agents who, after working hard to get me out of Fox, now could not cash in on the money I could be making. I devoted myself to being the perfect woman. I cooked. I made love any way he wanted it. Culinary and amatory arts I did not know I possessed suddenly blossomed in me. Sausages and mash, toad in the hole, shepherd's pie, Irish stew, bread and butter pudding, rhubarb and custard — I became an expert in these simple English dishes, and a regular customer at Sainsbury's Market on Marylebone Road.

I had fierce competition for his attention though. His mother, Grace, his manager, Terry, and various other sycophants were all vying with me and each other to be close to him.

His mother worshipped the very ground he walked on. She was a sweet, birdlike little woman who had given birth to him illegitimately, and had been made to pay the price for this (then) outrageous transgression. She had brought him up practically single-

179

handedly, and lavished all of her love, attention and adoration on him. He took this as his due, having women wait on him hand and foot and cater to his every whim. Although she had married finally during the war, nevertheless, each day she appeared regularly at his cosy, little shabby flat in Chatsworth Court, off Earls Court Road to make his breakfast, and then to stay for the balance of the day doing the housework, cooking, cleaning and just being in his orbit.

I first met her one wintry Monday morning when the door to Tony's bedroom opened at nine o'clock and a perky little face, not unlike his, but crowned with a mass of grey curls said, 'Good morning, Son, what would you like for your breakfast today? I've got some lovely kippers, Or, I'll do you some bacon and eggs and fried bread. Or would you rather have some nice porridge, seeing as it's such a nasty cold day?' She did not acknowledge that there was another person in the bed with him, and after he had placed his order for porridge, she scampered away without so much as a glance in my direction.

'Do you think I could have a cup of tea?' I asked meekly of the young 'Master', who seemed not at all surprised by this unusual confrontation — or lack of it.

'Oh — Flower, of course. Mum — Mum,' he called, and the little lady scuttled back in again, grey curls bobbing and wiping her hands on a dish rag.

'Yes, Son,' she said nervously.

'Mum. This is Joanie, and she'd like a cup of tea.'

'If it's not too much trouble,' I said hastily, trying to look innocent and beguiling, with last night's mascara crusted around my eyes.

'No — no. Not at all. How do you like it — er . . . Joanie?'

'Oh. Two lumps please,' I smiled sweetly, hoping she would think what a delightful daughter-in-law I would make.

'I'll come and help you make the porridge if you like.'

'No — No. That's all right. Not to bother dear. I'll do it,' and she disappeared again quickly, no doubt thinking what loose morals the girls of today's generation had. Later Grace and I became friends and, in fact, some of the feelings that I had for my own mother were transferred to her. But at the beginning she was highly possessive and jealous of any woman that Tony became involved with, and made them well aware of the fact too.

I became instantly great friends with Tony's best friend and collaborator, Leslie Bricusse and his beautiful wife Evie. It was rare to have a four-sided friendship in which any combination of the individuals involved got along like a house on fire, but we four did. At Leslie's and my urging we finally, one cold December week-end, forced Tony on a plane to Paris and away from his ever present entourage, to sample some of the delights of another environment. And he needed a lot of persuasion. It was hard for him to leave the comfort and security of his snug flat in London for 'foreign parts', even for two days, and the Gallic cooking did not agree with his sensitive stomach. But I was determined to make him get away from his bourgeois and hermit-like existence and get used to some of the better things in life.

One of the songs in the show epitomised the renaissance that Tony was experiencing with his new found success and acclaim. It was called 'I Wanna Be Rich'.

> I wanna be rich
> And have a big house.
> With hundreds of acres,
> And pheasant and grouse.
> An American car
> As long as the street.
> And the local birds will will be lost for words.
> It'll knock them off their feet.
> I want to be famous,
> And be in the news.
> Go out with a film star,
> Whenever I choose
> Give me half a chance in the South of France
> To make my pitch . . .
> And I'll be dirty, rotten, filthy, stinking RICH!!!

I fitted nicely into the 'go out with a film star' line, and indeed he was starting to acclimatise himself to a more lush life than before.

Leslie and Tony's idol was the Scandinavian film-maker, Ingmar Bergman. So admiring were they of his work that they adopted part of his name, and incorporated it into their names as a nickname, by which they still refer to one another to this day. Newley became NewBERG, and Bricusse became BrickMAN. Tony also referred to himself mostly in the third person — an affection only used as far as I can recall by the Queen, Frank Sinatra and various heads of state, but his ego was such that it actually did not seem quite as affected as it would on a lesser mortal with a more humble Id!

The four of us had wonderful times — marvellous fun and a great kinship, and I relied heavily on the camaraderie of this four-sided relationship to help me through the dark days of my mother's failing health and death.

Her death, early one May morning, was almost a relief, for she had been in great pain, had a lost a lot of weight, and must have known what was happening although we all desperately tried to keep it from her.

A few days before she died I sat at her bedside telling her gossip and jokes, and hoping to make her forget her pain. Suddenly she took my hand and looked me in the eye and with great lucidity asked, 'What are you going to do with your life? It's time you settled down. You're not going to be young for ever, you know.'

My mother never usually confronted me with these kind of questions. She had let me go my own way to live my own life for a long time now. So I was taken aback at this, for her, frank approach.

'Well, Tony and I will probably get married — when he gets his divorce,' I said, crossing my fingers and sounding confident.

'Aah — I'm glad darling. He seems good for you. He's stopped you from gadding about,' she closed her eyes and breathed deeply and I thought she had gone to sleep. I gently withdrew my hand from hers, but as I did she opened her eyes and looked at me with such gentle love in her face that I could hardly keep from crying.

'You'd be a marvellous mother darling,' she whispered. 'I hope you have a baby one day. I hope you have one soon,' she closed her eyes again and I gazed at her, the tears streaming down my face. If she only knew! If she only knew that I almost did have a baby. It would have made her so happy. Married or not, I don't think it would have mattered to her, and I mentally kicked myself for the fact that there was no way now that she could ever hold a child of mine in her arms. It was too late. I knew it was only a matter of days. Some of my tears fell on her hand and she opened her eyes and smiled at me.

'You're so easily led,' she whispered. 'And you're so strong too . . . it makes it difficult for you . . . difficult,' her voice trailed off and she closed her eyes and murmured as she drifted off to sleep. 'I hope you have one soon. Have it soon darling . . .' she loosened her hand in mine and slept. Her hand was so thin and vulnerable, the blue veins standing up like tiny rivers on the frail white skin. My mother. The only person really in my life who had ever cared about me. She was going. And I could do nothing — had done nothing. I went to my room and sobbed for two hours,

Young love in bloom — the official engagement portrait.

PAUL SCHUMACH, METROPOLITAN PHOTO SERVICE INC.

Living it up in New York. We had to pay for our dinners at El Morocco (top) but we got a free ride at the Harwyn (bottom).

On location for Warren's first starring role in *Splendour in the Grass*. Director Elia Kazan (centre) is flanked by two happy couples — Joan and Warren (left) and Natalie Wood and Robert Wagner.

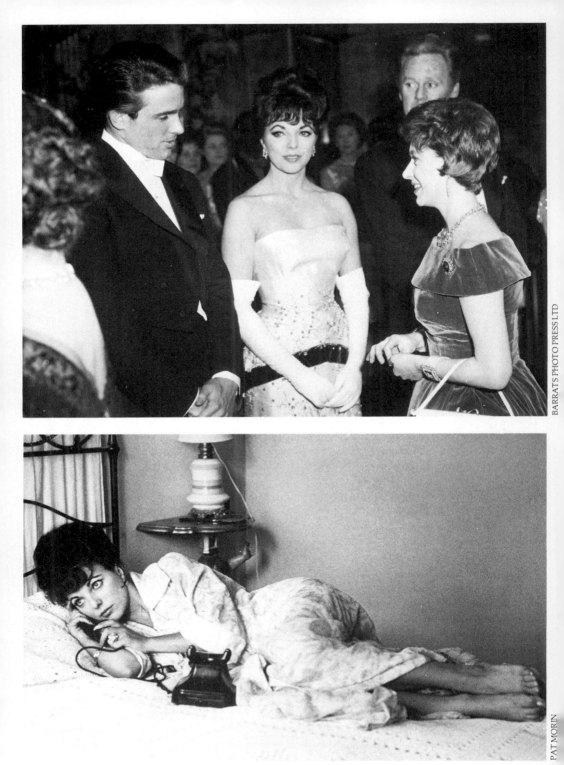

BARRATS PHOTO PRESS LTD

PAT MORIN

TOP: A Royal Command Performance. Princess Margaret seems quite taken with Warren — and vice versa. BOTTOM: Oh, those telephone bills to New York! Making *Esther and the King* in Rome, 1960 — and heavily featuring my new engagement ring.

TOP: Newly married to Newley, with best man Michael Lipton and matron-of-honour Cappy Badrutt. New York, 1963. BOTTOM: The Newmans and the Bricusses commiserate with Tony after reading the New York reviews of *Stop the World* . . . 1962.

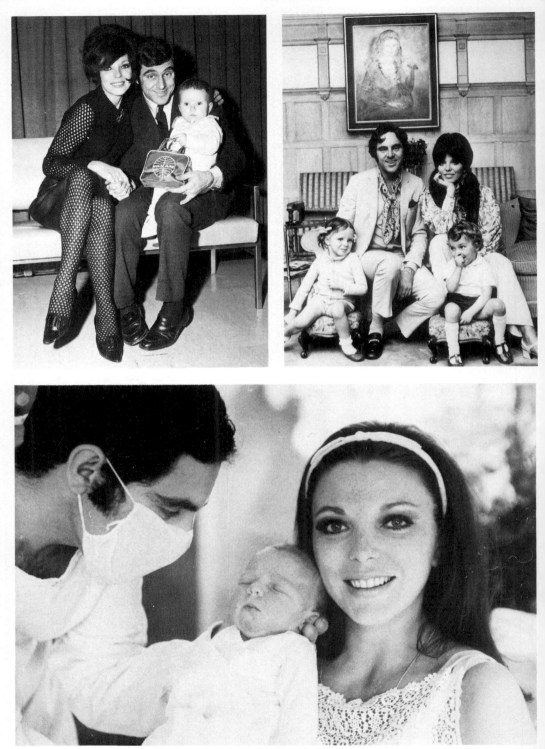

TOP LEFT: Tara's first trip. TOP RIGHT: Happy families — my own now. With Tara and Sacha — London, 1968. BOTTOM: Oh what a beautiful baby!

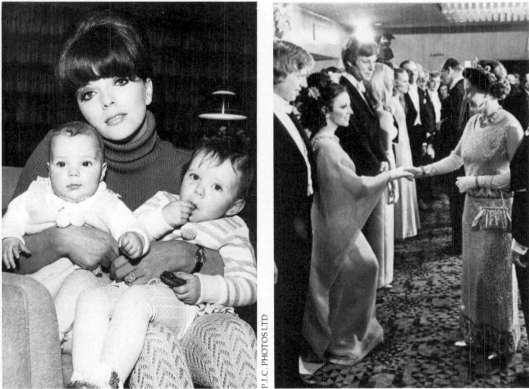

P.I.C. PHOTOS LTD

MARCO SCHIAVO

TOP: With Roger 'The Saint' Moore and Bob Monkhouse. BOTTOM LEFT: Me and my two smashing kids. BOTTOM RIGHT: The curtsies I'd learnt in *The Virgin Queen* came in handy here !

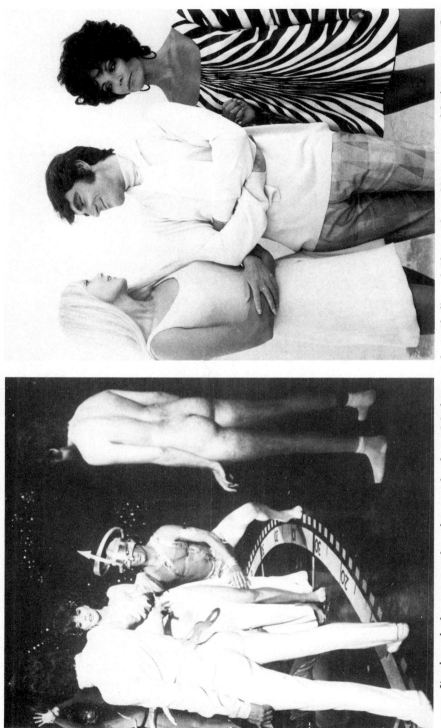

LEFT: I've heard of upstaging but this is ridiculous! My big number 'Chalk and Cheese' from *Hieronymus Merkin*. RIGHT: 'I think he's trying to tell me something.' Tony gazes admiringly at Connie Kreski, who played Mercy Humpe to my Polyester Poontang — Malta, 1968.

and made a resolution. If I did nothing else I was going to try and do something to please her and make her happy. Although I did not believe in an after-life, in some way I knew that if and when I had a child she would know about it and be happy.

I cried all my tears for Mummy that evening. When Daddy came into my room at 6.30 in the morning a few days later and said, 'She's gone,' I had already faced the loss and the tears had been shed. But the resolution remained. I had an ambition and a goal now. For her. And I was going to make it happen . . . come what may.

I rented yet another house in Los Angeles, and Tony and the Bricusses came to visit for two weeks. Cordell Mews was nestled in the Hollywood Hills behind the fabled Doheny Estates. It was a tiny jewel of a house, beautifully furnished in Chinoiserie and Melrose Avenue pseudo-English antiques. The master bedroom featured a giant bed, with an ornately scalloped, gold painted headboard. Just right for a 'menage à quatre' had we been so inclined. Tony took one look at this Hollywoodian masterpiece and fell on it gasping for breath. 'Ha, Ha!' we all shrieked. 'What a sense of humour the Young Master does have.' Unfortunately he was not being humorous — the dreaded flu bug had attacked him even as he had surveyed the palaces of the affluent during the drive to the house, and he was seized with simultaneous headache, stomach ache, throat ache and muscle ache.

'Oh God, Flower — I'm so sorry,' he moaned, as Evie and I scurried about bringing him aspirin and hot lemon and honey — his staple drink which usually warded off attacks on his ever-delicate throat.

'Never mind, darling,' I bustled, doing my best Florence Nightingale impression. 'It's just Jet-Lag. You'll be up and about tomorrow.'

'Please God,' he groaned pitifully, and sank back onto the carefully arranged pillows we had surrounded him with to protect his head from the wooden monstrosity looming behind him.

'I'll think I'll have a little kip,' he said, putting large wads of pink waxy substance in his ears and placing a black eye mask over his feverish eyes. He wore pyjamas — the only man I had ever met, other than my father, who did so, and had arranged a decrepit old camel-coloured scarf around his bony neck. He pulled the covers up to his nose and fell instantly asleep. Something he was always able to do anytime, anywhere. I looked at my exciting lover, on the brink of snoring and tiptoed out ruefully to join

Leslie and Evie in the living room. What a start to a romantic, whirlwind holiday.

I had planned dinner on the patio, where we could look at the twinkling lights of Los Angeles spread out like a sequined shawl, and listen to the newest Sinatra and Mathis records on the excellent stereo system. I has prepared my favourite dish, 'Pomme Paysanne' it was known at Les Ambassadeurs, where I had been introduced to it by Laurence Harvey. Actually 'Peasant Potato' was a cute pseudonym for a large baked potato oozing with fresh black Iranian caviar, butter and sour cream. With caviar at $50 an ounce, I had not stinted myself or my guests, and I managed to eat several ounces of the succulent black eggs and at least two potatoes trying to get over my disappointment at Tony's indisposition.

One could not be down-hearted for too long, however, around Leslie and Evie. They were young, fun and in love. Evie, with her flawless olive skin, huge dark eyes, lustrous black hair and hourglass figure was one of the warmest, kindest and funniest girls I had known. And Leslie, with his Cambridge blond English looks, owl-like glasses and biting humour was stimulating and witty enough to make me forget the 'Limey Jew', bedded with influenza and wheezing away miserably in the huge 'Hollywood' bed.

Leslie was a great planner. That evening, after several bottles of good white wine had been demolished, we plotted and planned our two week vacation every minute from dawn to dusk. It was organised with soldier-like precision. Like me, Leslie was a grabber of life, and each new day was an adventure to be discovered and savoured and enjoyed to the utmost. We both had new Polaroid cameras, which we used constantly on everyone. It got to the stage where one had to be sure the bathroom door was completely locked or you never what might get snapped! Because of the Bricusses, I saw Los Angeles and California through new eyes — discovering places and things about the city that I had not seemed to be aware of before. Life became a constant photo call. Not the boring uncomfortable sessions in the sterile portrait gallery at the studios but funny, spur-of-the-moment, helplessly giggly photos snapped wherever and whenever we felt the urge.

'Quick, get the Polaroid. Tony's drowning,' someone would squeal and off we'd go. Snap — tear — count to ten — pull — voila!

'Oh, it's good of you Evie' — 'Oh no, I look *awful* — but you look *great!*'

The coffee table was heaped with dozens of pictures. There we were mugging it up outside Dino's on the Strip — Tony wielding a large comb and trying to look like Kookie 'Lend me your comb' Byrnes. There we were at Disneyland, surrounded by Mickey Mouse and Donald Duck, and fractured with laughter. There were Evie and I in the bathroom, in the process of teasing our hair to immense beehives — fourteen or sixteen inches high, wearing only our bras and tights, caught open-mouthed with surprise. There was Tony by the swimming pool in Palm Springs wearing football boots, drooping black socks and disreputable grey shorts, lifting with mock effort a huge pair of dumb-bells.

There we were the four of us, joyfully clustered around Sammy Davis Jr in his dressing room in Vegas, our faces shining with admiration, for there was a mutual exchange of hero-worship between Tony and Sammy. Sammy often 'did' Tony in his act, and was Newley's and Bricusse's first and biggest booster in the States. He, not Tony, had the first big hit with 'What Kind Of Fool Am I'. Quite a few Newley/Bricusse songs were getting air play now in the States especially on KLAC. We would often hear the strident Cockney tones boom forth with 'Yes, we have no bananas', and 'Pop Goes the Weasel', but he was still a virtual unknown as far as most of America was concerned.

Leslie had the incredible knack of combining extremely hard, prolific work with a large measure of holidays, vacations and pleasure trips. He could make a simple outing to the zoo a gala event, and was able to turn the most mundane situation into a great adventure. It is a priceless gift he has and he has managed through the years to continue doing it, juggling his and Evie's and their son Adam's lives and balancing them with their several homes all over the world, and their dozens of friends, so that wherever he is there is always instant action.

All too soon the brief vacation drew to a close and it was time for them to return to London and for Tony to start *Stop The World* again for a few months until it was time to bring the show to New York for the fall season under the auspices of the 'King of the Broadway Producers', David Merrick. During his summer break Tony was also going to star in a very demanding role in a movie called *The Small World of Sammy Lee*, whilst also working with Leslie on two future projects for musicals — *Noah* and *Mr Fat and Mr Thin*. On top of that he was appearing in three or four TV specials, his own TV show — called 'The Johnny Darling Show' — and cutting at least two or three records. I figured that for the next few months the boy was going to be very, very busy indeed, and where I was going to be able to fit into his already crammed schedule was a puzzlement. Consequently I allied my fortunes with those of the Bricusses and we planned at least three trips during the spring and summer. I had made my own mind up as far as Newley was concerned. I had decided to marry him, and had made it clear to him that this was what I wanted the bottom line of our relationship to be. He was ambivalent and scared to death of marriage, but he was also terrified of losing me. His feelings vacillated back and forth like a yo-yo. One minute totally enamoured, could not live without me — life was empty — life was grey — I was the only woman, etc. The next minute, more or less careless indifference to my feelings and desires. Adamant that he would be a disaster as a husband and that we were from two different worlds . . . 'What can a rich, young, single film star see in a married Cockney, half-Jewish git?' he would ask me ruefully, sitting behind his shabby, top-heavy dressing table backstage at the Queen's Theatre, in his stained and moth-eaten navy blue dressing gown from Marks and Spencer, a brown hairnet scraping his heavy wavy hair off his white-lined forehead, whilst he scrubbed the cold cream around and around until his black and white make-up turned into liquid grey mud. I looked at his mournful spaniel eyes — so *English!* So long suffering — the more sunk in gloom and depression he became because of our relationship the more appealing he became. He was like an adorable, petulant little boy.

'I'm half-Jewish too, Newberg, and don't you forget it. A half-Jewish Princess from Bayswater Road via Sunset Boulevard. I think we make a great combination.' I put my head close to his and we studied ourselves in the fly-specked mirror. 'If our children have my looks and your brains and our half Jewishness there'll be no stopping 'em. It will be an *unbearable* combination!' He smiled faintly and gave me a greasy kiss.

'Ah, Flower, you always look on the bright side don't you?'

'You betcha,' I said — reapplying my lip gloss and feeling optimistic. 'Except, wouldn't it be awful if the children had your looks and my brains!' He gave his staccato laugh and did a bit of Sammy Davis Jr's appreciative stomping on the ground.

I felt confident we were going to work things out. He had started divorce proceedings against Ann Lynn, an actress from whom he had been separated for three years. The English courts were notoriously long-winded as far as divorces were concerned. It was unlike the States where divorce is as easy to get as a cold. I knew it would be a long haul and a difficult time but I felt I was on a winning streak and could almost see the finish line ahead of me.

Whilst Tony was rehearsing in New York for *Stop the World*, the Bricusses and I spent a week in Jamaica. It had been four or five years since *Sea Wife*, and I revisited some of the beaches and lagoons with nostalgic interest, whilst my own interest, unbeknown to me was whiling away his non-rehearsal hours with a blonde baby-faced twin. Leslie and Evie thought the idea of Tony and me married was super. Even when we sat one evening listening to the ominous tones of the radio announcing that President Kennedy was going to stand firm and not allow Russian bases on Cuba (we were holidaying right in the middle of the Cuban missile crisis!) I was still preoccupied with Tony. But finally we realised that Jamaica was rather too close to Cuba for comfort and that getting *out* of Jamaica and back to the States might be a trifle dangerous. We decided to fly back to New York.

Tony met us at the airport and was thrilled to see me but at the Philadelphia opening he was quite cool. First night nerves, the Bricusses assured me. He's scared to death; there's a lot on the line here. But things weren't the same between us. He confessed his 'thing' with Daisy. He realised it was an almost unnatural obsession; that she was in every way wrong — but there it was — and who was I to deny him that. The flesh is weak. I knew that too. We separated. With a heavy heart I flew back to Los Angeles carrying a French poodle called Ladybird that he had given me. Now she seemed destined to be my life's companion, but I had promised the Bricusses and Tony that whatever personal problems were going on between us I would definitely attend the first night of *Stop the World* in New York.

I flew back and stayed at the Drake Hotel. I was fulfilling my duties as a friend but I couldn't fight City Hall. If he preferred this child to me that was it as far as I was concerned. I had to get on with my life. I had offers of movies in Hollywood and Italy and could now reap the rewards for all the years I had spent doing Fox's potboilers. They were paying off in one way at least.

After the opening of *Stop the World* everyone went back to Tony's suite at the Navarro and waited for the reviews. They were awful. The critics, although admiring Tony's unusual talent, and the score, which was of course magnificent, did not like the show. They felt it was self-indulgent, egotistical and pretentious. Paul and Joanne Newman had come in from Connecticut and with Michael Lipton — Tony's best friend, Peter Charlesworth, the

Bricusses and a few other close mates, we sat reading the scathing reviews of Bosley Crowther and John Kerr and felt the kiss of death on the show.

I knew the Newley relationship was over. I wasn't about to put myself any more in yet another subsidiary and subservient position as I had with The General. This was it. Over. Finished. Done with. Goodbye baby and amen. Another year down the tube. I loved him, but that didn't seem enough. We all said tearful goodbyes to each other in the early hours. Leslie and Tony were convinced that Merrick, on the strength of the appalling reviews, would take the show off and that they would go back to London and perhaps start writing another one. I was going to accept one of the movie roles. Preferably one that would be 10,000 miles away from Newley. Gloom was rampant. Wine and whisky were consumed with abandonment.

But the next morning an amazing thing happened. There were lines around the block outside the theatre: hundreds of people waiting to buy tickets for *Stop the World*. This time the word of mouth of the public proved stronger than the critics' scathing words. The show was an instant hit.

I was happy for Tony, and for Leslie and Evie who were also staying at the Drake Hotel. We had a celebration drink to the show's success in the bar a couple of nights later, whilst Leslie excitedly told me about the great audiences and ovations they had been having. 'He still loves you Joanie,' said Evie sympathetically. 'He really *needs* you. He's miserable without you.'

'That's too bad,' I said calmly, watching my date for the evening come in. 'I'm not a groveller Evie, you know that.'

'We certainly *all* know *that* Jace,' said Brickman as the young man came over to our table and sat down and had a drink with us.

I introduced them to Terence Stamp. He was phenomenally handsome. More truly beautiful than most women. He had had a big success in William Wyler's film *The Collector* with Samantha Eggar, and having just played the title role in *Billy Budd* for Peter Ustinov, was in New York doing publicity and movie promotion.

'Well, we'll see you guys later,' I said after twenty minutes as Terry and I got up and left for dinner. Evie shot me several knowing and penetrating looks. 'God he's *gorgeous*,' she whispered to me. 'Tony will be *livid* when he hears.' I didn't care if he was. He had no right to be livid. If I was subconsciously going out with this amazingly handsome man to make him jealous that was perhaps a little bit of revenge for Daisy.

Terry was a Cockney boy, full of whimsical wit and cocky

assurance. His new success had not gone to his head and he found all the hoop la and hullabaloo 'a bit embarrassing'. He and Michael Caine had shared a flat when they were penniless actors a few years previously. Now Michael's career was starting to happen too. It was the time of the English actor. Albert Finney, Alan Bates, Pete Cook and Dudley Moore, Peter Sellars and now Terence Stamp and Tony Newley were taking America by storm. England was where it was, where the action was, and anything and anyone British was very appealing.

Terry was also staying at the Drake Hotel which was where we met. It certainly made life less complicated. Newley called three times that night. I didn't return his calls. I had other things to do. I was trying to get over him, and I wasn't going to jump through his hoop whenever he decided to set it up. After a dozen or so phone calls during the next two days in which he begged me to meet him to 'talk about things' we met on neutral ground, a bench in Central Park. It was a cold, blustery November day. The trees in the park were now stark and almost bare of leaves. A few brave people walked around with dogs and children. We sat huddled on a hard bench. The collar of his navy blue raincoat was turned up, and he wore his usual woolly scarf to keep his precious vocal chords, always on the point of giving up the ghost, warm. He came to the point quickly. He wanted me back. Under any circumstances. Whatever I wanted was fine by him. Anything.

What did I want? Looking at his strained white face with the almost permanently ingrained pained expression I felt great compassion and pity for him. 'I don't think you *really* love me Tony,' I said carefully. 'I think you're fascinated with me, infatuated, call it what you will, but I don't truly think it's love, do you?'

'I don't know Flower, I don't know what the bloody word *means* for Christ's sake.' He got up and strode up and down the path, the wind whipping his thick dark hair, his face a mask of agonised concentration. 'I've been fucking miserable the last couple of days. *Miserable.* You've been running around New York with Terry Stamp — all of my friends telling me about it,' he smiled bitterly. 'I think, I really feel, I can't live without you now, Flower.' He sat down next to me and put his arm around my shoulders. I was shivering. Whether from the cold or the emotion I didn't know.

'What about Daisy?' I said evenly. 'A month ago it was she whom you couldn't give up. How do you feel about *her* now?'

'I can't deny it Flower — I can't deny I find young girls attractive, very attractive. It's something I've had to live with all my life. I know it's a sickness — I know it . . . but . . .' He paused, groping for words — his dark blue eyes searched my face as though hoping to find the answer there. 'I'll try and . . . control it . . . I'll really try — if you try and help me . . . can you help me Flower?' I didn't know the answer to that one. I didn't know where altruism ended and ego began. But I knew what *I* wanted and needed out of life now. I wanted to marry and have a child. If it wasn't Tony it would be someone else eventually. I was in love with Tony but I'd been in love before. Love was like measles, you could get it again and again.

I told him that I would try and be understanding about his attraction to adolescent girls, and I told him that if he wanted me, truly wanted to be with me, that then we would have to marry. 'Otherwise I'm leaving for Rome next week to do a movie,' I said flatly. 'But you can't keep turning me on and off like a tap.' I had had my fill of selfish men. The General and Warren had between them taken over three years of my life. I had been an actress for over ten years. I wanted to be a mother now, have children, be a wife, settle down. Give up this life of furnished apartments and hotel rooms, locations and airports, living out of a suitcase. Stop the World — I want to get *On*. I want roots. I want to belong. I want to buy my own furniture, get my books and records out of storage and make a nest.

I told him and he understood. And he agreed. A week later we moved into a huge, unfurnished penthouse apartment in the Imperial House on 63rd Street. He started immediate divorce proceedings with Ann Lynn and we haunted Bloomingdales and furniture stores on 3rd Avenue for tables and chairs and beds to furnish our nest.

Six weeks later I was pregnant! The good years had begun.

9

A Most Peculiar Mother

Tara Cynara Newley was born at Mount Sinai Hospital in New York on October 12th, 1963. She was quite without a doubt the most beautiful creature I had ever set eyes on — from her perfectly shaped pink head, with just the tiniest blonde fuzz on it, to her enormous blue eyes, rosebud lips and perfect little body. She was so infinitely precious and wonderful that I sat and stared at her in wonderment for hours. She was mine. Ours. Our baby daughter. Tony had wanted a daughter, I didn't really mind as long as it was healthy, but I was overjoyed to see his reaction to this gorgeous elf.

I had her by natural childbirth and had done all the right things while I was pregnant: plenty of vitamins, lots of rest, tons of milk and eggs and fresh green vegetables; natural childbirth classes; special breathing exercises so that she wouldn't have to have any medication or anaesthetic in her while she was experiencing the trauma of birth.

Joanne Woodward had told me I *must* nurse her myself! Although I loved the symbolism of the whole thing, Mother Earth incarnate, I wasn't too sure whether I could really handle it. Having gained thirty pounds I was quite eager to shed it and get back into my clothes again, and nursing entails knocking back two or three quarts of milk or beer a day to keep everything on tap, so to speak. The nurse on my floor was surprised when I told her. 'We haven't had a mother do that for years — except in the wards of course,' she added hastily. The wards were where the poor Puerto Rican and Black women from Harlem went to have their young delivered.

I was on the third floor, where the private rooms were. Lovely young creatures having their first, second or maximum third child who would never consider defiling their svelte figures by anything as peasant-like as breast feeding.

But this was 1963 and a whole movement was afoot to

popularise not only childbirth, but a natural way of feeding the child too. I gritted my teeth and vowed to Joanne to do the best I could. I was quite a curiosity on the third floor as nurses and interns would pop in to see how the movie star was coping with suckling her young. It was a source of some amusement to them and to some of my friends, who couldn't believe I could do anything so plebeian.

'Joanie, I just can't watch this — it's too disgusting,' said horrified Sue Mengers — an agent friend noted for her outspokenness.

I persevered. Tara was yelling a lot. I was convinced that she was starving to death. I consumed enough beer to make a truck driver keel over. Hiccuping wildly I would attempt again to stave off the pathetic little creature's wails. When she was three days old the hospital sent us back home. None of this languishing about in bed eating grapes and being waited on hand and foot applied any more to modern day obstetrics. Drop it and go home was the new method. Just like a Chinese peasant woman in the rice paddies.

I called Joanne. I was in agony, and so was Tara. I had bosoms the size of watermelons, and the consistency of granite, and a four-day-old infant screaming her lungs out. 'I cannot do it Joanne!' I cried. 'Breast feeding is for the birds and the peasants, it's just not happening. Tara is dying of malnutrition.'

'Don't worry,' said the calm and assuring tones of my friend. 'It's always like this, the fourth day is the worst. Perseverance — I know it hurts like hell, but believe me it will be worth it in the end — you'll see.'

She persuaded me with some very telling information for 45 minutes, while I rocked the squalling, and by now terrifying babe in my arms, the slightest move her little head made against my congested chest causing me to wince in agony.

'Give it twelve more hours,' pleaded Joanne. 'I promise you it will get better — I've done it myself with Nell and Melissa. Don't give up on it my dear — it's worth it.' I gritted my teeth and hung on in. It was a sleepless night — Tara's wails and my discomfort made sleep impossible, but suddenly the next morning I was the perfect advertisement for Madonna and Child, propped up in bed behind my flowered pillow, hair flowing, everything else flowing — feeling pleased as punch and twice as frisky. What a magnificent feeling of achievement I had. It infinitely surpassed anything I had ever done on the screen. Tara and I were a team, we didn't need anything else to make the world keep turning.

She bloomed. When she was six weeks old she had a check-up

at the pediatrician. 'What have you been feeding this baby — she's enormous?' said the doctor in surprise, bending over the bonny gurgling princess, already aware of what was going on around her.

'Oh nothing, 'I said blushing modestly. 'Just the usual!'

I noticed as we drove home in a cab through the crowded New York streets that a lot of people were behaving strangely. Cars had pulled over to the sidewalk, and people were standing about in clusters looking worried and unhappy. I leaned over to the taciturn driver. 'What's happening, is there something going on somewhere?'

'Beats me lady,' he drawled in the lovable way New York cab drivers have.

As soon as I opened the apartment door I heard our cleaning lady weeping loudly from the kitchen. It sounded like a wake. Tony strode out of the study and beckoned me in. He looked sombre and on the brink of tears. Television was on full blast and an ashen-faced announcer was doing a news report.

'Kennedy's been shot, they think he's dying,' said Tony.

'Oh no — oh my God — it's not possible.' I sank onto the sofa, the little pink bundle cooing placidly in my arms. We listened and watched in stunned horror for the rest of the day. It wasn't possible that this extraordinary man — a symbol to Americans and the world over that America was trying really hard to create integration and to erase poverty and unemployment, who was endeavouring to make the nation truly a democracy, who really cared about people — had been assassinated. Friends came over. None of us could do anything other than watch the box, still unable to believe that this monstrous event had occurred. The reporters were interviewing 'the man in the street'. Everyone was shocked and sad. 'Well — y'know ah just figures these things could never happen in the United States. Ah mean in England, sure, or some foreign country but never here,' said some bigoted oaf.

'Shit,' said Tony, angrily switching off. 'Let's get out of here Flower — I want to go back to England.'

He wrote a song about that terrible day on November 20th, 1963. We were both tremendous admirers of the Kennedy family, especially the President. Tony's homesickness for England probably had a lot to do with his decision to leave the States. He had never felt as though he really belonged in America. Though he was idolised and admired each night by throngs in the audience and the hordes of fans who would wait backstage for a glimpse of him, he still felt more his own man in England. His ideal place to live was a little hut on the coast of Cornwall, and he would often talk nostalgically of his hut. It had no water or electricity, was in the remotest part of the coast overlooking the fierce coastline, and was made of tin! Probably left over from World War I.

I, more pragmatic about these things, did not indulge in his enthusiasm for the little hut. But the assassination brought home to him all the things he disliked about New York. He wanted out.

The show was to close soon after Christmas. We were going home again. Who says you can't?

We arrived in Paris on a frosty February day. We had to wait until the tax year ended on April 6th to enter England again, so we decided to stay in Paris for a couple of months, where Tony could relax and start writing his next show. It was sad getting rid of our apartment in New York. It had been my very first proper home. The first place for which I had actually bought wallpaper and carpets, had chosen, albeit not terribly tastefully, lamps, sofas and tables, and tentatively started my hand at interior decoration which was to become a minor passion and, in view of the future moves, a necessity in my life.

What to do with all of this stuff? Records, books, scrapbooks, all kinds of junk and mementoes of our years together. 'Sell it or ship it,' said Tony, leaving *me* with the problem of how to do that. I had called my agent in Los Angeles and told him I was going to England 'indefinitely' and that I wouldn't be available for work. He hadn't been pleased when six months earlier he had excitedly phoned to say that he had a firm offer for me to play Jean Harlow in the movie of Harold Robbins' sexy book *The Carpetbaggers*.

'It's a wonderful part, honey, a terrific role — and the money is great. They really want you.'

'Would they really want me if they knew I was six months' pregnant,' I crowed proudly.

'Joanie . . . whaat??' My agent was understandably aggravated. Actresses who got pregnant were a pain in the rear end.

'All the time and effort we spent getting you out of Fox. You can't blow that sweetheart. Not now — it's finally paying off for you.'

'It's too late now,' I said surveying my swelling centrepiece. 'My bulge would look awful in white satin.'

'You're crazy,' he said grimly. 'Crazy. You're too young to give

194

up your career. You've worked too hard to pay your dues — now it could be really happening for you. Don't you *care* about working any more sweetheart?'

'Yes I *do* care,' I answered truthfully. 'But my life, Tony, Tara, and our personal happiness have to come first. And right now my life is with him and wherever he goes I go.'

I thought about this as I wheeled Tara in her chic French pram down the boulevards of Paris each morning. After a wonderful and fattening breakfast of hot croissants and coffee, Tony would settle down to write for three or four hours, and Tara and I would take our morning constitutional. I felt very much the young bourgeois housewife as I sat in the Bois de Boulogne with the other mothers and babies and fed the pigeons and watched the older children on the swings.

Sometimes we would parade down the Champs Elysées and Tara and I would look at the giant movie posters outside all the cinemas. *Road to Hong Kong* had just opened, and there was a painting of me fifteen feet high outside one of the theatres. Bouffant hair, glistening red lips and eyes painted an unimaginable shade of grassy green. How far away that life seemed to be already. Pushing the baby carriage in a camel coat, sensible shoes and headscarf, with hardly any make-up, I was unrecognisable from that Movie Queen up on the billboards, and I was, for the first time in many years, content.

Tara brought me infinite joy. I had eschewed the idea of a nanny — I wanted to look after my four month old infant myself. Although we lived in a suite at the Hotel Grand Point nevertheless I still had to make and mix her formula myself. I'd quit feeding her at three months when she developed a gargantuan appetite for cereals, fruit, and anything else she could grab. I washed her clothes by hand, played with her, bathed her and did all the other dozens of things a tiny baby needs. I didn't want anybody else to do this for her. She was my baby and I was going to do right by her.

One night Tony woke me up with a sharp nudge. 'What's all that commotion?' I said sleepily. 'Sounds like a drunken orgy next door.'

'Sounds like they're breaking all the glasses and windows in the place,' he said jumping out of bed in his blue and white striped pyjamas. 'I'll see what's happening.' He opened the door of our bedroom which led to the hall and recoiled coughing violently. The hall was filled with smoke. He banged the door shut and turned to me trying to keep the panic off his face. 'I think there's a fire,' he said quietly.

'Oh Christ, what about Tara . . .' My knees suddenly turned to water. I leaped from the bed and rushed into the living room which separated her bedroom from ours. It was almost impossible to breathe in her room. Clouds of acrid smoke everywhere and I could barely see. 'My baby!' I screamed fearing the worst. She was in her cot, gazing with surprised blue eyes at this interesting substance floating around her room. Another minute and she could have suffocated. I grabbed her and fled back to our bedroom.

Tony was talking to the concierge on the phone. 'There's a fire . . . um . . . oui, un feu . . . er . . . Christ . . . un grand feu ici — help us — s'il vous plait.' His calmness hid the edge of panic he was trying to cover up. His atrocious French was not an asset. I heard the concierge yelling excitedly.

'Oui, m'sieur — oui, oui — je sais — nous croyons c'est un feu — we 'ave already called the fire department. Do not worry m'sieur, you will be rescued, I assure you.' He hung up.

I looked outside, it was not a reassuring sight. We were seven floors up. In the street stood a lonely fire truck surrounded by five lackadaisical firemen trying to connect the hose to a nearby pump. A knot of mildly interested Frenchmen, obviously on their way home from the local bordello, since it was four in the morning, stood idly by smoking Gauloises and offering advice. Some of them chuckled occasionally. Weird humour these frogs have. Several people were hanging out of windows above and below us screaming wildly. Flames were shooting up from the top of the building and smoke was spiralling from the top floor. The *ninth* floor was the top floor and we were on number seven. The people on the eighth were understandably hysterical and of the people on the ninth, there seemed no evidence. Dead? Or escaped? A middle-aged German man, naked except for a string vest and green socks, was on the balcony immediately above us, jumping up and down and yelling incoherently. I couldn't help having an hysterical giggle at the fact he was so unaware of his nudity — he seemed even more bizarrely naked because of his vest and socks.

Then I realised I myself was only wearing the briefest see-through blue nightgown and nothing underneath. I grabbed a pair of jeans, a sweater and my slippers and thrust Tara into Tony's hands. 'Gotta get her bottle.' I dashed into the living room, where smoke was already seeping in below the door, and snatched three bottles of formula from the fridge. I took my mink from the closet and my jewellery box from the desk. That was it — the rest could go up in flames, but baby had to be fed and mama had to be warm

196

in the evening. Although frightened to death, I still felt we would be saved at the eleventh hour. Finally finding all this happiness and then getting fried to death in a second-class hotel in Paris could not be my destiny. Or could it? Tony thrust the baby into my arms again and jumped onto the balcony like Errol Flynn in his heyday. 'Where are you going?' I screamed. Was my new bridegroom about to commit suicide, or was he going to scramble to safety alone — with me holding the baby? I stood shaking on the tiny balcony watching him manoeuvre round the side of the hotel to where the smoke seemed less dense. I was suddenly very alone and very frightened. 'Help! Help! Please help us!' I screamed.

A small crowd had now gathered in the Champs Elysées to watch with laconic interest sixty people die horribly. They ignored me. The firemen were still fiddling about with the nozzle of their equipment and my opinion of the French plummeted. Such disorganisation. They couldn't even get the goddamned water connected, we could all go up in flames and they would still be jerking off down there. 'Au secour! Au secour!' I yelled, hoping that the correct French would do more good than English. The French have always been snide about the British. Maybe the reason they were so indifferent to our plight was because they knew the hotel was full of German tourists. A petite revenge for their occupation. Maybe if they saw a poor young Frenchwoman clutching her tiny babe, a future president of the Republic peut-être, they might get their act together and put out this *fucking* fire.

The smoke was getting denser. Sparks were falling on us. A woman on the ninth floor let out a horrifying scream. My God her hair was on fire!! It was too, too horrible. A nightmare from which surely I must finally awake. After what seemed about a year, Tony scrambled back along the balconies, dishevelled, his face blackened from soot, and his hands cut and bleeding.

'The fire's in the elevator shaft,' he breathed shakily, gasping for air. He was not much of an athlete — he wasn't even into jogging yet. 'It's on the top floor and burning downwards — we've *got* to get out of here Flower!'

'I know, but how?' I wailed. Tara started to cry. The three of us held on tight together. Horror stories of mutilated bodies found in burnt-out buildings filled my mind. I could hear screams, and breaking glass — cries and groans from the floors above us. I saw the headlines on the *Evening Standard* placards in London: 'Famous Stars and Baby Die in Paris Hotel Fire!' That would sell a few papers. Everyone would want to know who the stars were

197

and how horribly they died, and circulations would soar!

We stood there forever. Trapped. If *we* were too young to die, what about Tara? Four months old — what a tragedy. I tried to imagine my whole life passing through my mind. Wasn't that what supposedly happened when people knew they were doomed. I couldn't think of anything, except my little baby's life hadn't even begun yet.

And then — crash! The door to the bedroom burst open and two burly firemen appeared in masks and heavy asbestos gloves. It was the most glorious sight I had ever seen. They yelled at us in French.

'Suivez — Follow us — down on your hands and knees — NOW — quickly — vite — VITE!'

One of them grabbed Tara and gestured us to follow him as he crawled on all fours down the corridor. They damped towels from a bucket of water, and made us cover our heads with them. The floor was burning hot, and an acrid smoke filled my lungs even with the wet towels. The ceiling was an ominous red, and bits of plaster and ash were falling on us like confetti. The noise was horrifying. In a dream I crawled behind the huge garlic-smelling fireman, who was clutching my most precious possession, Tara. We reached the stairs which were next to the lift. 'Allez! Allez-vous!' said the fireman pushing us to the stairs. I looked up the lift shaft and saw the whole top in flames. I have never 'allezed' anywhere as fast as we whisked down those seven flights.

Saved at the eleventh hour. Ben Gary strikes again.

I never again have stayed in any hotel room without checking thoroughly to see that the fire escape was within immediate access. Once burned, twice shy — you better believe it!

We left immediately for Switzerland. It was untenable to live in the suite. Everything was blackened by smoke, there was no hot water or electricity. The management begged us to be patient — normal service would resume shortly, but the event was so awful that we wanted out.

St Moritz in early March was just coming to the end of the season. It was the most exclusive, elegant and glamorous ski resort of the international set, and the Palace Hotel was where everyone congregated. My best friend Cappy was now happily — or fairly happily — married to Andrea Badrutt, the owner of the Palace Hotel. Cappy had become the doyen and social arbiter of the St Moritz social calendar. She knew everyone and everyone knew her. Niarchos, Onassis, Agnelli, Thyssen, Von Opel,

Gunther Sachs, Charles Clore. The cream of the jet set was partaking of the pleasures of the Palace — probably the least of which was ski-ing. Intrigue, romance, high finance, big business, deception, seduction — all took place, and had done for dozens of years beneath the portals of this magnificent hotel. Set in the middle of the quaint village of St Moritz where the simple villagers rubbed shoulders with international playboys and princes, the atmosphere was at once deliciously decadent and jolly healthy.

Into this hot house atmosphere, reeking of sex and sin and sport, arrived one British belle — with a deranged look about her, grubby and unkempt from twenty-four hours by train from Paris. One Cockney genius, already with a sore throat and incipient flu, who absolutely *loathed* anything to do with high society, and one adorable female babe — good as gold I must admit, probably because she hardly ever left her mother's side.

I took Tara everywhere. To lunch at the Palace Grill, where Madame Dewi Sukarno, elegance personified in the simplest of under-played après-ski clothes, would lunch with Madame Badrutt — a vision in sable ski hat and velvet trousers, Baroness Thyssen (the former model Fiona Campbell-Walter), lustrous red tumbling curls and beautifully cut simple shirts and jodhpurs — and me. I had not come prepared for the joys of skiing, and had to make do with some itchy hot polo-necked sweaters, too tight trousers and a John Lennon black leather cap. Not at all what the fashionables could consider haute couture. These were liberally sprinkled with baby food and crumbs, since parked on my lap, or nearby on her portable chair, where the waiters cursed angrily, little Tara would sit and gurgle happily away. The ladies did not exactly approve. The atmosphere was far too refined to have children around, let alone babies, who should only be seen by their parents between four and five pm for nursery tea.

'My God Joanie — you can't go on like this,' said Cappy. 'You can't go walking about St Moritz with that baby slung on your back like some African peasant woman. Get a nanny for goodness sake dear.'

'I don't *need* a nanny,' I said defensively, spooning up a trickle of cream of wheat oozing from Tara's little mouth, and realising as I got closer to her that it was time to change her nappy again.

'What's the *point* Cappy in having a child if you don't take care of it yourself?' Tara burped happily in agreement, and beat a little tattoo with her messy spoon on my grubby sweater.

'Look at you!' said Cappy. 'Look at your hands — you've

ruined them by washing her clothes, and whatever else it is you wash.' She had glanced distastefully at the beautifully decorated marble bathroom now festooned with drying nappies and tiny garments of all descriptions. 'The role of hausfrau does *not* become you,' she said sternly. 'Neither does this role of camp follower to your husband. You must settle down darling and get a house and home and some roots, and you should *work*.'

'I know we need roots,' I said ruefully. 'But we can't go back to England until April because of Tony's tax situation, and honestly Cappy, I *enjoy* looking after the baby — I really do. And as for work — who needs all that standing around on sets — all day — I've done it since I was 16 — it's fantastic to be free.' I picked Tara up and threw her over my shoulder to burp her — then down on the bed to change her.

'I find this delightful domesticity a little hard to take,' said Cappy, glancing at her patrician features and elegant body, fetchingly clad in a grey fox hat and co-ordinated pale grey ski-clothes. 'I don't exactly consider you free, dear. At least I hope you can get a baby sitter tonight so you can come to the party at the Corviglia Club.'

'Darling, I promise you I will not arrive at your party with egg yolk down my dress and dishwater hands.' Fortunately I was able to make the transformation from harassed housewife during the day to soignée sophisticate at night with little effort. Geminis thrive on changing roles. It was much more fun to be the perfect mother all day and a glamorous vision at night. However, playing one of those roles all the time could get monotonous.

John Crosby of the *Herald Tribune* wrote an article about me in St Moritz called 'A Most Peculiar Mother'. He said,

St. Moritz — There's a very peculiar mother here named Mrs Anthony Newley, otherwise known as Joan Collins, a movie film star of some renown, who takes care of her own baby.

In this citadel of the rich, this is a throwback to primitive behavior patterns almost unknown in these parts since they introduced the Roman alphabet.

Other mothers in St Moritz, who are barely on a first-name basis with their babies, stare at Miss Collins in considerable awe: 'Washes her own bottles' they whisper to each other. 'You know, the things they feed the baby with.'

'All the women here think I'm mad,' said Miss Collins. 'If they have one child, they have one nurse, two children two nurses. Three children, three nurses.' . . . Joan Collins's peculiar behavior started in Paris when she assumed

executive control over Tara Cynara, washing bottles, changing nappies and all the other unnatural practices for mothers.
The story continued in that vein — I thought it most amusing.

On April 7th, 1964, Tony and I, and all the rest of the English performers, writers, sportsmen and others who had gone non-resident for a year returned to London. I rented Keith Michell's house in Hampstead and Tony and Leslie Bricusse plunged themselves feverishly into writing a new show, *The Roar of the Greasepaint, the Smell of the Crowd*. Evie had just given birth to a little boy, Adam, and the six of us were now playing 'Happy Families' together. Except I hardly ever saw my husband. He was besotted and completely enslaved by his work. He scribbled away morning, noon and night with little thought for much else. Although I now hired a housekeeper, I was still preoccupied with the baby and my new-found domesticity. I spent days looking for houses in the country but near to London, and finally found a wonderful house at Elstree, full of character and charm, an old Edwardian mansion, with three stories, stables, grounds — just right for the large family we planned on having. I was expecting another baby and although I thought it was rather too hot on the heels of Tara, nevertheless I was happy and fulfilled, and busy as a little bee.

Friars Mead the house was called, and it needed a monstrous amount of renovation and decoration to make it habitable. It had cost the astronomical sum, in those 1964 pre-inflation days, of £20,000. Tony thought this was far too expensive, but I had convinced him it was worth it as we now planned on living in England for ever. The days were full. Playing with Tara who was becoming more adorable and delightful all the time, consultations with architects and Robin Guild, interior decorator, and shopping, for wallpapers, fabrics and furniture for this new home. Goodbye Gucci suitcases — hello roots. Tony moaned about the cost of everything, his humble background had not accustomed him to the fact that things cost money, but he was learning to like the better things in life, not all of which unfortunately are free, and I was certainly an expert teacher. My own bank balance, however, was diminishing rapidly. Always used to making money, I was equally used to spending it. Tony was not financially secure, certainly not in the league of being able to fully support a wife who liked buying her clothes at St Laurent and Thea Porter.

So when an offer materialised for me to go to Rome and star

opposite Vittorio Gassman in an Italian comedy, he persuaded me to do it. I had lost the baby I was expecting and was feeling blue. Tony was on the road in Manchester, Birmingham and the sticks, working hard on out-of-town try outs for *The Roar of the Greasepaint, the Smell of the Crowd.* Leslie and Evie and Tara and Adam and I were of course all there too.

Tony was directing, but having considerable trouble with his star, Norman Wisdom. Wisdom seemed reluctant to be doing this show. Leslie, and Bernard Delfont, who was producing, were doing their best to persuade Newley to play the role of Mr Thin, a role for which he was far more suited than Wisdom, but Tony has a stubborn streak in him a mile wide. He wanted to direct and write, he hated to perform and he refused to play the role. Little Mr Wisdom, I felt, was a parody of what Tony would have been had he played it. He also disliked the show, and said so — to reporters and on television.

Tara was one year old when I left for Portofino, Lugano and Rome to make *La Conguintura.* It was the first separation since our marriage and I was unhappy about it. Although fairly pleased with the idea of getting back to work again, and realising that to live the life I had been accustomed to for the past several years I needed money, nevertheless I had a foreboding that even with Tony's protestations of, 'Yes Flower, do it — you know it'll be good for you. You know you love to work,' that he did not *really* mean it. Deep down I think he wanted a wife who would stay at home, cook for him and take care of his needs. You can take the Boy out of Brixton but you can't take the Brixton out of the Boy.

La Conguintura turned out to be one of the most successful movies I made. At least in Italy. It was number eight at the box office the following year. Unfortunately, for some reason it was never shown in England or America. A pity, because I was doing my favourite thing, comedy. Tara had a wonderful time on location. She even appeared in a scene in her pram when Gassman trips over her in a mad dash around the hotel in Lugano. When Tony, Evie and Leslie all came to Portofino after the London opening of *Greasepaint* their faces told the sad story.

Disaster had struck. The critics had given the show every nasty epithet in the book. We were deeply hurt, because a lot of love, care, time and talent had gone into it. Tony was even more upset. He had discovered that his tax structure was such that it was impossible for him to live permanently in England without paying 90 per cent of his income to the government, and to top it all, David Merrick, having come to Manchester to see the show, had made an offer they could not refuse. Tony was to play Mr Thin in *Greasepaint* on Broadway.

The camp follower immediately did all the right things. Sold the house at Elstree — we had never even moved in, and it was so beautiful now — my dream house at last — I had spent many hours lovingly planning every detail of it. I begged Tony not to sell it. *I* would pay the £20,000 to keep it, but he was adamant, and so was his tax man. Neither of us could own property in the UK. Even though I had been a resident of America for seven years, it could seriously disrupt him tax wise if we kept it.

Out came the 29 Gucci cases, and once more, amidst tearful farewells to friends and family, we flew to New York. I was pregnant again and liked getting on planes less and less, and I was deeply upset by this latest move. This time we moved into a furnished apartment on 72nd Street. With Tony's mother Grace now as Nanny-cum-housekeeper I once again found myself living in someone else's house surrounded by someone else's possessions, and several families of giant cockroaches. At nearly 30 I still owned *nothing* except my clothes, books and records. Would I ever have roots?

Alexander Anthony Newley was born on September 8th, 1965. In the same hospital and the same room as his sister Tara. It was unbelievably thrilling that I now had a boy child too. He was exactly what we had ordered. We were now a perfect little family unit. Indestructible. Or so I thought. I dismissed from my mind the time I had arrived unexpectedly back stage in the last month of my pregnancy, to be greeted nervously by various members of the cast looking sheepish as I waddled through the narrow corridors to the 'Young Master's' dressing room. Dismissed the fact that his dresser, embarrassed, tried to stop me from going in immediately and said in a rather too loud voice, 'Oh good evening Mrs Newley — Mr Newley will be out in a minute.' Dismissed the fact that a pretty young blonde and Newley jumped apart and looked at me guiltily when I entered. I was too involved with my all-consuming role of wife and mother to let petty and imaginary jealousies cloud my life.

Things were going well for us. *The Roar of the Greasepaint* starring Tony and with Cyril Ritchard playing the other part, had opened to mixed reviews, although the praise for Newley's performance was high. He had developed a huge fan following and was a major draw on Broadway now, but our living arrangements were less than satisfactory. That summer we had rented a house in Long Island where I lazed around happily playing with Tara, swimming, sunbathing and barbecuing on weekends for the cast. Tony would leave for the theatre around 4.00, and I would have the rest of the evening to read, write, think and generally be a great, placid, bovine lump. My friends were amazed at my transformation. From an energetic, volatile, high spirited and vigorous creature, who was only happy doing, going and being where the action was, I had turned into a contented cow, happy to laze away the days. The high spot of my week was a visit to the local supermarket, wheeling baby Tara in the basket.

A week before 'Sacha' was born, we moved into Paul and Joanne Newman's apartment on 72nd Street and 5th Avenue. It was a beautiful, airy, tastefully furnished apartment, filled with early American furniture and English antiques — a tribute to Joanne's excellent taste. I had visited her in the hospital a couple of months previously. Her third baby Claire was born three months before Sacha. Now my fear of flying had become an obsession. Although we were in Toronto, Canada, on tour with the show, I preferred to take the overnight train to New York and back rather than spend two hours in a plane. We had a bad experience on a short jaunt from Boston to Cleveland in a blinding snow storm. As the jet, its wheels already descended, was coming in for landing, it suddenly, 200 yards from the runway, zoomed back into the air again. My stomach gave a sickening lurch, and I felt as though I had lost the three month old scrap inside. The stewardesses all went pale green, and when I asked one of them what happened she replied shakily, 'Probably something on the runway.'

'Probably something on the runway!!!' What, pray, I wondered, could that something be? Another plane? A stewardess taking an afternoon stroll? A stray dog? It was too horrible to contemplate that 100 tons of metal carrying sixty or seventy pieces of flesh, blood and gristle could be wiped out by 'something on the runway'. How close we constantly were to death. When the plane finally landed I made a silent vow to never fly again unless there was no other alternative. Now with Sacha's arrival and Tony's full houses each night, I hoped that there would be no plane trips in the foreseeable future.

If having one little baby and taking care of it yourself was a novelty and fun, suddenly two little babies, one a few days old, and one 22 months old, both in nappies, became much, much too hard to handle. I hired a German nanny, Renata. She came with excellent references and arrived a few days before the new baby, to start getting used to Tara.

The hospital as usual briskly sent me home when Sacha was only three days old this time. They obviously believed that the more kids you had the less time you deserved for lying about. With terse instructions to 'get into bed and take it easy for at least a week' I entered purgatory. As soon as 22 month old Tara — the pampered and adorable apple of her parents' eyes — got a glimpse of brand new, excitingly different, proud-faced and magnificently masculine Sacha she smiled, stroked him and begged to be allowed to touch and fondle him.

But as soon as he was settled comfortably on my lap in bed, propped up against the Porthault sheets, she became a raging mini nag. She wanted to be up there where he was. On the spot, looking over my shoulder whilst I attempted to feed the poor little mite, piteously meouing for his dinner. When I held him she wanted to be held, when I changed him, she wanted to be changed. Suddenly the potty training of the past six months went to pot. I couldn't let him sleep in a crib in our room as I had done with Tara in the early days, because *she* wanted to be allowed to sleep there too! So he slept downstairs with her and Renata. My German treasure obviously had cloth ears, for the children could cry and scream all night and she would not be roused. Staggering downstairs at 10.00 or 11.00 at night, Tony at the theatre, Renata dead to the world, I would carry the baby and drag little Tara by the hand up to my bedroom and try to placate them both. Tara got a cookie, Sacha got Mummie, if he was lucky. I was so exhausted he sometimes had to settle for a bottle. At 3.00 or 4.00 am the same thing, and yet again at 9.00 or 10.00 in the morning. The only time Renata was conscious it seemed was between 11.00 in the morning and 9.00 at night. The poor girl needed her sleep — but so did I, and all this traipsing up and down the stairs was a strain. After a week I woke up one morning feeling like death. The doctor, on examining me, came right to the point.

'You're lucky,' he said. 'A few years ago this disease carried them off like flies, in the wards.'

'What disease?' I said weakly. I had never felt worse.

'Puerperal fever — or childbed fever as it's called now,' he said briskly, injecting me with some wonder drug. 'Yes it's a terrible thing my dear — *was* a terrible thing I should say, only ten per cent survived. We don't see much of it nowadays — only . . .' He looked at me suspiciously, 'with those mothers who *do too much*.' He looked quite accusing, 'Have you been doing too much young woman?' I nodded weakly. 'Keep the children away from her. It can be dangerous to the baby,' he told Newberg, 'and better get a nurse for her and a new nanny for the children no doubt.' He had caught a glimpse of frail, white-faced Renata, hovering on the landing clutching a whimpering Tara by the hand. And Sacha's demanding yells for lunch were issuing from the downstairs bedroom.

The new nanny turned out to be a capable treasure. We stayed on in New York for a few more months. We were friends with a girl who had become the toast of New York in *Funny Girl*, Barbra Streisand and her husband, Elliot Gould. Elliot was a good actor but finding it hard to get work. His wife's astonishing and well deserved success had not rubbed off on him yet, and he was in the unenviable position of being 'Mr Streisand' to the hordes of fans who clustered around her stage door each night and inundated her with their idolatry. Barbra did not take too kindly to giving her autograph. She would sweep disdainfully through the crowds to her waiting limousine and rarely deign to scribble her signature. We had seen her just a year and a half earlier at the Blue Angel club where she was starting out, and the magnificence of her vocal talent, and originality as a performer swept New York instantly. She became a 'must see' for anyone and everyone. Barbra and Tony had a mutual admiration society together. They were similar in temperament — high-strung, hard working, dedicated to the perfection of their craft. We often had dinner together after their curtains had fallen, talking and laughing and joking late into the night. With her eloquent Romanesque nose, bouffant hair and porcelain skin, her unusual, sometimes quaint and kinky, and sometimes the highest of haute couture clothes, she was an imposing and arresting looking woman, and made more so by her exceptional, extraordinary talent. She was about to make her first movie *Funny Girl* and questioned me at length about make-up techniques and all matters pertaining to motion pictures. She was like Brando with her thirst for knowledge. Her mind was a sponge — it soaked up everything and she had an intense desire to learn and improve herself in every way.

I found these qualities admirable and enviable. My mind was more like a sieve — the more that went in the more went instantly out with the vegetable water. Although I was an avid reader, and went to the theatre, concerts and movies constantly, I still, due to my mercurial tendencies, was hard pushed to remember anything I had read, seen or listened to, for more than a couple of weeks afterwards. I could learn an entire script in an hour — memorise it by heart — and a month later not a line would I remember. Same with crews — I knew all the names in two days — a year later — 'who dat?'

Negotiations had begun for Tony to appear in a major musical for my old alma mater, Twentieth Century-Fox. It was to be a mammoth spectacle for which Leslie Bricusse was writing the book and lyrics. It was *Dr Doolittle* from the favourite children's book by Hugh Lofting. Rex Harrison was playing Doolittle and Tony was excited about being in such an important production. He wanted to act in films now — to direct and to write. He vowed that in 'Greasepaint' this would be the last time he would appear theatrically.

We took the train to California. It took three days. Newley wrote, and I stared at the scenery and his mother. Tara loved dashing through the carriages and stopping at all the stations to buy souvenirs. At two and a half she was a tiny, beautiful little girl. Bright, funny and alive, and wonder of wonders she and her baby brother actually *liked* each other!

Tony was perfectly content to reside in the rented house in Bel Air that Leslie had found for us — but I insisted we *had* to have our own house. We could not keep on dashing all over the globe, with two children, seventy-four suitcases, nannies, mothers-in-law and crates of books and records in storage all over the world. I didn't have a dress without permanent creases all over it.

I started to look at houses in Beverly Hills. Tony was working on another project. Tara started nursery school, Sacha was well taken care of by Rosie our nanny, and I suddenly felt rather useless. I started to think about work, and my career — which had been sublimated for over three years with the exception of the Italian film — began to become important to me again. Maybe this was because I was once again living in Hollywood, where everyone eats, sleeps and breathes motion pictures. Television now was a major industry force, instead of the poor relation to the movies it had been during my days at Fox. The William Morris Office contacted me. Would I be interested in doing some guest shots on TV in various dramatic shows? Why not indeed? I looked as good as, if not better, than when I arrived in Hollywood ten years previously, and I certainly was a better and more experienced actress. If I was going to continue acting at all I had better start now by stretching myself and getting back in the saddle again.

It's too easy not to work, to let things slide and 'think about that tomorrow'. Suddenly tomorrow arrives, and it's too late, baby. People in the motion picture industry have memories as short as matchsticks. I had made a series of mediocre to good films a few years ago, and then evaporated to England and New York, in virtual retirement as far as they were concerned. It wasn't going to be particularly easy to get back anything like the position I had had before. A whole new generation of actresses had arrived — Candice Bergen, Julie Christie, Faye Dunaway, Raquel Welch, Samantha Eggar, Barbra Streisand. These were the stars of the mid-to-late-sixties. As far as America was concerned I was practically an unknown again.

'Who's that pretty girl?'

'Oh that's Anthony Newley's wife — didn't she used to be an actress?'

'Oh yeah — Joan something-or-other. Whatever happened to her?'

Stardom had never been something I strove to obtain. I enjoyed acting tremendously. The creation, portrayal and characterisation of another being. I loved the studios, wandering in the back lots, awed by incredibly complicated and minutely detailed sets that still remained standing after years. They were used over and over again in movies and then in the ubiquitous TV shows. (This was before studios got ambitious and started shooting everything on location.)

When Tony and I lunched at the Fox commissary I was amazed at what had happened to the giant back lot. It had been sold for an astronomical fee — no doubt to pay back to the stockholders some of Fox's debts, a few of which surely must have arisen from the turkeys I had appeared in. I felt a strong need to work again, even if only in a lesser way. I knew my energy and enthusiasm should be channelled into some sort of creative direction. If not acting then interior decorating or perhaps writing. Much as I adored my children I knew that I was not the sort of woman to whom home, hearth and family was the be all and end all of existence. Tony, whilst not discouraging me, was so absorbed in what he was doing that it was preferable to him to have me occupied and out of the way often enough so that he could concentrate on his writing. Tara and Sacha had Rosie Riggs, their fresh-faced English nannie, to look after them and, although I adored playing with and being with my children, the day to day grind of cooking, washing-up, changing nappies and feeding was no longer as enthralling as it had been at the beginning.

Ah fickle Gemini! Only another Gemini can truly understand the vagaries of the Mercury-ruled mind. The compulsion to do too much — to take on too many projects and not finish them — to be able to do six things at once and still have time for one more — the way the mind flitters like a butterfly from one subject to another, from one project to another — and — oh, evil thought — from one man to another.

We are the 'butterfly' sign of the zodiac — we are youthful in spirit, and often in body, we are open to the new — the novel, the unexpected. Routine is the killer for the Mercurial sign, and much as I hated to admit it, I needed the stimulation that acting gave me.

The signs had been in the air for some time that Tony was perhaps not the most faithful of husbands. Even when he stayed with my father during the time I was filming in Italy I heard rumours that he was on the town several times in the company of various young dollies and with his friend and partner in crime, the redoubtable 'O.F.', a gentleman of somewhat sinister and oriental appearance who specialised in finding little things to make Tony happy. I knew that girls had been phoning him at Harley House while I was away, but like all things that upset me I did my Scarlett O'Hara act and 'thought about it tomorrow'. It certainly was an excellent device for me to avoid dealing with the realities of misery and disappointment and unhappiness. By putting off the moment when I had to analyse and evaluate a particular situation, I successfully managed to never have to think about it all. Even the most traumatic experience of my life — the death of my mother — I did not completely realise and mourn for until several years later.

It was, and is of course, a great way of getting through life as happily as possible, and, for an actress whose lot is often heartbreak, rejection and frustration it kept me sane. But marital problems must be sorted out. Festering sores should be discussed, however painful. Tony's ostrich, head-in-sand attitude, not wanting to rock the boat and to keep everything on an even keel, and my 'keep it on ice for another day' attitude, guaranteed that important issues in our marriage were buried as deep as the Pharaoh's treasure.

Of course we talked, discussed, sorted out, even argued in a very mild way, but he hated it. We never dug deep enough to explore our most intimate psyches and emotional problems, and in the end this lack of communication, added to his infidelity, began corroding our marriage.

In New York while crossing the street one night in the pouring rain with my sister Jackie we almost got hit by a bus, because Tony darted ahead of us paying no heed to how *we* were crossing.

Later, when I told him off, he sulked for the rest of the evening. Consequently in the future to prevent the sulks I would not speak out and making no waves became the *modus operandi* of our marriage.

In his biography for *The Roar of the Greasepaint* in the programmes for that show, Leslie Bricusses' ended with '. . . and he is married to beautiful screen actress Yvonne Romain'. Tony's ended with no mention of his marriage and children at all. He thought it 'stupid', although practically all Broadway stars write down some details of their personal lives. Whenever I asserted myself with him he called me 'bossy' and a New York Yenta Housewife. He could not seem to understand that my feelings and ideas were of value too and each time we disagreed the gulf between us widened imperceptibly.

We went to live in California again. Once more the lure of the palm trees and the sweet smell of success beckoned us to tinsel town where I attempted to finally put down those longed for roots and make a permanent home for our two children.

Tara was now three, and old enough for nursery school and I desperately wanted her to have some stability in her life at last. Born in New York she had spent more than half her short life in hotel rooms all over America in the never ending *Greasepaint* tour, and the rest in rented houses and apartments everywhere from London to Paris, Rome, Portofino, Lugano, Liverpool, St Moritz — God, her passport looked like that of an international playgirl. I was determined she should have what most other little girls of her age have. A pretty nursery in which she could display her dolls, collected from all over the world, and to be able to play with her toys, secure in the knowledge that this was her *home* and here she would stay, hopefully for a long long time. Sacha, at one year old, was still too young to feel the effects of the constant changing of scenery but I knew that he, the most gorgeous hunk of blond curly-haired baby, needed his own security too.

Hollywood in the late sixties had not changed much from when I had first arrived ten years previously. The same lavish and star studded parties were still being given by the now diminishing ranks of the movie moguls. Darryl Zanuck was gone, and Fox was desperately trying to get itself back on its feet after horrendous losses over the past several years. Spyros Skouras — the wily old Greek — was dead, so was Lew Shrieber, my mentor and father confessor during my contract days. Harry Cohn, feared head of Columbia Studios who ruled the lives of Rita Hayworth and Kim

Novak with a rod or iron, was long gone, and his place had been taken by a corporate executive.

A young actor called Bob Evans, under contract to Fox at the same time as I, had taken over the reins at Paramount Studios and proved to be infinitely better at running a studio than he had been as an actor.

Jack Warner was still the boss at Warner Brothers, but the studio was in the process of changing its name and calling itself The Burbank Studios. Because so many independent productions — both TV and motion picture — used the Burbank lot they changed the name to a more non specific one, so as not to invite petty jealousies from other independent studios.

Universal, home of the tacky sand and sin pictures, was now the biggest force in television production. Strongly controlled by the redoubtable Lew Wasserman, former President of MCA and a shrewd and clever businessman to boot, Universal Inc had amalgamated with the octopus-like MCA agency which at one time seemed to represent ninety per cent of the top theatrical talent in America.

The contract system had virtually finished, except for the signing of likely prospects for TV series at salaries of around $200 a week, and now the big stars were commanding gigantic amounts of money to appear in movies. Newman, Steve McQueen, Barbra Streisand, Clint Eastwood, Charles Bronson . . . were superstars on a level not seen previously and their agents were now having unprecedented power with the studios. And what do you know, even my old ex-fiancé Warren Beatty was having a phenomenal success with *Bonnie and Clyde* which he produced and starred in, and was on his way to becoming a multi-millionaire. After his initial impact with *Splendour in the Grass* he had made a series of indifferent films, but now he was on the crest of superstardom, as well as becoming the most talked about stud in the Western Hemisphere. The shyly myopic, pimply-faced skinny boy, who had caused much mirth amongst my acquaintances when our romance had first started, was now a handsome, mysterious charismatic sexy movie star, and a brilliant producer to boot. He had become irresistible to throngs of girls and women. No woman 'twas said, could resist the blandishments of those baby blue short-sighted eyes. His charm and success with females of all ages had become a legend, and his prowess between the sheets was the subject of much Hollywood tittle-tattle. Although he had always had a 'live in lady' in his life, he apparently was able to cram in an endless amount of extra curricular activity, and was on his way to becoming the successor to Errol Flynn as a ladies man and lover *par excellence*.

'God, I must be the only woman in LA and New York that Warren hasn't tried to "shtup"!' said my agent Sue Mengers laughingly. It seemed to be true, although Warren was clever enough to never admit his conquests — thus was a legend born.

It was all coming true, just as my astrologer Ben Gary had predicted. Warren's fast rise to fame, fade-out for a few years and then wham-bam Charlie super-star stud, and thank you ma'm too. So was my marriage to 'actor-or-writer-or-director' Newley — he was all of those things. And there were the two children: Tara petite, Sacha husky, almost the same size and, since I often dressed them alike, they were often mistaken for twins. And the gypsy existence Ben predicted, that had also come true. I didn't want to think about his last prediction though, that my marriage would last seven years. We were barely making it through the fourth.

10

Libra and Gemini Haven't a Chance

The Daisy was a Beverly Hills discotheque that overnight became a mecca for everyone in town. Perhaps they were trying to compete with the 'Swinging Sixties' syndrome in London, but as the mini-skirt rode thigh high, and the gentlemen's hair began to curl gracefully over the collar, a dancing frenzy gripped Hollywood the like of which had not been seen since Joan Crawford charlestoned her way to fame in the 1920's movie *Her Dancing Daughters*.

Every night the Daisy was jammed with the beautiful and the trying to be beautiful people and the not-so beautiful people in Hollywood. Even Arthur Loew, arch enemy of the dance got married there. Starlets, agents, writers, producers' wives, flabby legs flashing madly beneath crocheted micro-minis, balding, breathless producers, all crammed on to the dance floor to 'dig the action', 'let it all hang out' (and it often did) or to sit and just watch. It was certainly interesting to observe. Much better than television. A sort of madness gripped everyone. Outrageous clothes and extraverted behaviour were suddenly the norm. No dinner party was complete without a trip to the Daisy afterwards. Everyone was doing the Monkey, the Funky Chicken or, for the older folk, the Bossa-Nova and the just-moving-it. It was sheer madness — but delightfully served.

Even Tony would occasionally deign to accompany me there, although he was now busy rehearsing for his role in *Dr Doolittle* and also writing a new script tentatively based (yet again!) on the story of his life. On the evenings when we had dinner together at home he would immediately return to his study after dinner to work on the script again, or to stare at the TV set with blank eyes. We had virtually no communication; he was completely wrapped up in himself, and anything else — even the children — seemed an intrusion.

213

I was not happy. The beautiful house in Beverly Hills, complete with pool and all mod cons, and the two gorgeous children, the light of my life, couldn't make up for the emptiness of my marriage. When, like pulling teeth, I managed to extract a conversation from him about our problems he would become irritated and talk about the immense problem he had in *himself* in relating and loving and giving. Yes, he loved me in his own way but what was I? An attractive stranger who shared his bed and to whom he said 'thank you' after making love. 'Thank you?' That was carrying British politeness too far.

'You don't have to thank me,' I exclaimed bitterly. 'I didn't make you a cup of tea!'

When we gave dinner parties I could never be sure he would attend. We had a sit-down dinner for fourteen in honour of Peter Sellers, which I had spent several days planning and organising. He pleaded a stomach ache and stayed in the bedroom, leaving thirteen for dinner, and me making excuses for him and getting fiercely drunk in front of a monosyllabic Sellers.

Newley started letting me go out on my own. He didn't like dinners or parties anyway, even though they were, as ever in Hollywood, part of the social scene, and so I would go out with a platonic man friend, or a couple, or a glamorous gay, and since I loved dancing I became a fixture at the Daisy.

A young man asked me to dance one night. He looked vaguely familiar: brawny, Irish blond, good looks, tall, a face like a handsome boxer, he looked as though he might get his nose broken one day, or maybe some of those perfect white teeth. He was obviously an actor, although tight blue jeans and a shirt open to mid-diaphragm showing a well-muscled chest didn't necessarily mean in Hollywood that he had to be. Physical perfection was the achievement of all in Beautiful Beverly Hills — agents, writers, producers. The gyms were full of them flexing well tanned biceps and heaving their way through fifty sit-ups a day. The hair stylists couldn't keep up with the demand for the romantically tousled long haired look, copied from 'swinging London'.

Ryan O'Neal had it all going for him in the looks department — and he wasn't lacking in the charm and humour department either. Or the dancing department, or the sex appeal department. He was the first man I'd been attracted to for a long long time. It was an interesting feeling, and we kept on dancing. Knowing looks were exchanged among the members of our group when he sat down with us after an energetic hour or so on the floor. Mick Jagger was singing 'I can't get no satisfaction'. It sounded like the title song of my marriage.

The fact I was married didn't seem to faze Ryan one bit He wanted my number, but I wouldn't give it to him. Tony would just love that. The double standard was rife in our household. OK for him — no-no for her. But Tony must have subconsciously realised that letting me go out alone two or three nights a week to the Daisy was asking for eventual trouble. A nun I had never been — only in the movies — and I liked, and needed attention. I certainly wasn't getting my ration of it at home.

Ryan was funny and endearing. He had an open boyish personality and a droll self-mocking attitude towards himself. He was part Irish — with a name like O'Neal what else — married and divorced and had coincidentally two children Tatum and Griffin the same age and sex as my two. What fun — he could bring them over to the house and we could all go swimming together. One day, maybe. That was a fantasy because attractive and cute and sexy as he was, my marriage vows still meant a lot to me, and I was not going to open up this can of beans, however inviting the label.

The next afternoon idly flipping channels to find cartoons for the kiddies I came across him again, all teeth and brawn, being boyish and sincere with Mia Farrow in the serial 'Peyton Place'. I watched with interest. He had definite star quality. I had believed in my forte for being a good casting director. I could pick a winner, and this boy had charisma, (and great pectorals). It flashed across the screen, along with sizzling sex appeal, even with the banal plots and dialogue of 'Peyton Place'. I sighed and switched the channel to the cartoons the children were clamouring for. That was forbidden fruit.

I hankered to play the main female role in *Dr Doolittle* — that of the haughty British belle who falls for the Cockney-Irish charm of Newley, but although this was a Fox film produced by our friend Arthur Jacobs they didn't think I was right and the part went to Samantha Eggar. My movie career appeared to be kaput in Hollywood. Although I received scripts from England, Italy and Spain I could not get a film part in the States. I'd been away too long and was no longer a new face. Thank you Warren. Thank you Tony. She gave it all up for love. Shmuck! But television offers came aplenty. I had my pick of the top shows and I accepted most of them. Now I could be a wife, a mother and an actress all at once. A neat little package deal. I was trying to please Tony but I really wasn't pleasing myself because guesting on episodic TV shows was not tremendously fulfilling. Most of the movies I'd made had not been too fulfilling either, but the plots and the actors were better.

The truth was I enjoyed working — why did I feel pangs of guilt when I admitted it? Why wasn't I just content, like most of the young Beverly Hills matrons I knew, to be a faithful wife (albeit an ignored one) and a dutiful mother? Content to run the house with my trusty Portuguese couple, lie by the pool and ruin my skin and then go to the facialist, and the dermatologist to repair it; go to the analyst, the hairdresser, the manicurist, the gynaecologist, the numerologist, the group therapy session, the tennis lessons, the tap dancing classes, the Kaffee Klatches, the hen party lunches, the backgammon games and the beach — Why? Why? Why?? Young Beverly Hills matrons had a *slew* of things to do with their day.

Apart from the above there was always *shopping* — a major occupation for a Californian lady of leisure. God forbid one didn't pop into Saks or Magnins at least once a week and blow thirty or forty dollars on some new lipsticks and skin creams, meander upstairs to 'lingerie' and buy a few cute robes at eighty or ninety dollars a piece, and top it off with a bauble or two from the cut price jewellers on Beverly Drive. A solid gold his 'n hers key for 'their' house — a solid gold 'ankh' for good luck, very popular that year, everyone was wearing them, or the latest rip-off from Tiffanys — whatever it was. Money well spent meant time well spent. Certainly the average 'nut' of the moderately wealthy was close to a quarter of a million dollars a year. The proceeds of the toil of the business men and actors in this town went through their wife's sieves as fast as it came in. The men dropped dead of heart attacks and stress younger and younger, whilst their widows pushed, pulled, tucked, trimmed and taped (no-one over sixty-five ever looked a day over forty), collected the insurance money and paid it over and over again to Saks and Magnins, and the boutiques on Rodeo Drive.

I wondered why everyone had such huge closets overflowing with finery never worn, when the usual invitation was 'Come to dinner but don't bother to dress'! But there were moans and groans of anguished protest if a brave hostess had the temerity to suggest 'Come to dinner — black tie'! It was a paradox I couldn't fathom. Why did they buy all these clothes if they never wore them? Everyone looked more or less the same. The teens, the twenties, and the actresses in jeans and T-shirts, the thirties and forties in linen pants and silk shirts, the over forties in polyester

216

and dacron permapress pant suits, with plenty of co-ordinated accessories. I sat in Century City shopping complex one day, one of the few places in LA where people walked about and watched the people busy as bees doing their daily thing — shopping.

I surveyed my large closet, choc-full of the latest in ladies' outer wear. I didn't need a thing. I had everything to wear. I didn't want to learn to play tennis, backgammon or tap dancing. I didn't intend to ruin my skin at the beach or pool, didn't need the analyst and the gynaecologist and didn't believe in numerology or group therapy sessions. Girls' lunches I liked, but once or twice a week was enough. I wanted to work — the roar of the greasepaint — lights, cameras, action! The need for these things never leaves you.

So I worked. I did 'The Man from Uncle' with my ex-classmate from RADA, David McCallum; and 'Batman' — that was a kick — I still get residuals today; and 'Mission Impossible' with stalwart Martin Landau and impeccably groomed Barbara Bain (the hairdresser combed her hair 109 times a day). And 'Star Trek', the cult show of all time. The one I did became the most popular. As Edith Cleaver, a young mission worker for down-and-outs in [*Keeler!*] New York in the Depression, I try to prove to the world that Hitler was OK. Bill Shatner as Captain Kirk falls in love with me, and Dr Spock — he of the ears — allows me to get run over by a [*Mr!*] truck, lest my teachings lead the world to total destruction. Good clean fun.

In the evenings I came home and frolicked with the children, and Tony and I gazed sombrely at each other across our Wedgwood dinner service.

One night I got out all the letters we had written to each other and read them. Yes, I had really tried. My letters were full of love and care, compassion and understanding. 'Please try and understand me,' I cried out in red ink on Beverly Hills Hotel notepaper. 'The only thing I want is for us to be together — to communicate with each other — I understand your problems — I want to help you — I love you — please let's not blow it.'

It was food for thought. Try as I might, the contact, the humanness, the oneness, the communication weren't there. Had they ever been?

I gazed at my perfectly made-up face in the dressing table mirror. Flawless skin, helped along by Revlon, Clinique and Estee Lauder; arresting green eyes, all the better for double sets of eyelashes from the Eyelure company; and a weak chin. I narrowed my eyes and gazed at my chin; yes, it was definitely the chin of a coward and a weakling; a person unable to make decisions, solve problems or obtain the love of her husband. I slammed the make-up drawer shut and stalked in to my tender loving husband. He was curled up on the sofa in his study, wearing his usual black sweater, grey flannels and, for Christ's sake, a plaid blanket covering him up to the chin! It was already May!

'We're late,' I said sternly, as he looked wearily up from the script of *Dr Doolittle* he was studying. 'We're late for Arthur's party.' Since Arthur was Arthur P. Jacobs the producer of *Dr Doolittle* I expected him to attend this one.

'Sorry Flower,' he said, a smile attempting to flit across his face and failing. 'I'm beat. Why don't you call Brickman and Eve and go with them?' He sighed and turned back to his script. The troubles of the world seemed to sit on his bony shoulders, and I didn't feel like shaking them.

'OK,' I said flatly, not showing any of the emotion that he so detested. 'Arthur won't be too pleased you know. After all you are one of his stars, and Rex and Samantha and Dick Fleischer will be there — are you sure you're too tired?'

'I'm exhausted luv,' he rubbed his eyes and yawned as though to emphasise his fatigue. His face did look white and strained — but then he never took the sun. Probably too much time at the office with the cute secretary, I thought, evilly.

'Go on Flower, have a good time. I'll see you in the morning.' He gave another sigh — I knew he wanted me out of there. We brushed cheeks together and he went back to his script and I went to make my by now inevitable phone call to the Bricusses.

After Arthur's party it was Daisy time. I hadn't been for several weeks, but even the usual excitement that the place generated couldn't get me out of my depressed lethargy. I gloomily sipped a Brandy Alexander and surveyed the frenetic scene. Legs, legs, legs — a veritable forest of them, kicking and stomping and pirouetting to the latest Beatles and Stones and Supremes discs. With every song that was played I seemed to be able to find some special meaning in its title. 'Can't buy me lo-ove' sang McCartney and Lennon, their young voices cascading in a crescendo. 'She loves you — yeah, yeah, yeah,' they wailed and I cynically yeah yeah'd myself into my third Brandy Alexander. She loves *you* all right, although it's evaporating rapidly these days. As if to answer my thoughts Newley's voice crooned over the sound system the words to his most famous song, and the one which made me realise now what he was all about:

What kind of fool am I
Who never fell in love
It seems that I'm the only one that I have been thinking of
What kind of man is this?
An empty shell
A lonely cell in which an empty heart must dwell.
What kind of lips are these
That lied with every kiss
That whispered empty words of love
That left me alone like this
Why can't I fall in love?
Like any other man?
And then I'll know
What kind of fool I am?'

My eyes misted over. The words applied to him totally. I had *known* it though. He had warned me what he was, but I had thought my love could change all that. What kind of fool was *I*?

'Like to dance?' Ryan stood there looking arrogant and nervous at the same time. I got up.

'Sure.'

'Haven't seen you around lately.'

We gyrated in front of each other amidst the flashing lights and the flashing legs.

'I've been working a lot,' I explained, now caught up in the music and the dancing. It started to blow the blues away. Jagger was intoning suggestively 'Under my thumb'. It was good. He was good. Ryan looked *very* good. Just what the doctor ordered for a dissatisfied wife. We danced the rest of the night away. Blues, Brazilian, fast, slow — he had enormous energy, and he had to be on the set of 'Peyton Place' at seven in the morning.

He was an Aries — that's where the vitality came from. They were very compatible with Gemini because of their tremendous energy.

My group left. We danced on — it was closing time. Ridiculous early Californian licensing laws dictated that all drinks must be off the table by 1.45. I, like the song said, could've danced all night. He insisted on driving me home, after I insisted on not going up to his apartment on Doheny Drive for a nightcap.

'I bet you've got etchings there,' I joked feebly.

'No, just 8 x 10 glossies,' he twinkled.

I was nervous in the car going home. God forbid Newley decided to look out of the window and see his dutiful wife arriving home at two in the morning with a goodlooking blond actor.

'Give me your number,' he said urgently as we approached the driveway. 'We can have lunch, or tea. You English ladies always have tea don't you?' His blue eyes twinkled. He was definitely adorable. But trouble. Trouble I did not need.

'Bloody liar,' said the inner voice of Joan Collins. 'Do you a world of good.' I took *his* number and promised to call him sometime.

'Promise!' he leaned over the steering wheel to kiss me and I avoided it as if he had foot and mouth disease.

'I promise, I promise. Cross my heart and hope to die,' I said hastily, saying the first thing that came into my head.

'I'll be waiting then,' he called and the little sports car made a 100 degree turn, a screech of brakes and was off down the hill.

I didn't call. I couldn't. I wasn't a teenager calling a boy for an innocent date. If I called him it meant I wanted to go to bed with him. He knew that, and I knew that, and I was a Sadie-Sadie married lady, even if it wasn't a perfectly great marriage and my husband thought about fifteen-year-old girls when we were making love.

I had had my fill of other men, and running around and getting involved, bruised and rejected — those were the bad things — but aah, the good things! For sheer out and out, heart in mouth, appetite killing excitement, nothing replaced the opening act of a new relationship.

Newley went to New York for a few days and I went to work at Universal guesting on 'Run for your Life' with Ben Gazzara. It was the usual cops and robbers shoot 'em up TV trash, and I played the usual beautiful villainous spy with a heart of brass.

Tara came to visit one day, and after watching a scene in which an actor screams at me angrily for not being a good enough spy, or whatever the hell I was supposed to be, her baby voice piped up indignantly: 'Don't you talk to my Mummy like that you rude man!' The crew broke up — Tara was showing her mettle at an early age.

Ryan showed up and dragged me to lunch at a Chinese restaurant on Ventura Boulevard, where for forty-five minutes he was captivating, witty, and triumphant that we were lunching at last. He was enormously appealing in a roguish way. Not to be taken seriously by any means but he had all the sparkle that was lacking in Tony's personality. He positively glittered with exuberance and enthusiasm.

'What about dinner?' he said as we drove through the gates of Lew Wasserman's big black glass film factory.

'Never,' I said faintly and unconvincingly.

'What are you doing tomorrow?' He never gave up. The butterfly in me liked that. His net was always out.

'Tomorrow's my birthday and Tony's coming back from New York. We'll probably celebrate with a hot dog in front of the TV set,' I said firmly, surprised by the bitterness in my voice.

'I'll call and wish you happy birthday then.' I jumped out and went back to Ben Gazzara and Co, feeling lighthearted. He made me feel good.

Tony never did make it back in time for my birthday. Whatever it was that he was doing in New York was taking longer than expected. He sent a large bunch of flowers and a gift wrapped automobile which, since it was rented from a car-hire firm, did not belong to me at all, but it looked cute — the little white Mustang sitting in the driveway with a vast red ribbon perched on the hood.

'Happy Birthday English lady — where's your husband taking you tonight?' said the husky familiar tones, the sound of which were by now making me somewhat weak in the knees, and I didn't want the crew of 'Run for Your Life' to notice that.

'He's not,' I said simply, 'He's stuck in the Big Apple, with only his record producer for company.'

'Oh you poor kid,' he clucked sympathetically. 'Well . . . er . . . we wouldn't want you to be alone on your birthday would we?'

'No we wouldn't.' There was a pregnant pause, I suddenly decided what I wanted for my birthday present. A girl should get the best she deserves on her birthday. And he was.

A few weeks later my sister Jackie married for the second time, Oscar Lerman, an American businessman. Her first husband had died in tragic circumstances and I really hoped that now she would find the happiness she truly deserved. Certainly it had eluded me most of my life. Oh yes, there had been passion and infatuation and what, for months or sometimes years, had passed for love, but as I stood behind Jackie and Oscar at the simple wedding ceremony at our house I realised definitively that nobody had ever really loved *me*. I know I had loved *them* — some of them — and they had professed to love me, but when the chips were down none of it had meant a damn thing. But *I* had picked these men, hand picked them — for what? I had had dozens of choices and I'd usually picked a bummer. A guy whose interests were always self-serving.

And I knew why too — that was the irony of it. I *had* to pick the toughies — the ones who couldn't, wouldn't, didn't know *how* to commit. The guys who cheated on their wives but wouldn't leave them, who used women on their climb up the ladder, who basically hated the whole bloody female sex. And *why, why* did I do it? To get Daddy. That's why. Because he was remote, and cool and undemonstrative. I never felt he loved me or cared. If I could get an impossible man to fall in love with me (because underneath all the façade we are all still seven years old) *then* I could say, 'Wow! I really made it. I'm a worthwhile person at last.'

If I had any guts I'd end my marriage to Newley. His love for me was as shallow as a pan of water. He professed a lot of love when I was being a good little, sweet little, warm little, home loving obedient Joanie — Flower. But let me show one of the other sides. The strong side, the determined side, the aggressive side, the argumentative side and he couldn't *stand* me — and he admitted it. And it was the same with all the others. Total false adoration when I was behaving myself and no understanding at all when I wasn't what they wanted me to be.

God knows I had my faults, and I knew them. But show me a faultless person and I'll show you a bore.

I decided to go back to my shrink, who I thought I had quit for good when I met Newley, and sort myself out again.

Newley left for England and *Dr Doolittle* locations. I stayed on for a few weeks. I was rather enjoying being an adulteress — that wonderful biblical word. Ryan was a terrific, imaginative and inventive lover. In fact inventiveness was one of his strong suits. He had a tiny apartment on Doheny Drive not far from where Nick Hilton had lived, and the afternoons absolutely flew by.

Several people suspected the relationship by now since, although we had been discreet, we had been in each other's company often. We daringly went to dinner with newly-wed Lermans — but I realised I was playing it too close to home when I read the blind item in a gossip column one morning:

Mr X, talented British born performer seems unaware that his sexy actress wife Mrs X is doing more than just polishing her dance steps with handsome Mr Z, up and coming star of one of America's favourite soap operas . . .

'Nobody ever looks at the face of a nun!' My last line in the film *Sea Wife*. 1956.

TWENTIETH CENTURY FOX

TOP LEFT: Shipwrecked on a desert island with Kenneth More in *Our Girl Friday*, 1954. TOP RIGHT: Bob Hope, Bing Crosby and Dorothy Lamour's replacement on *The Road to Hong Kong*, 1962. BOTTOM LEFT: With June Allyson in *The Opposite Sex*, 1956. BOTTOM RIGHT: *The Virgin Queen* with Richard Todd and Bette Davis, 1955.

TWENTIETH CENTURY FOX

I.T.C.

PETER W. DICKENSON

TOP LEFT: With Robert Mitchum in the 1977 remake of *The Big Sleep*. TOP RIGHT: In *Rally Round the Flag Boys*, 1958 — my favourite comedy role. BOTTOM LEFT: *The Man who came to Dinner* with Orson Welles in the title role. For N.B.C. Television, 1973. BOTTOM RIGHT: With Susannah York in Noël Coward's *Fallen Angels*, 1974.

SANDERSON-SCOPE

EDDIE SANDERSON

RON KASS

TOP: With 'Starsky and Hutch' alias Paul Michael Glaser and David Soul. BOTTOM LEFT: Four patriotic English ladies. Jane Seymour, me, Juliet Mills and Samantha Eggar celebrate the Queen's Silver Jubilee, and my own twenty-five years in movies. BOTTOM RIGHT: Hard at work trying to fit in time to write this book! — whilst on location in Hawaii for 'Starsky and Hutch', 1977.

TERRY O'NEIL

Party time! London, 1974. FROM LEFT TO RIGHT: Alice Cooper, Ryan O'Neal, Dewi Sukarno, Tessa Kennedy, Princess Fyrial of Jordan, Roger and Luisa Moore, Fiona Lewis. SITTING: Tatum O'Neal, Ron and me, Marisa Berenson.

TOP LEFT: Pregnant . . . TOP RIGHT: Married . . . BOTTOM: 'Our gang' — his, hers and theirs. The cast, clockwise from the bottom of the picture: Sacha, David Kass, Jonathan Kass, Tara, Ron, Robert Kass and me with sweet, six-week-old Katyana Kass — Marbella, 1972.

EDDIE SANDERSON

EDDIE SANDERSON

DAVID STEENE

How things have changed! Making movies today often involves dropping one's inhibitions, along with one's clothes, and having lots of physical stamina. TOP LEFT: Trying to keep the goose bumps from showing and putting on a happy face for *The Moneychangers*, 1976. TOP RIGHT: In the midst of the Florida swamps for H. G. Wells' *Empire of the Ants*, 1977. My feet and legs got covered with infected cuts, in spite of the elegant Wellingtons! BOTTOM: A somewhat more unusual way of swinging than the way it was in *The Girl in the Red Velvet Swing*. With Mark Burns in *The Stud*, 1978.

TERRY O'NEILL

TOP LEFT: Oliver Tobias as 'The Stud' — London, 1978. TOP RIGHT: Another Gemini — Katyana Kennedy Kass visiting Mummy on the set of *The Stud*, January 1978. Another future actress? BOTTOM: Sisterly collaboration on *The Stud*. Jackie wrote it and I was in it.

Oh my God — if *she* knew about it, that meant it was almost in public domain. Although I knew of Tony's infidelity I didn't particularly relish him becoming the town cuckold.

I packed the bags, the children and the nanny and flew to join him in London. My little fling was over, I had to now really work out whether there was any hope or life left in our marriage before the rot totally set in — for my sanity and for the sake of our precious children.

Rumblings had obviously reached Tony about Ryan. He had in fact brought Tatum and Griffin up to swim several times. He did as many tricks with them in the pool as he came up with in bed. People weren't blind. We'd been seen together often. Tony wasn't stupid and he had obviously realised my dissatisfaction and the possibility of losing me. He was aware I was highly attractive to men, more now than in my Rank and Fox days. He made a genuine effort to become the loving husband he had been at the beginning, and we sailed through the next year on more or less calm water.

With Paul Newman, Sammy Davis, Peter Lawford, our friend Ronnie Buck and two or three other businessmen Tony went into the discotheque business. 'The Factory' became an overnight sensation. It was on the top floor of an old disused factory on Robertson Drive, and decorated in a melange of Art Deco, Art Nouveau, English antiques, stained-glass windows and flashing disco lights. With a live band augmenting the recorded sounds it was flash, fun and fabulous. The opening night was jammed with major celebrities from Hollywood. The huge dance floor was immovable. Word gets around fast in Hollywood, and at 350 dollars membership, everybody wanted to join and did. Night after night the most illustrious and glamorous people — people who had never ever set foot in a disco before — sat and stared at the incredible goings on. Marlon Brando was there, Barbra Streisand, Steve McQueen, Loretta Young, Liza Minelli, Dean Martin, Peter Sellers, Bobby Kennedy, Vanessa Redgrave — a veritable who's who couldn't do it justice.

We couldn't believe how quickly the success happened and just as quickly as it happened it faded. Too much too soon. Goodbye Sweet Factory. In a little less than a year its vogue had passed — just like many a Hollywood career, and we were back in London again.

Tony was achieving his life's desire to write, direct and star in an erotic musical-comedy-fantasy, based on his life story — *one more time!* It was succinctly call *Can Hieronymus Merkin ever forget Mercy Humpe and find true Happiness?* and it was an avant garde satirical movie about a successful actor-director (Newley-Merkin) who, at the age of thirty-eight, sits miserable and bitter on the beach outside his Beverly Hills mansion screening a montage of film clips from his life, whilst showing them to his two tiny children and his old Cockney mother. His main fantasy in the film revolved around a deliciously nubile sixteen-year-old blonde, Mercy, for whom he has been searching all his life. He considers her his suppressed desire, the penultimate sexual object and complete female. A divine child goddess. She is of course a slave to his every whim. He is torn between his love for her and for the beautiful, headstrong, raven-haired Polyester Poontang who becomes the mother of his two children and goes through the film putting up with his philandering with every Jane, June and Jenny who crosses his path or, as they were more poetically named, Filigree Fondle, Trampolina Wham Bang, and Maidenhair Fern!

Incredibly I decided I had to play this part. Who, more than I, could play it better? Since our two children — now four and a half and two and a half — had been cast at the insistence of Tony as the film's children, Thumbelina and Thaxted, I would have to be in London and Malta in any case for four or five months, being a stage mum.

Tony wrote a song for Polyester to sing to Hieronymus. It was a good song and he even dedicated it to me since it was based absolutely on us. Before the song there was a symbolic scene where the two meet for the first time. Polyester looks at the mask (Newley — Merkin's alter ego) and says:

POLYESTER
(sympathetic as she looks at
THE MASK)
Typical Libra. You bruise so easily.
HIERONYMUS
(leering to himself)
Typical Gemini . . . you gonna get it.
(They stare at each other in a kind of mutual fascination.)
POLYESTER
You realize, of course, we have absolutely nothing in common . . .
And POLYESTER sings.

Libra and Gemini Haven't a Chance

How did you get into my horoscope
You funny irascible lovable dope.
Isn't it clear from the stars that you haven't
a hope with me?
Anyone else would have known in advance,
Libra and Gemini haven't a chance.
Anyone else would have seen at a glance it could
never be —
Chalk and Cheese we're as different as Chalk and
Cheese.
Were there ever two people more out of step before
More unalike if you please
Souls apart, we are opposite, poles apart.
When I think about me and you saying, how do you do?
Maybe it wasn't so smart.
Me, I'm bright, got a groovy scene.
I like to be where it's at!
You're up-tight as a tambourine
What kind of music is that?
Chalk and Cheese — who would ever blend things
like these?
On the other hand people say love is here to stay
Hurray for the birds and the bees!
I'm a fool maybe — but I don't mind chalk with
my cheese.

I performed this little ditty clad in a clinging white Grecian gown, whilst Tony (talk about upstaging) wore nothing except a giant toy key sticking out of the bottom of his spine since he was playing his alter ego and a man next to him with a completely blank face was dressed in his clothes. A motley selection of hankies and camera tape covered his full frontal which was never actually revealed to the camera in this scene — but which one could catch glimpses of later in the sensuous graphic underwater love scenes with the virginal Miss Humpe, played by flaxen-haired *Playboy* centrefold Connie Kreski after a search rivalling that of the quest for Scarlett O'Hara.

Tony and Connie became extremely close on this movie. Since she was a novice on the film set he obviously had to coach her a lot, and they spent many an hour together on and off the set going over their scenes.

She, however, was not the only pebble on the beaches of Malta. Women featured heavily in Hieronymus Merkin's life and there were dozens and dozens of girls to be interviewed, talked to, coached, rehearsed, prepared, and built up for the many roles in the film.

I was beginning to get an inkling, yet again, as to why when Tony took the lease on an office he insisted he always had a bedroom attached to it. Casting couch be damned! Who needed that when a comfy double bed was next door. I had a sick horrible feeling when I first read the script of *H.M.* He seemed to have spelt out the death of our marriage with this totally revealing picture of his life, and how little he cared for me.

Hieronymus has a sidekick producer and mentor, Good Time Eddie Filth (Milton Berle), who encourages him in his philanderings. Newley-Merkin has a scene where he sits on top of the mountain having the following dialogue with God —

There has never been a woman who commanded a moment of my regard after I'd made love to her. I realise I have no respect for women — I really believe I hate them, and take my revenge in sex. The ritual murder, forever stabbing and re-opening the divine wound.

After this speech Good Time Eddie dressed as Satan, officiates at a ceremony in which dozens of robed candle-holding monks surround an altar bed on which lies a naked woman. Hieronymus is ceremoniously derobed and mounts both the altar and the girl to ritual moans.

The finale of the movie finds Hieronymus at dawn, still on the beach surrounded by his paraphernalia — skips, wardrobe hampers, sky high cans of film and scrapbooks, mementoes of his career, and his whirring projector. The two kids are asleep on Grandma's knee. Hieronymus sings a plaintive ballad summing up his misery and disillusionment with life. It was called 'I'm all I need':

I'm all I need, if I got me — I got rainbows
If I got me — just you see how the rain goes away
'Cos I've got somebody who cares
Someone who likes my company
While I've got me — I've got a sky full of blue birds
When did you see someone as lucky as me?

He continues in this vein and as the song finishes a squad car approaches on the beach and disgorges two Los Angeles cops and

226

a distraught Polyester-Joan who has been calling throughout the movie for her husband.

She rushes towards him, gathering Thaxted-Sacha in her arms and Thumbelina-Tara by her tiny hands and a torrent of words pour out. 'Darling are you *crazy* . . . have you been here all night . . . I've been calling . . . didn't you hear me calling? I didn't know what to think. I called the police. Your agent called the police, I called the hospital. You do this sort of thing, you do it all the time. You don't think and you don't care. Well I've had enough. I'm taking the children — yes I am — I'm taking them back to Europe and this time I mean it. This time I *really do mean it* — I really do.' Exit Polyester-Joan sobbing hysterically, Thaxted-Sacha, and Thumbelina-Tara, leaving Hieronymus-Newley unmoved and slightly puzzled.

The playing of this scene affected me so violently that during and after each take a positive torrent of real tears and anguish burst forth — all the tears and the anger I had been hiding for six years. It was true. Our marriage was badly cracked, and when I finally saw the film in a private screening room in London a few months later I knew there was no hope for us ever to live normally together again.

11

Aries and Gemini Have!

'This is Ron Kass.'

My heart did a couple of flip flops. It had done so before, of course, but this was a definite lurch. The man sitting on the couch in my living room in London was a devastatingly attractive American — tall, fair hair worn happily somewhat shorter than the current vogue for shoulder-length locks, amazing green eyes in a deeply tanned face, an extremely sensual mouth and a warm, open and endearing smile. He was a sartorial dream, in a beige suit and black sweater — dressed, I guessed correctly by our introducer, the tailor Doug Hayward, who had been a close friend of Tony's and mine ever since Evie Bricusse and I used to go with our respective husbands to his tailoring shop, then in shabby Shepherds Bush, and shock the hell out of the staff by being in the changing rooms with Tony and Leslie whilst they were fitting. We 'oohed' and 'aahed' in breathless girlie voices whilst the customers listened horrified to the scandalous goings on of these flighty 'show-biz types'. Now Doug was the trendy top tailor of the Swinging Sixties London set, with a chic emporium in elegant Mount Street, near Park Street, where Newley and I were temporarily living whilst he cut and edited *Hieronymus Merkin*, and hello, hello! a mere two blocks away from elegant South Street where Ron resided. We were all within a stone's throw of each other, were we of a mind to throw stones, which indeed I was not after meeting the extremely attractive Mr Kass.

We had dinner at the Club dell Aretusa, the fashionable Italian restaurant-disco on Kings Road, where rock stars rubbed shoulders with MPs and debutantes, models, managers, photographers, and actresses clustered nightly. Wall to wall glamour. Anybody who was anybody was usually there and it was a heady and amusing place.

Evie Bricusse was Doug's 'date' for the evening, I was with

Tony, and Ron was alone. He was recently separated from his wife of several years. She and their three sons were living in Lugano, whilst he was in London, managing director and president of Apple records, the Beatles' recording company.

It was a fairly sparkling evening at Aretusa as usual. Michael Caine was there. So was Jean Shrimpton, London's top model, with Cockney photographer David Bailey, the hottest behind the camera man in town. The 'Swinging Sixties' were regretfully drawing to a close and many of the people who had made it happen seemed to be at Aretusa that night. Bailey dropped by the table. He wanted to arrange to take a picture of Tony and me for his book to commemorate the dizzy decade. Seven years after publication nearly all the couples Bailey pictured in *Goodbye Baby and Amen* were divorced or separated by some tragic circumstances — Susan Hampshire and her French husband, and Roman Polanski and gorgeous ill-fated Sharon Tate among them.

Tony was not unaware of the interested looks I was trying not to exchange with Ron, but shortly after dinner he excused himself and telling me to 'have a good time Flower', left to work.

Doug, Evie, Ron and I sat sipping sambuccas in the discotheque. With Tony gone the atmosphere lightened up considerably. Tony had started drawing on the napkins and tablecloths in restaurants when he was bored and more and more recently at the end of dinner the table would bear the fruits of his felt pen. Some restaurants took kindly to this quaint habit and framed them, and some did not.

I was attracted to Ron, not only for his warmth and easy personality, but also for a pulsating energy that emanated from his whole being. He was, of course, an Aries. Not only that, his birth *date*, 30 March, was exactly the same as Sydney Chaplin and Warren Beatty! Surely the chances of that were two million to one at least.

We started to see each other casually just for lunch or tea at first. I was treading extremely warily. I didn't want to upset his apple cart either. Aside from the extreme physical attraction I also felt he was a man who could be a friend, with whom one could talk about any subject under the sun, exchange ideas, explore each other's minds. He was mature, although only thirty-three. An enormous enthusiasm and zest for life pervaded his character. He was a match for my physical energy and stamina. Seemingly indefatigable, he ran the Beatles' company, jumped regularly on a jet to New York, Rome or Geneva at least twice a week, and was able to stay up until three or four with no jet-lag even after a sixteen hour day.

He was a doer and an organiser, as well as a very dominant male. The first truly *dominant* man I had ever been involved with. He was also the first man I had become involved with who was not either an actor, a playboy or connected with the film or television world. He was in fact a supervisor, businessman and executive with a Bachelor of Science degree in business (as a graduate of U.C.L.A. business school), an Associate of Arts degree in music, and with a keen and intelligent mind. He always knew what he wanted and usually got it. And what he wanted was me.

But butterflies, especially married ones who have difficulty in making decisions, are not so easily caught, and our relationship had stormy waters to ride. He was the first man I had met who thought of me first, and himself second. This was an exceptionally novel experience — even for one so experienced as me. He literally swept me off my feet, and try as I did to stem the tide I found myself becoming more and more attracted to him, not only in an emotional and supportive way but in the need we discovered in each other as human beings and friends. I grew to depend on his advice more and more.

Because Newley was still completely enmeshed in his work I was able to see Ron while we were in London, often. Since I was not asked where I went, I had considerable freedom, and with Tara and Sacha now both at school, and my supply of American TV shows not in evidence, we managed to spend time discovering each other. And the more I discovered the more I liked. We did not launch into a flaming affair immediately. Perhaps now, my subconscious was finally realising that here was the man I had been searching for all my life, and it led me more carefully than previously. I didn't want to injure our blossoming friendship and love by jumping instantly into bed, and so we lunched at the Connaught, tea-ed at Claridges, met for drinks at Trader Vic's and bided our time.

I went to Trieste to make an 'intellectual' film. At least my Italian agent had assured me it was an intellectual film. 'Not much money, Cara, but aah — the *prestige!*' The director was a devout Communist, the crew numbered a mere seventeen — my salary was minimal, and I was not allowed to smile once on film, since the director considered smiling a cheap and shallow Hollywood device.

'Do you see smiles in a Bergman film?' he roared. 'Or an

Antonioni film? Maybe only *one* smile, when you are very, *very sad*, si?'

I played a desolate young widow who becomes involved in a love affair with a seventeen-year-old boy. For this I had to do my first nude scene which scared the hell out of me. It was nearly 1970. Nudity on the screen was in-in-in, all the rage — yes sir. No more the ruby in the navel, and the flower in the too plunging neckline. Goodbye chaste kiss and fade out to sensual violins. Hello, get your knickers off and jump into the sack, or the sofa, or the back of a truck — wherever it would be the most 'artistic' to shoot it. Our director finally decided after mulling it over for days that the scene would perhaps play better in bed (thank heaven for small mercies). And so one freezing winter afternoon in Trieste, which is on the border between Italy and Yugoslavia and one of the most dismal and depressing cities I had ever been to, I took off my all for art.

Mathieu Carrière, the twenty-year-old actor playing the seventeen-year-old, was not quite as nervous as I, perhaps because he was allowed to keep his shorts on. Whilst I had on a vast assortment of tights, woollen socks, leg warmers, underpants, to keep out the freezing air (Michael Caine always told me he wore Wellington boots for his love scenes in *Alfie*) I still had to be bare above the waist. Since the director had assured me repeatedly that as this was an 'art' film he was not interested in showing anything as vulgar and commercial as a nipple, but he just needed the two bodies in the throes of sexual throbbings, I decided to cleverly camouflage the basic bits with camera tape. Camera tape, unlike ordinary sticky tape, is very strong and is usually used to attach weights to cameras, and the 1001 other uses it has in the studio. Italian camera tape is also bright blue. In my dressing room I carefully attached a neat X of camera tape in the middle of each breast. 'Great ad for "Blue Cross",' I thought, glumly surveying the surrealistic image in the mirror.

Mathieu arrived with a bottle of brandy, thoughtfully sent by the director to 'warm us up'. Whether for the love scene or to keep out the bitter cold we knew not. Half a bottle of brandy later I found myself drunk and panicky, tucked in between the sheets with young Monsieur Carrière who was, if anything, even drunker and more panicked than I. Peering hopefully at us behind the hand-held camera was Il Regista, sizzling with artistic fervour. The Italian crew lounged nonchalantly around, pretending indifference to the simulated coupling they were about to see. I still had on my robe, while the director tried to get the perfect angle for this piece of celluloid passion. Mathieu appeared to have fallen asleep — it was comfortable in the bed and one tiny snore escaped from his beatifically smiling countenance. I nudged him awake. We were clutching each other stolidly like two great hunks of wood, neither of us about to do anything remotely sensual until the magic word 'Actione!' was screamed. It was usually screamed in Italian films. The director imagines that this electric word will galvanise his cast into dynamic performances. It usually made me jump.

'Va Bene — Va Bene — Allora Joan.' He turned to me, 'Take off the roba.'

'Shit,' I muttered, the moment of truth had come — what the fuck was I doing here, thousands of miles from my loved ones, making a lousy uncommercial Italian art film which no one would probably see anyway. Here in bed with a young lad barely past puberty, with blue camera tape over my nipples. Oh the degradation! I bravely stripped off the robe and threw myself onto Mathieu's scrawny chest to cover my by now embarrassing blue crosses.

'OK — ACTIONE!!' screamed the director excitedly. The whirring cameras could not keep up with the sound of his yelled excitable instruction 'KEEES . . . Beeg beeg keees.' I pressed myself even more fervently to Mathieu and we locked lips and simulated lust. 'More *sexy!*' roared Romana. 'You *woman,* he *boy* — ees veree veree beeg *thrill* for you.' God, this was like making silent movies. Sound was not important in Italian pictures, everything was dubbed later, but our director was going a bit far even so. His vocal efforts were causing me to giggle, I tried to prevent it by biting my lip. and found Mathieu's there instead.

Squirm, squirm — wriggle, wriggle — pant, pant — we wrestled around on the bed. I felt as passionate as a cat on a cold tin roof. And to top it off, my suppressed giggles caused me to get hiccups. I was determined to keep back to camera at all times, but the staccato heaving of my shoulders every three seconds caused the director to yell 'CUT!' We disengaged lips — a thin line of saliva connected us — I disconnected it — giggled and hiccuped. Mathieu was dissolved into hysterical drunk laughter. We disengaged arms. I tried to back off from his chest and found I couldn't. The edge of one of my blue crosses had attached itself to Mathieu's chest. Suddenly we were Siamese twins. I thought of the courting couples who are found locked in the throes of sexual embrace and who, unable to separate, have to be taken to hospital while they put them under a cold shower or administer non-stimulating drugs to cool their ardour. Mathieu, aware of what had happened, became even more hysterical and, hiccuping wildly, so did I. The crew were puzzled, until they saw what had happened and guffaws abounded — except for the director who remained aloof and cold. He hated people to smile, let alone laugh. The wardrobe lady separated us and I put on my robe and staggered, still hiccuping, to my dressing room to recuperate.

'We will shoot the rest of the scene tomorrow,' said the director coldly, 'when you both 'ave sobered up.' He stalked off briskly, moustache bristling.

After a strong expresso was brought I proceeded to try and remove the tape. Solid as a rock! It would not budge. Alarmed at the thought of permanently blue nipples, I rushed back to the hotel and after a soak in a hot bath for an hour attempted to pull off the offending tape. The agony was such that, after it was finally removed, and my bosoms emerged red and raw from the pulling, I vowed to hell with modesty — in the future if I had to do any nude scenes I'd let it all hang out.

Newley and I by now had an unspoken 'arrangement'. He went his way and I went mine. I was in a tremendous dilemma. I wanted to be with Ron, I felt he was the man I had been searching for always — combining the qualities of leadership, dominance and intelligence with loving warmth, communication and compassion. I loved Tony still, but in a completely different way, and I felt enormous sisterly compassion for his inability to give himself totally to anything except his work. He was the father of my children, and this was the biggest problem. I dreaded having to break up the children's secure and happy home. To take away their roots, which I had fought hard to get for them. Every time I made the decision to separate from Tony, I changed my mind again because of the pain and hurt it would bring the children, who were the most important things in my life. How could I ruin their innocent lives. It was selfish and rotten of me; yet at the same time, I knew that living in a house without love was probably even worse for them. I agonised for months, completely torn, completely unable to decide one way or another. I hated myself for being so weak, for not being able to take the decisive initiative and end the marriage, which I knew was as hollow as a chocolate Easter egg. Meanwhile I juggled my quadruple lives of wife, mother, actress and adulteress and tried to put on a happy face.

I had always had a hankering to be a singer. At one time I took extensive singing lessons in Hollywood before auditioning for a Broadway musical, which luckily I didn't get since it closed after three performances. My voice was quite good but weak (rather like my character), I had though crooned a passable duet with Bing Crosby in *Road to Hollywood*, a little ditty by my Oscar-winning friend Sammy Cahn called 'Let's Not be Sensible' and I had also sung the notorious 'Chalk and Cheese' opposite my naked husband in *Hieronymus*. Now Tony's record company in London had approached him about the possibility ot him producing and writing an album on which I would perform. The irony of this close working relationship commencing at about the same time our marriage was going down the drain did not escape us.

We were in the process of an amicable 'trial separation' whilst still residing in the same house 'for the sake of the children'. I had now told him about Ron. I knew about Connie Kreski and various others — we were going to attempt to live through this exceedingly difficult period as normally as possible. It was naive of us to think it could be so.

The album was to be tentatively called *And she sings too!* and would feature on the sleeve an enormous portrait of me looking as seductive as can be. Somewhat like the cover of this book! My voice was a cross between Claudine Longet and Astrud Gilberto — sort of breathy, sexy and girlish. Streisand definitely did not have to worry. Tony wrote a song which he gave to me, and which I sang for the album. It was a hard driving rock song, better performed by someone with the vocal strength of Petula Clark. It was called 'Why do you try and change me?' and it said it *all* about our marriage —

> You tell me you love me
> But if you love me Baby
> Why do you try and change me?
> I don't want to change you baby
> You know you have faults as well
> I accept them 'cos I really love you.
> You can lead a horse to water
> But you'll never ever alter me.
> I'm free — I'm me . . .
> Life is a Mardi Gras and I refuse to miss the party.
> I want to dance the night away —
> You want to keep me home a perfect little
> household pet.

But I don't want to be your mother
Take me as a friend and lover
That's the only way I want us to be.
Strange, when I think at first
You seemed to be so mad about me
Why should you suddenly complain?
If you go on and on insisting that I do thing
                              your way
You are going to drive me from you
After everything we've gone through
Tell me what you want
I wish that you'd say.
Didn't I change my name for you?
Didn't I play the game for you?
Didn't I make it wild for you?
Didn't I make a child for you?
Take me the way I am or leave me alone
Didn't I stay at home for you?
Didn't I give up Rome for you?
What do I have to do to show you I care?

I awoke at six o'clock with a distinct feeling of foreboding. I was having a dream of such reality that I forced myself to awake from it. Could it be true? I had to find out immediately and the only way to do that was to make a phone call to Brazil. To Rio de Janeiro, where Ron had gone for the annual song festival. He had wanted me to go with him and I had been sorely torn. For weeks I anguished about the ramifications a trip to Rio, where half the jet-lag world were congregating, would bring. But I wanted to go. Travelling — experiencing new places, smells, sounds, vibrations — was one of my greatest pleasures, and Rio had always been at the top of the list of places I wanted to visit. To go with Ron would be an extra added bonus. But although Tony was aware of my relationship with Ron it simply wasn't cricket to openly attend a highly publicised music festival, at which the press of the world would be, with my lover. I was popular in Latin America, and if we went to the festival together it was tantamount to taking an ad in *Variety* about our affair.

Evie Bricusse, whose marriage to Leslie was also going through a rough patch, was considering going too, and we spent anxious hours discussing the pros and cons of our projected visit. But reason prevailed. I still needed time — time to think about my children, and what divorcing their father could do to them. I couldn't decide. I knew what I wanted: I wanted Ron. But I was trying to have my cake and eat it too, a practical impossibility.

I drove later that morning to Ron's rented house on Coldwater Canyon to phone him in Rio. There was a four hour delay and I fretted, anxious, uptight. Finally his voice came through, faint and surprised yet happy to hear from me. I didn't beat about the bush. The dream was too vivid in my mind.

'Who's this dark haired, twenty-six-year-old socialite you've been going out with?' I said, rather more sharply than I had intended. Diplomacy and tact were never my strong point.

'Whaat??' his voice from a distance of more than six thousand miles sound fuzzily amazed. 'How do you know about her? Who told you?'

It was true. God it was true then. My dream was a reality. 'I just know that's all,' I battled on bravely. 'How long has it been going on?'

'My God Joan.' He was the only man who had ever called me by my proper name. A good sign. maybe he saw the real me, and not some plaything or imaginary Goddess. I had always been Honey, Sweetheart, Babe, Joanie-bird, Butterfly, Flower, or Jaycee before Ron.

'It hasn't really been "going on". I met this girl — she's a lovely girl —' I gritted my teeth, the green-eyed monster convulsing me. 'But we haven't gotten really involved or anything — yet.'

Yet! Yet! Oh, my God I was a fool, an absolute fool. I had let this exceedingly handsome man of thirty-four go off to Rio telling him, after over a year of knowing each other, that I 'had to have more time to think things over' and expected him to keep the faith. He was only human. Who, more than I, could empathise with that!

A torrent of feelings and protestations burst from me. Realisation that I was getting close to losing him. The only man who had ever really understood me. The only one with whom I had a true communication.

We talked for an hour. An hour in which I finally resolved my horribly ambivalent feelings and faced up to what losing him would mean. I knew now what I wanted and needed and what he wanted too. We had to be together. It was the only way.

If anyone imagines that divorce, for an actor or actress is easy, let them think again. This parting was infinitely more terrible than my divorce from Maxwell Reed because I really did still *care* about Tony, and my conscience was sorely affected by what I was doing to my two innocent children. But the sparks of love between Tony and me were not enough to re-kindle our marriage. We liked and sort of respected each other, but living together any more was out of the question. The split was amicable. Painful, hurtful, but amicable. I wasn't the right woman for him and he knew it. We had been staying together for the children's sake for far too long. Even they, at the tender ages of six and a half and four and a half, were aware of it.

The beautiful house on Summit Drive went on the market. I took no alimony — only a property settlement derived mostly from the sale of the house — which was bought by Sammy Davis Jnr. We agreed on a realistic sum for the children's support. They were my responsibility now, and since I had let my career take a more than secondary position for seven years, the prospects of me earning enough money to support them were dim.

Ron already had a wife and three kids in Lugano to whom he had to pay alimony and child support and sign away his Swiss house including all of the furniture, paintings and books that they had accumulated in their ten years of marriage. I could hardly ask him to support my two children as well.

Marriage to Tony had lasted seven years just as Ben Gary had predicted. It was uncanny!

I assured him that he could see the children whenever he wished. The last thing I wanted was to ever have them hurt, or used as a pawn in the marital upheavals as I had seen so many selfish spouses do. But for some reason, in spite of my efforts to remain on friendly terms, he became exceedingly bitter towards me in the media.

'I work for an organisation that supports Joan Collins,' he announced sarcastically on a TV talk show one afternoon. My English tea and biscuit stuck in my throat. 'I keep Joan Collins in the style to which she became accustomed during her marriage to me.' Other hurtful remarks too. 'Women who get money from men after they divorce are worse than whores.' It was unpleasant and unfair. I had devoted seven years to him and to raising our children. The money I possessed when we married was put into a joint bank account. Never one to take a free ride, I resented his attitude that it was through him and only him that I was able to continue to live well. He put himself forth as a martyr on the cross of my monetary gain and I found it sickening.

I returned, yet again, bags, baggage, furniture and children to my beloved London.

Ron was now president of MGM records and Robins Feist and Miller Music Publishing Company. He had two plush offices in New York, and spent much time commuting between continents. I refused, for the children's sake, to move into Ron's Mayfair town house with him, and instead took a horrible, cramped and exceedingly overpriced furnished flat around the corner. I plunged into getting my children settled in new schools, and setting up my career yet again in a different country and generally sorting out our lives. I was deeply in love with Ron, although we fought like dog and cat. We both always said what was on our minds. No beating about the bush. It was instant combustibility! But honest. I knew that at last — after a long search! — I had found a true, dedicated and supportive love in Ron. However, I did not wish to traumatise the children even more by a new 'Daddy' suddenly appearing on the scene. My main concern was to take care of their needs and adjust them as well as I could to this totally new and strange life. London is very different from sunny Beverly Hills with a swimming pool in every backyard.

It was the spring of 1970. Ron bought me a cute new Mini. My birthday 'present' from Tony had to go back to the car rental agent in Los Angeles after our divorce. It had never been mine to own in fact. I raced around London looking yet again for a suitable house. Ron wanted us to marry, but I was convinced that, as Oscar Wilde said, 'One should always be in love — that is why one should never marry.' Two attempts at marriage had made me realise I wasn't very good at it — although I realised my choices had been bad. And it was too soon. The ink hadn't dried on my divorce papers yet.

Luckily I was able to start working in films and TV immediately. In quick succession, in the early part of the 1970s, I made *Three in the Cellar*, the last film in the States before I left for England. It was a comedy — a rather abortive one. I also made *Quest for Love* and *Revenge* for Rank at my old stamping grounds, Pinewood Studios. Over fifteen years had passed since the 'coffee bar Jezebel' had crossed those hallowed portals to portray floozies and sexy delinquents. Now I was playing lovely leading ladies, with a touch of mischief or evil thrown in for extra added interest. None of these films were by any means either box office bonanzas or works of art, but an actor acts and I needed the bread.

Then came a quick series of horror films which were euphemistically referred to as 'psychological melodramas' — *Fear in the Night, Tales from the Crypt, Dark Places* and *Tales that*

238

Witness Madness. I became known as Queen of the Horror Flicks — a title I was not madly keen on. But I was nothing if not resilient. I considered myself lucky to be working so much after such a long period away from the British screen. And the critics were kind. 'Miss Collins — an actress always better than her material' said the *Evening Standard* — and 'Joan Collins is an actress who only improves . . . and brings beauty, luminosity and compelling charm to the screen.'

I was a survivor! And thanks to Ron, I had faith in myself at last.

I had always thought that if my acting career collapsed I might become a casting director. I could see the potential of some obscure unknown actor or actress and say to myself: 'There's a future star'. It first happened at MGM whilst making *The Opposite Sex*. A young guy, about my age, who worked in the mail room, and sometimes delivered my fan letters, used to whistle at me as I sailed in my tight-boned Helen Rose creations to the commissary for lunch. One day I stopped to chat. He was really cute — very young and boyish, black curly hair, wide blue eyes, a sense of humour and a certain offbeat sex appeal. He had a lot of confidence in himself for he asked me for a date which I refused. He told me he was an actor, and his name was Jack Nicholson.

I thought I saw invisible Kleig lights over his head as I locked eyes with a handsome, tousle-haired, black-eyed slightly wild looking young actor, dressed in Russian peasant clothes. He was at the far end of the Pinewood dining room, lunching with Topol and Norman Jewison who were making *Fiddler on the Roof*. I was at the other end lunching with Roger Moore, David Tebet, a vice-president of NBC, and a good friend, and my Gemini girl-chum Judy Bryer.

'Look at the guy,' I whispered to Judy, 'don't you think he's magnetic?' She looked him over. She, being a true Gemini, immediately realised his potential, and agreed he was indeed attractive.

Topol came by our table and introduced him to us. His name was Michael Glaser which he soon changed to Paul Michael Glaser and hit the heights of TV superstardom with *Starsky and Hutch*.

This summer I went to Hawaii to film a special two hour episode of *Starsky and Hutch*. Paul was sitting on the lawn of the location paradise we were shooting in. Palm trees waved and lush tropical plants shimmered in the hazy morning heat. He was absorbed in a technical brochure on cameras, and although wearing an outrageously unflattering outfit of baggy Bermuda shorts, cheap printed Hawaiian shirt, red ankle socks and tennis shoes, managed to look charismatic and handsome. He had a slight look of Charlie Chaplin and Tony Newley in their prime. David Soul brought him over to say hello and he remembered instantly the day we met at Pinewood, five years previously.

I enjoyed working with David and Paul in *Starsky and Hutch* — more than with many of the dozens of actors I worked with. They were both craftsmen, excellent actors, considerate gentlemen, always concerned that what they were doing was the best, the absolute *best* they could make it. It was rare and refreshing to be involved with such energy and enthusiasm — in spite of the fact that the scripts of the shows were far from their ideal. Theirs was the frustration of talented actors, who care deeply about their craft, being used as fodder for the great TV machine. They both wanted out of the show, to pursue films, and in David's case also concerts and records.

Paul ruefully remarked that by the time he finished his five years on the show he'd be thirty-seven: 'That's a little old to start a career as a screen leading man.' I thought him wrong. I am sure he will have a tremendous screen career whenever he starts it.

I'm now making a movie of *The Stud*. It's a project dear to my heart ever since Jackie wrote the novel six years ago. 'I MUST play Fontaine,' I told Jackie as soon as I'd read it. 'It's a great part and I would be fabulous,' I added modestly.

After several years of trying to get it off the ground, oh the *problems* of being a producer, I never realised them before, we are finally making it with Ron producing which he does with great flair although I am convinced one day he will wake up with a phone permanently attached to his ear!

The young actor who plays 'the stud', Oliver Tobias, has a cornucopia of moody sex appeal, brooding good looks, charisma and talent — a better looking Alan Bates with a strong measure of the young Brando thrown in. After this movie every one believes he will become very successful.

We interviewed many actors for this part and only Oliver fitted the role exactly and Jackie and Ron and I knew it as soon as we saw him. Success has a lot to do with being in the right place at the right time. Talent is not enough. Luck is not enough. It's all in the lap of the Gods, and if they smile upon you at the right time you're in clover.

We finally found the perfect house we had been searching for. It was, from the outside, a rather ordinary looking semi-detached 1930s house, not unlike the forty or fifty others in the same avenue, but it was exactly what we wanted. A lovely warm family home into which Ron, Tara, Sacha and I happily moved, and with the added excitement of a new addition expected to our already large family. Ron's three husky young sons — David, Robert and Jonathan — visited us each summer and Christmas, at our house in Marbella and when baby Katyana arrived we had a his, hers and theirs brood.

Ron and I sat with friends Paul Wasserman — Ron's best friend, an American publicist with a dark and saturnine wit — Pete Kameron, and Burt and Maxine Kamerman in Mr Chows ten days before baby was due. We doodled on the paper tablecloth possible names. Ron desperately wanted a girl — after three boys who wouldn't? Pete was sure it would be a girl. Pete was one of Ron's closest friends — a sort of father figure. Wealthy from his thirty-five years in the music business and with 'The Who' group he had given up up most of his material possessions and spent several years travelling the world and searching for the truth. He explored India and China and Africa examining, analysing and experimenting with many different kinds of religion and philosophy and searching for the truth.

He had just returned from a trip to India and meeting with the extraordinary Indian, Saha Baba, an Indian holy man held in the highest esteem. Pete had a small phial of grey dust, and he dabbed some of it on my forehead and cheek-bones. It was a substance that Saha Baba created himself — out of thin air literally, and it had, so I was told, powerful properties. Pete was a great believer in getting your 'Karma' right. He was a strong influence on me to eliminate from my life many people and situations which were time consuming, non-supportive, back biting and useless. I was going for the reality in people rather than the bullshit I'd been absorbing for so many years.

After he applied the ashes he told me that the baby would be a blessed child, possessed with immense personal magnetism, intelligence, beauty and luck. 'You'll have her tomorrow,' he said gravely, convinced it was a girl.

'Nonsense — it's not due for at least ten days,' laughed Ron. We wrote down some names — mostly Russian from his ancestry for his original family name was Kaschenoff — Tatiana, Katya, Katyana. I wanted something completely original, with a Russian flavour. Four hours later, after consuming an immense Chinese meal, and Ron consuming a powerful sleeping pill I went into labour. Unable to rouse Ron from a deep sleep I poured three cups of strong coffee through his groggy lips before he could get himself together enough to drive me to the nursing home!

I was having this child again by natural childbirth, helped along by Ron's encouragement, and a fierce 'Scrabble' game which lasted almost until the birth.

When James Schneider, my obstetrician said excitedly: 'It's a girl!' I argued with him. 'You're just staying that to make Ron happy,' I said. 'He always gets what he wants and you don't want to disappoint him.' Ron was there too, beside himself with joy, helping me, and Katyana Kennedy Kass brought us closer together than ever.

I was extremely concerned what the effect of a new baby would have on Tara and Sacha. It hadn't been easy for them at all adjusting to a new country, new friends, new house, new school, new stepfather. I remembered how horrible I had felt attending all those different schools and having to make new friends when I was a child. But they adored Katy instantly and seemed to adjust to their new situation.

Ron and I had waited a long time to get married. Waited in fact until three months before Katy was born! My sister, a very observant lady, and now a successful novelist, was completely stunned when we informed her we were leaving for Jamaica to marry and that she was going to become an aunt again imminently! I had been working up until March, without anyone having a clue about my condition. I made an expensive commercial cleverly draped in a flowing shirt, just before we left to get married.

Katy was born on 20th June 1972. Being a Gemini, too, she and I probably understand each other better than anyone else in the world.

I was now in what without a doubt was the happiest time of my life. If one can measure the highs and lows of one's life, the years between 1970 and 1975 were as almost perfect as anything could be. I loved my husband. I adored my children. I was happy living in England with my family and working on some things I really enjoyed.

Buzz Kulik, who had directed me a few years earlier in a ghastly potboiler *Warning Shot* with David Janssen, asked me to play Lorraine Sheldon in *The Man who came to Dinner*.

This was a prestigious NBC Hallmark Hall of Fame two-hour special and although shot, for some obscure reason, in England it was to be shown in America for Thanksgiving.

Lorraine was a divine part based on the character of Gertrude Lawrence. Flamboyant, gutsy and eccentric. And it was a comedy. Marvellous! And just the sort of role I could sink my teeth into hook, line and sinker.

Buzz gathered an excellent cast. Lee Remick was to play Maggie, Sheridan Whiteside's loyal secretary, immortalised in the screen version by none other than Bette Davis. Marty Feldman was a mad Groucho Marx character, Don Knotts the catatonically shy doctor, Peter Haskell the journalist and last, but definitely not least, Mr Orson Welles himself as Sheridan Whiteside. *The* man who came to dinner.

He comes to the house of a respectable middle-aged Connecticut couple and stays, creating havoc, turmoil, and humour. Sheridan Whiteside was one of the best (and longest) comedy roles ever written for an actor. He dominates every scene, is bitingly witty, ruthless, scheming and hilarious. Hallmark felt they had a major coup in getting this giant (literally and figuratively) of the entertainment world to grace them with his august presence in this role, and he was treated like an emperor.

We rehearsed for three weeks, during which time Mr Welles consumed vast quantities of burgundy-coloured liquid from tea cups, and read every one of his lines from massive cue cards, 3' x 3' wide, which were held in place by two wide-eyed, nervous young students from RADA.

I felt like a wide-eyed nervous young girl from RADA myself in the presence of Welles. He was immense and frightening, and his reputation for not letting anyone get the better of him preceded him. I practically bobbed and curtsied and would have pulled my forelock reverently — as did everyone — such was the awe he instilled in us. Was this not the boy wonder of the movies who, at the age of twenty-five, had made the unforgettable *Citizen Kane*, one of the greatest movies of all time? Awesome Orson I called him. Since I was playing a poised, sophisticated, glamorous actress, whom nothing fazed I had to steel my nerves whilst working with his magnificence.

He was performing a longish speech to me one afternoon. I was standing on my correct mark when he suddenly ended the speech with . . . 'and I can't read the rest of the lines because MISS

243

COLLINS is standing in front of the damn cue cards!!'

'But I'm standing where I'm supposed to be,' I muttered feebly, catching a sympathetic grimace from Lee Remick. It didn't matter that he was in the wrong. I blocked his view of his lines so I must be placed in another position where his Highness could view them without obstruction. I meekly did what I was told. Mr Welles looked triumphant and his secretary brought him another cup of 'tea' — which he insisted was coca cola but which we later discovered was red wine, and not even vintage.

Peter Haskell, however was not so intimidated. He bounded in the following day with an airy speech about it being a beautiful Christmas day and the snow was on the trees and the frost on the ground, and Welles boomed in his stentorian tones: 'You read that just like a goddam faggot.'

'What did you say?' said Peter menacingly quiet, and advancing towards Welles with measured stride.

'I said you read it like — a — er — faggot. But dear boy I was only joking, I assure you — ha ha ha! Dear boy, sorry.' His huge laugh boomed and rocked the draughty rehearsal hall. Some of the technicians laughed sycophantically and Peter, slightly placated, continued the scene. Orson seemed to admire him after that. They became quite chummy. He obviously enjoyed people standing up to him, and relished putting the fear of God into lesser mortals.

Don Knotts was not so lucky. Lee and I sat in the transmission room watching a dress rehearsal on TV. Don had his best and funniest scene cut to ribbons by Welles. He insisted on restaging, so that all Don's best lines were shot on the back of his head, and cutting anything that he felt detracted from his own performance.

During the three-day studio taping, which drifted into five and a half days, whilst another TV company stamped their feet in frenzy outside our studio door, Mr Welles read *every single line* of his part from the cue cards. Kulik tried to remonstrate with him. Welles always insisted on being placed centre stage facing the camera (and his cards). Kulik suggested that perhaps some of the other actors should get a look in or a close up occasionally. Welles boomed at him, 'I am the star. This play is all about Sheridan Whiteside. The rest of the troupe are just supporting players!'

Buzz retired crushed and Welles did it his way. Needless to say it was one of the un-funniest productions of *The Man who came to Dinner* ever done.

I received a great compliment from Kitty Carlisle, the wife of co-author, Moss Hart, who came to visit the filming. She told me that I was the best Lorraine Sheldon she has ever seen and she had seen every actress play it since the forties.

The Man who came to Dinner was notable for introducing me to one of the brightest, warmest and most talented dress designers the English theatre possessed. Someone whom I grew to love dearly, almost like a surrogate mother figure. Beatrice 'Bumble' Dawson had been Vivien Leigh's closest friend and confidante when we met ten years previously whilst I was with Warren on *The Roman Spring of Mrs Stone*. At that time she had intimidated me and we barely spoke.

A lady, although not young, with an enthusiasm and zest for living that put people half her age to shame, she had immense vitality and, although suffering from severe arthritis, zipped about in her little Mini, shopping with the actresses she loved to dress and design for.

Ron and I were instrumental in getting her to do the clothes for *Fallen Angels* and *The Adventures of Tom Jones*. Alas, during her return from a fitting at Pinewood she was involved in a serious traffic accident and although she recovered, she died six months later.

Her death was a blow. Although my quest in life had been for a father figure not a mother figure I was sorely conscious of the lack of a mother in my life, especially with three beautiful children to whom having a granny would have meant so much. The family unit was most important to me now, and I missed my mother. What a pity it took me so long to realise it. I found I thought about her more and more, especially as Tara grew older, for I could identify only too vividly still with my own childhood feelings. Indeed I sometimes even felt that Tara was me, little Joan eight or nine years old, and I, the Joan of today, became my mother.

My feelings for my father were not as strong now. I realised his weaknesses and failings but I still cared about him and felt compassion without the sense of loss he had engendered in me for so many, many years.

He had married again and had another child. His wife was coincidentally also an agent and artists' manager. Irene was about the same age as me, which was quite funny really. I wondered if she had ever searched for a father figure too?

But my mother's image still haunted me and I dreamed about her more often. Jackie has become enormously close to Mummy in the years before her death, and I regretted that I had not been able to because of leaving for America whilst still too young to appreciate

245

her. A boy needs a father some of his life, but a girl needs a mother all of her life. Or is it the other way around? In any case I prefer my version.

I finally fulfilled one of my major ambitions. To play in a Noël Coward comedy. Ron obtained the rights to several Coward plays amongst them *Fallen Angels*. *Fallen Angels* had been produced in New York in 1927 with a young Tallulah Bankhead and Edna Best in the leading roles of two women, best friends for life and now happily, if boringly, married to dullards, who shared a mad passionate romance in the past with a devastatingly attractive Frenchman. It was a *tour de force* for the two actresses, and Tallulah and Edna made enormous successes on Broadway. Since then the play had been constantly revived, but always, for some reason, with older actresses in the roles which should have been played by women in their late twenties or thirties. Perhaps managements thought that only these actresses could play these roles, which were extremely funny, bawdy, and juicy. Hermione Gingold and Hermione Baddeley had played them, amongst others.

For the first time I started to become instrumental in the production side of the entertainment business. Ron was producing, and with my casting director's hat on I suggested that Susannah York would be perfect to play Julia, and Sacha Distel, the French heart-throb, to play Maurice. This role, probably because it was small, has usually been played by some lackadaisical nonentity but it was, I thought, extremely important to the plot that if Susannah (Julia) and I (Jane) spent three quarters of the play extolling the virtues of this divine Frenchman, with whom we were both still secretly in love, by the time the audience see him he had better be a knockout.

The play, for Anglia Television, worked extremely well. Susannah and I got along like a house on fire, indeed I got on better with her than with some of my male co-stars, and Sacha, a long time friend, looked suitably stunning as the devastating Frenchman. It was screened over the Christmas holiday and received excellent reviews, not to mention ratings.

Bumble did the clothes. She scoured the antique shops looking for authentic twenties frocks. They were beautifully made, the quality, fabric and workmanship so much finer than anything of today. My nostalgia for the twenties was in full flower.

'SOAK THE RICH!' screamed Chancellor of the Exchequer Denis Healey in the headlines of the British papers. 'Tax them till they bleed. Squeeze them dry!!'

It was ominous. Too ominous for us. Ron, American and living in Europe for over ten years would feel the crunch badly. He was now President of Warner Brothers Records, UK, with offices in the middle of Soho, happily involved in the music business with people like Paul McCartney, Mo Ostin and Joe Smith. People and activities he adored.

There was nothing for it but to escape from Healey's claws. I had worked hard all my life. The possessions I had accumulated — a house, furniture, car, jewellery, some paintings and my collection of Art Deco objects and 1920s figurines, would, it seemed, subject to an immense wealth tax each year. It wasn't just. The newspapers editorialised that England would lose much of its creative talent by this governmental blunder, but Healey was adamant. He wanted his last pound of flesh.

With astonishing alacrity, dozens of writers, directors, producers, sportsmen and actors speedily left England as fast as they could. Some Americans, English residents for twenty years, were on the next plane.

I was desolate. Destroyed. I couldn't *bear* the thought of yet again packing up everything, taking my children from the schools and friends to whom they had become so attached, and hitting the long and winding road to Hollywood, California. My *third* permanent move there in twenty years!

Ben Gary's prediction for me in 1961 came terrifyingly true yet again: 'You will *always* be a gipsy. You will strive to have roots, but you will constantly be on the move somewhere again, and have to put down new roots.' It was in the stars. Ben was uncanny. Could he, I wonder, see from his grave how accurate he had been about my entire life?

'You are amazingly resilient,' he said to that young girl back in 1961. 'You will always adapt, and you will always adjust to what life has in store for you. You must work — it is essential for you to be involved and creative, and nothing will ever get you down or depress you for long. You will always make money and have a measure of happiness because you are a happy person — one of life's survivors.'

And as I look back on my short, yet crowded life I realise that Ben was right. My past was not perfect, very little really ever is, but the future looks promising and I have (I hope!) a lot of time ahead of me. I think these words that Robert Browning wrote

apply beautifully to *my* life:
    'How sad and bad and mad it was,
    But then, how it was sweet!'

THE END

EPILOGUE

London, 14 December 1977

As I sit now in London finishing this book I realise what an amazingly unpredictable year 1977 has been for me. After making four TV shows early this year. I then made three movies in a row — *The Big Sleep* with Robert Mitchum for Lord Lew Grade (I finally worked in a movie for him): *The Day of the Fox* in Vienna and Italy, and *The Stud* in London for which we all have high hopes and which is the best role I have played in many a moon (thank you Jackie!).

I have written on aeroplanes, in the endless LA to London and back again flights; in draughty dressing rooms in Putney and Chelsea — in the swamps of Florida huddled in a camp chair swatting mosquitoes — in cramped humid trailer-caravans in Hawaii — in the back room of the discotheque 'Tramp' whilst a hundred extras hovered nearby — under the hairdryer whenever possible! — thank God no phones can ring there — flopped on my bed in Beverly Hills, surrounded by the joy of having my three children around me, with the TV going full blast on cartoon time and the phone, as usual ringing constantly and sometimes — oh bliss! — alone in my living room, just me and my felt pen.

I have, of course, adjusted yet again to my new-old life in Beverly Hills. I do it well, adjusting that is. I think I have finally found out who I am. Writing this book has helped a lot, almost a catharsis, I realise how fortunate I am and really always have been.

I am no longer insecure, nervous and afraid of what people might think of me. I am confident in my craft, which I intend to continue as long as I can — even if they have to push me in front of a camera or behind the footlights in a wheel chair. I like people, and I love life and my family.

Some wise person once said if you want to be happy you must not live in the past but in the *now*. This I truly believe. It's taken me a long time to grow up, but I think I'm almost there!

FILMOGRAPHY

YEAR	FILM	STUDIO	DIRECTOR	CO-STARS
1952	I BELIEVE IN YOU	Rank	Basil Dearden	Laurence Harvey Celia Johnson Cecil Parker
1953	DECAMERON NIGHTS	Mike Frankovich	Hugo Fregonese	Joan Fontaine Louis Jourdan
1953	THE SQUARE RING	Rank	Basil Dearden	Stanley Baker Maxwell Reed Bill Travers
1953	COSH BOY (THE SLASHER — US)	British Lion	Lewis Gilbert	James Kenney
1953	TURN THE KEY SOFTLY	Rank	Jack Lee	Yvonne Mitchell Kathleen Harrison
1954	THE GOOD DIE YOUNG	Romulus Films	Lewis Gilbert	Laurence Harvey Stanley Baker Gloria Grahame Margaret Leighton
1954	OUR GIRL FRIDAY (THE ADVENTURES OF SADIE — US)	Independent	Noel Langley	Kenneth More George Cole
1954	LAND OF THE PHARAOHS	George Minter Prod. Warners	Howard Hawks	Jack Hawkins Sydney Chaplin James Robertson Justice
1955	THE VIRGIN QUEEN	Fox	Henry Koster	Bette Davis Richard Todd
1955	THE GIRL IN THE RED VELVET SWING	Fox	Richard Fleischer	Ray Milland Farley Granger
1956	THE OPPOSITE SEX	MGM	David Miller	June Allyson Dolores Gray Ann Sheridan
1956	SEA WIFE	Fox	Bob McNaughton	Richard Burton Cy Grant

Year	Title	Director	Studio	Cast
1956	ISLAND IN THE SUN	Robert Rossen	Fox	James Mason Harry Belafonte Joan Fontaine Dorothy Dandridge Stephen Boyd
1957	THE WAYWARD BUS	Victor Vicas	Fox	Dan Dailey Jayne Mansfield
1958	THE BRAVADOS	Henry King	Fox	Gregory Peck Lee Van Cleef Henry Silva Albert Salmi
1958	RALLY ROUND THE FLAG BOYS	Leo McCarey	Fox	Paul Newman Joanne Woodward
1959	SEVEN THIEVES	Henry Hathaway	Fox	Rod Steiger Eli Wallach Edward G. Robinson
1960	ESTHER AND THE KING	Raoul Walsh	Fox	Richard Egan Denis O'Day
1962	ROAD TO HONG KONG	Norman Panama	UA	Bob Hope Bing Crosby
1964	LA CONGUINTURA	Ettore Scola	(Italian)	Vittorio Gassman
1966	WARNING SHOT	Buzz Kulik	Paramount	David Janssen
1968	SUBTERFUGE	Peter Graham Scott	English Independent	Gene Barry
1968	CAN HIERONYMUS MERKIN EVER FORGET MERCY HUMPE AND FIND TRUE HAPPINESS?	Anthony Newley	UI	Anthony Newley Milton Berle
1969	THE EXECUTIONER	Sam Wanamaker	Columbia	George Peppard Keith Michell
1969	DRIVE HARD, DRIVE FAST	Douglas Heyes	UI (TV)	Brian Kelly
1969	STATE OF SIEGE	Romano Scavolini	(Italian)	Mathieu Carrière
1970	IF IT'S TUESDAY IT MUST BE BELGIUM	Mel Stuart	UA	Suzanne Pleshette
1970	THREE IN THE CELLAR	Ted Flicker	AIP	Larry Hagman
1970	QUEST FOR LOVE	Ralph Thomas	Rank	Denholm Elliott Tom Bell
1971	REVENGE	Sidney Hayers	Rank	James Booth Siobhan Cusack

1971	FEAR IN THE NIGHT	Hammer	James Sangster	Judy Geeson Ralph Bates Peter Cushing
1972	TALES FROM THE CRYPT	Cinerama	Freddie Francis	Ralph Richardson Richard Greene Ian Hendry
1973	DARK PLACES	(English)	Don Sharp	Christopher Lee Jane Birkin Jean Marsh
1973	L'ARBITRO (THE REFEREE — US)	(Italian)	Louis Phillipo D'Amico	Lando Buzzanca
1973	TALES THAT WITNESS MADNESS	(English)	Freddie Francis	Michael Jayston
1974	ALFIE DARLING	EMI	Ken Hughes	Alan Price Jill Townsend Annie Ross Georgia Brown
1974	THE CALL OF THE WOLF	(Spanish)	Robert Lynn	Jack Palance
1974	ADVENTURES OF TOM JONES	UI	Cliff Owens	Nicky Henson Trevor Howard
1975	I DON'T WANT TO BE BORN	Rank	Peter Sasdy	Donald Pleasence Eileen Atkins Ralph Bates
1976	THE MONEYCHANGERS	Paramount	Boris Segal	Kirk Douglas Christopher Plummer Helen Hayes
1977	EMPIRE OF THE ANTS	AIP	Burt Gordon	Robert Lansing John David Carson
1977	THE BIG SLEEP	OA	Michael Winner	Robert Mitchum James Stewart Oliver Reed Sarah Miles
1977	THE DAY OF THE FOX	Franz Ante Prods.	Stelvio Massi	Mauritzio Merli Gaston Mascine
1977	THE STUD	Brent-Walker Film Prods.	Quentin Masters	Oliver Tobias Emma Jacobs Sue Lloyd Mark Burns

252

379